About this Book

Worldwide more and more governments have begun to buckle under a variety of strains, including the ongoing pressures of economic crisis, followed by structural adjustment programmes and the impact of declining legitimacy, often resulting in the outbreak of civil war. In this study of aid policy, Joanna Macrae argues that the disintegration of state authority and civil order has created acute problems in aid management. Largely ignored by major aid organizations, insecurity and failures of governance are now the major obstacles to aid reaching those in most need.

International aid has traditionally assumed the existence of stable, sovereign states capable of making policy. In a number of developing countries, including post-conflict regimes like Cambodia, Uganda or Kosovo, this is no longer the case. The big donor agencies have usually responded by suspending development aid and substituting some kind of emergency or relief assistance. Now, as the author shows, there are calls to make relief more development-oriented and for it to address the underlying conflicts which cause these crises. But she concludes from her investigations on the ground in a number of countries that relief and development aid are very distinct processes. In the absence of public policy-making authorities, aid becomes highly fragmented, often inadequate in scale, and certainly not capable of building local sustainability for particular programmes.

The international aid system, Macrae concludes, faces real dilemmas and remains ill-equipped to respond to the peculiar challenges of quasi-statehood that characterize chronic political emergencies and their aftermath.

An important book for policy makers, scholars and students of the development process wrestling with 'real world' issues of aid delivery.

About the Author

Joanna Macrae is a Research Fellow at the Overseas Development Institute. Over the past decade she has conducted a wide range of research and evaluations looking at how aid works in conflict settings, and how these responses reflect wider changes in international relations. In addition to extensive work on donor policy in this area, she has also conducted fieldwork in the Balkans, Cambodia, Ethiopia, Sudan and West Africa. She is co-editor, with Anthony Zwi, of *War and Hunger: Rethinking International Responses to Complex Emergencies*, and with Helen Young of *Disasters: The Journal of Disaster Studies, Policy and Management*.

. . . .

Aiding Recovery? The Crisis of Aid in Chronic Political Emergencies

Joanna Macrae

. . . .

Zed Books

LONDON AND NEW YORK

in association with

Overseas Development Institute

LONDON

Aiding Recovery? The Crisis of Aid in Chronic Political Emergencies was first published by Zed Books Ltd, 7 Cynthia Street, London N1 9JF, UK and Room 400, 175 Fifth Avenue, New York, NY 10010, USA in 2001.

In association with the Overseas Development Institute (ODI), 111 Westminster Bridge Road, London SE1 7JD

Distributed in the USA exclusively by Palgrave, a division of St Martin's Press, LLC, 175 Fifth Avenue, New York, NY 10010, USA

Cover designed by Andrew Corbett
Set in Monotype Dante by Ewan Smith, London
Printed and bound in the United Kingdom by Biddles Ltd, Guildford and King's Lynn

A catalogue record for this book is available from the British Library.
Library of Congress Cataloging-in-Publication Data: applied for

ISBN 1 85649 940 5 cased
ISBN 1 85649 941 3 limp

Contents

List of Tables, Figures and Boxes / vii
Acknowledgements / ix
Abbreviations and Acronyms / xii

1   *Introduction*   1

2   *Aid, War and the State: 1945–89*   7

Decolonisation, developmentalism and the invention of aid, 1945–70 /9   Developmentalism and the economic crisis of the 1970s /13   Adjusting to quasi-states: aid and the Cold War thaw /15

3   *Aid Beyond the State: The Emergence of a 'New' Aid Orthodoxy*   24

The need for a new aid paradigm /24   The evolution of a new orthodoxy: relief, development and war /31 The new orthodoxy: a preliminary critique /37

4   *The Context of Recovery: An Overview of War and its Impact in Cambodia, Ethiopia and Uganda*   48

War, the state and international relations in Cambodia /50 War, the state and international relations in Ethiopia 1974–91 /53   War, the state and international relations in Uganda /58   Public health: needs and response in quasi-states /61

5   *The Legitimacy Dilemma: Aid in a Vacuum*   73

In search of a constitution for decision-making: Cambodia /74   International aid for health sector rehabilitation in Ethiopia /87   International aid for health sector rehabilitation in Uganda /103   Different folks, same strokes: issues and implications /110

6   *The Sustainability Dilemma*   *120*

Defining sustainability and its determinants / 122   Public
finance and international aid: the determinants of financial
sustainability of the health sector in Cambodia, Ethiopia
and Uganda / 122   Investing in development? / 132
Maintaining the myth: systems and strategies of rehabilitation
planning / 143

7   *Conclusion*   *154*

War, peace and politics: from 'post'-conflict transition to
chronic political emergencies / 155   'Linking relief and
development' aid: towards a political analysis of aid in
conflict / 158   Operational implications / 162
A healthy peace? Lessons for public health policy / 164

References   *173*
Index   *186*

Tables, Figures and Boxes

Tables

4.1 Direct and indirect impacts of political violence on health and health systems 61

4.2 The impact of political violence on health services 62

5.1 Conditions of sovereignty and legitimation in the immediate 'post'-conflict period in Cambodia, Ethiopia and Uganda 111

6.1 Summary of key factors determining the availability of national health resources in Cambodia, Ethiopia and Uganda compared with average least developed country 129

Figures

3.1 Official emergency aid flows (excluding food aid), 1980–96 26

3.2 Emergency aid as a percentage of total official aid flows (excluding food aid), 1980–96 27

6.1 Military and public health expenditure in Cambodia, 1989–95 124

6.2 Aid to Cambodia from socialist bloc and OECD countries, 1970–95 125

6.3 Total receipts of official development assistance to Uganda, 1971–95 126

6.4 Total net receipts of official development assistance to Ethiopia, 1971–94 127

6.5 Ugandan Ministry of Health expenditure for selected years as a proportion of the 1979 budget 127

6.6 Cambodian government expenditure on health, 1989–95 128

6.7 Government of Ethiopia total recurrent expenditure on health 128

6.8 Government and aid expenditure on health in Cambodia, 1992–95 131

6.9 Government and aid expenditure on health in Ethiopia, 1989–93 131

7.1 The political and aid continua 156

Boxes

5.1 The goals and objectives of health policy in Cambodia, 1992 80

5.2 Main tenets of Ugandan Ten-year Health Plan, 1991 106

For my parents,
Garth, Freya, Myles and Catherine,
and in memory of Charles

Acknowledgements

The research reported here was started in late 1992. During the course of the series of studies it reports, I have been extraordinarily privileged in terms of the colleagues with whom I've worked, the opportunities to visit Cambodia, Ethiopia and Uganda, as well as Europe and the USA, and the people met there.

Without the support of Anthony Zwi, there would be no book. He took a risk in supporting me at a critical stage of my career, for which I will always be very grateful. Other colleagues in the Health Policy Unit at the London School of Hygiene and Tropical Medicine were also generous in the time and intellectual energy needed to develop a new area of work. In particular: Anne Mills, Lucy Gilson and Gill Walt. Felicity Cutts, also at the School, provided an important opportunity to contribute to teaching on health and complex political emergencies. The ensuing contacts with students who brought with them a wealth of experience provided an important testing bed for some of the ideas presented here.

Moving to the Overseas Development Institute (ODI) in 1995 enabled me to put ideas regarding health systems in unstable environments into the broader context of humanitarian policy. John Borton has proved an invaluable mentor over the last five years, persuading me to overcome my fear of numbers and to use them, and to value history and geography as much as philosophy! Since 1996, the Humanitarian Policy Group at the ODI has expanded considerably, and my newer colleagues have proved patient as I have repeatedly buried my head in the sand of the doctorate that is the basis of this book. I am also grateful to Simon Maxwell, who allowed me to absent myself from the office for five months, enabling me to tie the final strands.

The fieldwork for this study could not have been undertaken without the support of the following people. In Uganda, Lucie Blok and

Martin Bottelier opened their home and generously shared their ideas; Jacqueline Hoojimaijers and the local HealthNet staff in Soroti proved very generous hosts; Dean Schuey and Henry Bagarukayo of AMREF facilitated fieldwork in Luwero. Tom Barton of the Child Health Development Centre, Makerere University, provided access to an invaluable collection of documents. Frances Mwesigye, Sam Okounzi and David Kistu Kewessa all provided critical comments on drafts, adding further insights and clarifying interpretation.

In Cambodia, Stephen Lanjouw acted as the principal field investigator, thoroughly trawling a seemingly endless primary documentation and conducting a large number of interviews. His wife Choo and son Nick provided hospitality and entertainment during my all too brief visits. Penelope Key and Julian Lob-Levyt of what is now the UK Department for International Development (DFID) provided crucial logistical and financial support for the study. Georg Petersen, Country Representative of the World Health Organisation (WHO) was uniformly hospitable and encouraging, as were Mauritz van Peltz and Mit Philips of Médecins Sans Frontières (MSF). Most particular thanks are due to Dr Oum Sophal, director of the National Centre for Health Research, for hosting the study.

In Ethiopia, Abdelhamid Bedri Kello, at the Institute for Development Research, Addis Ababa University, hosted the study. Dr Wedson Mwambasi, Country Representative of WHO, became a friend and avid supporter of the work, as did Sandro Loretti. Gebre ab Barnabas also shared his family, history and his passion for Ethiopia and for the future of its health services. Christian Gunneberg, Save the Children Fund-UK in Harar, kindly welcomed us to his home and provided great insights into emerging health policy in the region. Oxfam, Save the Children Fund and UNICEF all contributed to the costs of a small workshop to launch the study in July 1995, for which the research team was most grateful.

More broadly the research draws on a patchwork of projects and associated funding. David Daniels and Egbert Sondorp, then of HealthNet International, enabled us to make the first tentative steps in the research in Uganda in 1993. David Nabarro, then head of Health and Population of what was then the Overseas Development Administration (ODA), enabled us to follow this up with funding for a more generic review of health sector rehabilitation aid, so funding the first round of interviews with the donor community in 1994 and the preparation of the Cambodia study. The European Commission funded the Ethiopia case, which formed part of a comparative study with El Salvador. The Cambodia case study was funded by the Health and Population Division, ODA. Although not originally planned, the research benefited from a second round of interviews with donor agencies and international organisations, conducted as part of a study commissioned by UNICEF in 1998. Many thanks are due to the Emergency Health Action team at WHO – in particular Dr Harald Siem – which funded the five-month sabbatical that gave me the time to complete the analysis and writing up.

Over the past five years there have been a number of people who have shaped my analysis profoundly and without whose insights this would have ended up a very different piece of work. Most particularly, Mark Bradbury, Mark Duffield and Nicholas Stockton. Barbara Hendrie cast her critical eye over earlier drafts, helping to refine and clarify the analysis at a critical stage. Catherine Spencer has been infinitely patient and generous in her support; in addition to reading drafts, she and Charles put up with repeated invasions of their house as I sought peace and space.

My most grateful thanks go to my supervisor, Kelley Lee, who has shown the most extraordinary commitment to this research. Her stamina, intellectual rigour and unfailingly generous support have sustained the process. Finally, all my love and thanks to Garth Dixon, without whose encouragement, patience and practical support I would have given up long ago.

Abbreviations and Acronyms

AMREF	African Medical Relief
CFSP	Common Foreign and Security Policy
CGDK	Coalition Government of Democratic Kampuchea
CHA	Community Health Agent
CoCom	Coordinating Committee (for health in Cambodia)
CPP	Cambodian People's Party
DAC	Development Assistance Committee (of the OECD)
DANIDA	Danish International Development Agency
DFID	Department for International Development (formerly Overseas Development Administration) – UK
DHA	Department of Humanitarian Affairs (United Nations)
DP	Democratic Party
EC	European Commission
ECOMOG	Economic Community (of West Africa) Monitoring Group
ELF	Eritrean Liberation Front
EPI	Expanded Programme of Immunisation
EPLF	Eritrean People's Liberation Front
EPRDF	Ethiopian People's Revolutionary Democratic Front
ERA	Eritrean Relief Association
ERP	Emergency Rehabilitation Project
ERRP	Emergency Relief and Reconstruction Programme
ESAF	Enhanced Structural Adjustment Facility
FHP	Family Health Project
FUNCINPEC	United National Front for the Independent, Neutral and Peace Cooperative Cambodia
IASC	Inter-Agency Standing Committee
ICRC	International Committee of the Red Cross
IDA	International Development Association
IMF	International Monetary Fund

KNUFNS	Kampuchean National United Front of National Salvation
KPNLF	Khmer People's National Liberation Front
LDC	less developed country
MOH	Ministry of Health
MSF	Médecins Sans Frontières
NATO	North Atlantic Treaty Organisation
NGO	non-governmental organisation
NRA	National Resistance Army
NRC	National Resistance Council
NRM	National Resistance Movement
oda	official development assistance
ODA	Overseas Development Administration (UK)
OECD	Organisation for Economic Cooperation and Development
OFDA	Office of Foreign Disaster Assistance – USAID
OLF	Oromo Liberation Front
OTI	Office of Transition Initiatives – USAID
PA	Peasants' Association (Ethiopia)
PHC	primary health care
Prococoms	Provincial Coordinating Committees
RC	Resistance Committee (Uganda)
REST	Relief Society of Tigray
SAF	structural adjustment facility
SCF	Save the Children Fund
SEPHA	Special Emergency Programme for the Horn of Africa
SIDA	Swedish International Development Agency
SNC	Supreme National Council (Cambodia)
SOC	State of Cambodia
SRSG	Special Representative of the Secretary-General (of the United Nations)
TAC	Technical Advisory Committee (of the Supreme National Council, Cambodia)
TGE	Transitional Government of Ethiopia
TPLF	Tigrayan People's Liberation Front
UK	United Kingdom
UN	United Nations
UNAMIC	United Nations Advance Mission in Cambodia
UNDP	United Nations Development Programme

UNHCR	United Nations High Commissioner for Refugees
UNICEF	United Nations Children's Fund
UNOCHA	United Nations Office for the Coordination of Humanitarian Affairs (formerly DHA)
UNTAC	United Nations Transitional Authority in Cambodia
UPA	Ugandan People's Army
UPDA	Ugandan People's Democratic Army
UPC	Uganda People's Congress
USA	United States of America
USAID	United States Agency for International Development
WFP	World Food Programme
WHO	World Health Organisation

Probably the most important things about post-conflict situations is the particular psychology attached to them. Everyone thinks we must do something now. But all of this ceremony doesn't mean anything has changed. It is still the same. It will continue to be awful despite this frenetic activity.

Interview, World Bank official, Washington, DC, June 1994

CHAPTER I

. . . .

Introduction

§ It is a truism that the Cold War was a primary force in shaping the evolution of the international aid system. For nearly five decades confrontation between the superpowers, the USA and the Soviet Union, provided part of the rationale for official development assistance (oda). It also influenced the distribution of resources and determined the rules according to which they could be given. It is no surprise, therefore, that the end of the Cold War effectively removed many of the conceptual and operational pillars on which aid had been built. Most fundamentally it raised the question of why aid was needed at all.

The inability of the aid establishment to answer this question convincingly was reflected in the relatively sharp downward trend in oda flows during the late 1980s and into the 1990s. In this context, the international aid community has sought a new justification for continued assistance.

This search for a new aid paradigm (OECD 1993) has taken place in an environment characterised, if not by an increasing number of wars *per se*[1] (Sivard 1993; Wallensteen and Sollenberg 1995), at least by chronic and worsening insecurity in many recipient countries, particularly in Africa. In addition, the break-up of the Soviet Union spawned a new wave of conflicts, some of them very near to the doorsteps of Western European powers.

The ending of the Cold War provided new space to acknowledge the problem of violent conflict, an issue that had remained virtually absent from the aid agenda during the previous 'development decades'. This was despite the fact that over 23 million people died as a direct result of war between 1945 and 1992, and that the peak in war-related mortality occurred in the 1950s, not in the 1990s (Sivard 1993).

As international debate has grown regarding conflict and its impact on development, so the end of the Cold War has also opened new space for aid action in conflict zones. Freed from the straitjacket of bipolar politics, international actors, including aid actors, stretched previously unused muscles and initiated a series of experiments that sought to identify tools to prevent and resolve armed conflicts, and to mitigate their effects. These have included new military and political instruments, such as sanctions (for example, those against Iraq and Serbia); peace enforcement (for example in Bosnia Herzegovina after 1994, and in Sierra Leone after 1996); regional peace-keeping (for example, in Liberia and Sierra Leone); culminating in the 'humanitarian' war in Kosovo, fought by NATO (the North Atlantic Treaty Organisation) against the Federal Republic of Yugoslavia in 1999. With the partial exception of Iraq, all of these interventions have been undertaken in response to conflicts taking place *within* the borders of sovereign states.

Albeit selectively, these interventions have signalled the tentative, and sometimes faltering, emergence of a greater consensus within the international community, or at least among Western governments, that extensive violation of human rights by governments is not acceptable. Where governments are implicated in such violations, their sovereignty no longer protects them absolutely from international intervention. Rather, state sovereignty has become conditional, and may be violated by international actors claiming a 'just cause' (Clapham 1996).

This context of international political experimentation, and of chronic instability in many aid-receiving countries, has shaped the formation of what has been described as a 'new' aid paradigm during the 1990s. Until the mid-1980s, the primary response of the aid community to conflict was to provide emergency assistance. This was designed primarily as a palliative for the humanitarian crises associated with contemporary wars. During the 1990s, however, an orthodoxy emerged that aid can and should play an active role in responding to conflict (Macrae 1998). In addition to its palliative role, new claims have been made regarding its potential contribution to the prevention and resolution of conflict (see, for example, Boutros-Ghali 1992; European Commission 1996; OECD 1997). These claims regarding the role of aid in conflict management have become intertwined with a parallel debate regarding the relationship between emergency assistance and more developmental forms of aid. Again, a consensus is emerging that aid can and should seek to fulfil a more developmental role in conflict situations and that, in so doing, it may play an important role in addressing the root causes of conflict.

This book is about this emerging orthodoxy: namely that international aid can and should play a role in the management of conflict, and that, in conflict situations, it can and should adopt developmental principles and approaches.

The book adopts a two-pronged approach to analysing this orthodoxy. The first, more theoretical, strand traces the evolution of this area of aid policy, situating it in historical context and analysing comparatively the increasingly vast array of policy documentation emerging from official agencies in relation to aid and conflict.

This analysis, discussed primarily in Chapters 2 and 3, draws on three main sources of evidence. First, there is an extensive review of secondary sources on development and humanitarian aid, and their role in conflict management. Second, a wide-ranging review of primary sources of aid policy statements and reports has been carried out, focusing primarily on the United States, the United Kingdom, the European Commission, the Development Assistance Committee of the OECD and the United Nations (UN). A comparative analysis of these sources forms a primary focus of the original research. Finally, primary and secondary sources of material have been complemented by extensive, semi-structured interviews with key informants in key bilateral as well as multilateral aid agencies (the United Nations and Bretton Woods institutions) at headquarters level in the United States, the United Kingdom, Switzerland and Belgium.

A key objective of this strand of the analysis was to identify more precisely the novelty of the 'new aid paradigm', and to scrutinise its conceptual base. It thus presents a critical history of development assistance with an emerging literature concerned with the changing nature and conceptualisation of statehood. In doing so, it establishes an analytical framework within which the findings of the case studies (see below) can be understood, which should prove useful in assessing future aid policy and practice in unstable settings.

Specifically, the research has drawn upon the work of Robert Jackson (1990) and Christopher Clapham (1996), both of whom describe the changing nature of Third World states and the way in which their international relations are conditioned by evolving interpretations of sovereignty. These authors highlight the fact that, during the Cold War, international relations were mediated by an unconditional respect for sovereignty. This respect derived in part from the conditions of decolonisation, and assumed that newly independent countries would replicate the Western norms that were seen to define sovereignty, namely control of territory and the ability to raise and redistribute resources for the public good. Both these aspects of sovereignty – juridical and empirical – have been severely tested by political and economic circumstances in developing countries, and by changes in the geopolitical landscape.

While the normative conclusions of Jackson's (1990) work are not shared by this research,[2] as a descriptive tool, the concept of quasi-statehood he proposes provides useful insights into the debate regarding aid policy and practice in conflict-affected countries. 'Quasi-states' are those states whose capacity to govern their territory is compromised to a greater or lesser extent by a lack of resources and institutional failure. The legitimacy of these states is often questioned internally, particularly in those situations where governments are responsible for widespread repression and human rights abuses. At the most extreme, the lack of legitimate and competent government is associated with violence against the state itself. As Clapham (1996) argues, the idea of quasi-statehood may also be applied to state-like entities, for example rebel movements, which control territory and carry out state-like functions, but lack the juridical status of sovereign governments.

In brief, and as explained in greater depth in Chapters 2 and 3, the problem for aid policy-makers working in conflict-affected countries is that the aid system lacks the legal, institutional and operational tools to engage effectively in 'quasi-states'. Like other aspects of international relations, the conceptual and organisational basis of official aid remains premised on the assumption that a benign, sovereign government is in place within the recipient country that has the legitimacy and the capacity to distribute aid resources. As these chapters describe, since the mid-1980s the aid system has adapted in some significant ways to respond to the reality of the problem of quasi-statehood. However, the critical analysis of current aid theory and policy presented here identifies a number of significant weaknesses in current claims regarding the role of aid in conflict-affected environments. In particular, it argues that the transition in aid from relief to development mode implies a resolution of the issue of statehood and the legitimacy of incumbent authorities.

Having laid out the theoretical framework, and described and analysed the current global aid policy context, the book presents a series of case studies that highlight the challenges of providing aid in unstable settings. This second major strand of the research focuses on a particular subset of unstable settings, namely those where, following a lengthy conflict, there has been a process of transition to relative peace, signalled by a negotiated settlement or change of regime by force. These contexts, often referred to as situations of 'post'-conflict transition, can be seen as a particular type of quasi-state.

Reviewing the experience of three countries (Cambodia, Ethiopia and Uganda), the research focuses on the role of international assistance in the rehabilitation of public health services. Looking at international support for public services in situations of 'post-conflict transition' provides a number of insights into many of the current questions facing aid policy-makers and practitioners in situations of weak and contested statehood. The case studies analysed how priorities for rehabilitation assistance were identified and by whom, and on what basis aid resources were allocated to different types of intervention and institutions. In other words, what constitutes 'public policy' and who makes it in situations of 'post-conflict transition', where statehood is contested and public institutions are weak? Further, in the context of weak state structures, the legitimacy of which is often questioned by external actors, what mechanisms were used to coordinate international assistance? How significant were international resources in financing health sector rehabilitation, and to what extent did these investments contribute to the emergence of sustainable health systems? And finally, how did relief and development aid instruments and institutions link together in terms of their objectives, working methods and in relation to specific projects?

The research has adopted a comparative approach, looking at the workings of rehabilitation aid in three countries: Cambodia (focusing on the period 1989–93), Uganda (focusing on the period 1986–92), and Ethiopia (1991–94). In each of the three case studies, extensive semi-structured interviews were undertaken with government officials from relevant ministries, the United Nations agencies, the World Bank and bilateral agencies and with representatives of NGOs at headquarters in the respective capitals, and in selected districts.

The material from the case studies is presented in Chapters 4, 5 and 6. Chapter 4 describes the context of transition in the case study countries, providing a brief history of the conflicts and their impact on the national political economies. It continues by analysing the nature of the challenge of 'post'-conflict rehabilitation.

Chapter 5 focuses on what is described as the 'legitimacy dilemma'. In situations of 'post'-conflict transition, and in countries experiencing chronic political emergencies more generally, aid actors are faced with the difficult question of identifying who has the legitimate authority to make decisions regarding the allocation and control of international assistance. It analyses the political conditions under which international assistance was provided, and in particular the process by which the regime changes in the three countries were legitimised by international actors. It argues that it was these political questions of juridical and empirical sovereignty and of international legitimation that determined the form of aid provided, the channels through which it was disbursed and the systems for its management.

Chapter 6 analyses how the particular nature of rehabilitation aid determines the sustainability of aid interventions in contexts of 'post'-conflict transition. It concludes that rehabilitation aid is inherently unsustainable, raising the question of who should be responsible when rehabilitation interventions prove difficult to finance in the medium term. Chapter 7 draws together the theoretical and emprical strands, identifying key lessons for future aid theory, policy and practice in unstable settings.

Notes

1. Wallensteen and Sollenberg (1995) note that the definition of war is that there are more than one thousand battle-related deaths. Their analysis of trends in warfare during the 1990s is that the number of conflicts actually declined, rather than increased as is commonly perceived. Their data are significant in highlighting the problem of defining war (perhaps accounting for the more commonly used synonym of 'conflict' in many aid policy documents) where many of the deaths are of civilians rather than soldiers, and where the distinction between the two is often breaking down.

2. I am grateful to David Moore for his comments regarding the interpretation of Jackson's work.

. . . .

CHAPTER 2

Aid, War and the State: 1945–89

§ Since the early 1990s, the aid community has published an almost bewildering array of policy statements and held innumerable meetings and conferences claiming a new-found role in conflict management and new opportunities for developmental approaches to relief in conflict situations (see, for example, Boutros-Ghali 1992; Buchanan-Smith and Maxwell 1994; Netherlands 1993; OECD 1997; Overseas Development Administration 1996). While differing to varying degrees in their terminology and objectives, NGOs and the bilateral and multilateral aid bodies are moving towards a consensus regarding the links between aid and conflict prevention and resolution, and between relief and development assistance.

The concepts of 'human security' (Boutros-Ghali 1992, 1994; OECD 1993) and 'structural stability' (OECD 1997) are now widely used to describe the goal of official development assistance. These terms aim to capture the interlinkages between the political, economic, social and environmental aspects of development, and claim to go beyond the economism that previously dominated the development discourse. They also seek to place the issue of development within the wider, political framework of international security in the post-Cold War era.

This chapter aims to place these concepts of human security, and the subsequent claims regarding the role of aid in those situations where security has broken down, into historical context. It provides a framework against which to assess the extent to which claims regarding the role of aid in the management of conflict represents a significant paradigmatic shift in development theory and practice. In adopting such an historical approach, it aims to test the claim implicit in many current policy statements that the problem of conflict is new, or at least that there is a new role for aid in responding to it. If, as appears to be the case, aid has *always* claimed to serve a role in the regulation of conflict but has achieved limited success in so doing, it will be important to understand why, if its effectiveness is to be enhanced.

A theme running through this chapter is that the organisation and objectives of the international aid system have been a function of broader international political and economic relations. Not only have aid objectives been shaped by the foreign policy and commercial interests of major powers, the modalities of aid have reflected the goals and rules of international relations. In other words, it is not only the *content* of aid policy that has been influenced by international political considerations: its very *form* – its instrumentation and legal basis – derives from key assumptions about the conduct of inter-national relations.

During the Cold War, international relations were largely regulated by the principle of state sovereignty. Aid relations were also organised according to this principle and assumed the existence of a benign and sovereign state. In the post-Cold War era the political landscape has changed, challenging fundamentally the goals and working methods of aid agencies, particularly in conflict-affected countries.

There is now growing recognition of the crisis of statehood in many aid-receiving countries, characterised by weak public institutions, the limited ability of governments to raise and redistribute revenues, varying ability to control all territory and maintain law and order and, in a considerable number of cases, extensive violence perpetrated by different groups including governmental authorities. In other words, the sovereignty of governments is being challenged *de facto* by their perceived illegitimacy and inability to govern effectively.

Coinciding with these changes in the political formations inside aid-receiving countries, the post-Cold War era has seen major changes in the rules guiding relations between sovereign states, particularly those between North and South. Unconditional respect for sovereignty acted as the conceptual cornerstone for the regulation of international relations during the Cold War. Its removal makes for a volatile and potentially unpredictable international political economy.

The task of this chapter is to articulate how the paradigm that has dominated development assistance for five decades – developmentalism – has been underpinned by a conceptual and operational reliance on the state. This reliance reflected the wider political context of the Cold War. Chapter 3 describes and analyses the evolution of aid policy in conflict situations in the post-Cold War era.

Decolonisation, Developmentalism and the Invention of Aid, 1945–70

'Sovereignty': its meaning and function in the post-colonial era A sovereign state is defined as a bordered territory occupied by a settled population under effective government (Jackson 1990: 38). The sovereignty of states comprises two elements: juridical and empirical. While the juridical element is absolute, the empirical element is not. Jackson expresses it as follows:

> The language of sovereign statehood is categorical and not contingent. This is consistent with legal language generally. To say that sovereignty is an absolute condition, for example, is the same as saying that marriage or any other formal relationship is absolute: one either is or is not a married person, a baptized Catholic, a Bachelor of Arts ... Legal language is different from sociological language in the same way that marriage differs from sexual relations, baptism from submersion, a BA from learning ... the first category invokes a status, whereas the latter is merely description. (1990: 33)

The empirical element (the ability to govern) is more complex, implying at a minimum an ability to control all the territory within the defined borders of the state, to exercise law and order in order to protect the population, and to raise and redistribute revenue.

As Clapham (1996) points out, both these criteria of statehood were idealised, and did not correspond with the reality of statehood in the imperial powers themselves, whose only history of statehood had been extremely volatile, often characterised by oppression by governmental authorities. However, he argues, important in shaping internal relationships between societies and their governments, and between the governments of different countries are not only the reality of sovereignty and statehood, but perceptions of what they are and ought to be.

The end of the Second World War sounded the death knell of colonialism. The right to self-determination, embodied in the Charter of the newly established United Nations, removed the empirical condition of 'capacity to govern' in defining sovereignty. It provided for the handover of colonially defined states to national and political authorities on the basis of equality of nations (Clapham 1996; Jackson 1990). Decolonisation signalled a massive expansion in the number of players in the international system. By the mid-1950s, 87 of the total 122 member states of the United Nations were developing countries (Spero 1977).

The newly sovereign states played the game of international relations on equal terms with their former colonial rulers, at least in juridical terms. While they were lacking in economic power, what the newly independent powers shared were the valuable rights associated with 'negative sovereignty'. Negative sovereignty is the expression of the right to self-determination. It can be seen as the corollary of the juridical and external component of sovereignty. The right to non-intervention in internal affairs derived from an explicit rejection of the colonial claims of legitimate intervention (Jackson 1990). Clapham (1996) argues that the principle of self-determination of all states – in other words, unconditional sovereignty – was not simply a triumph of idealism over the racism of colonialism. Rather, this idealism coincided with the requirements of a new world order, characterised by the Cold War.

Respect for sovereignty can be seen to have provided a means of regulating the conduct of the Cold War militarily and politically. In political terms, the equality of states provided under the new rules of sovereignty proved mutually beneficial to the superpowers, enabling them to generate spheres of influence through the pure weight in numbers of sovereign allies backing their positions in international forums such as the United Nations. Militarily, respect for negative sovereignty also provided a means of curbing overt invasions of second countries and so reducing the risks of direct military confrontation by the superpowers.

The recognition of the legitimacy of a sovereign body, expressed in the right of non-interference, is, as Clapham puts it:

> not just an empty formula, but gives access not only to seats in international organisations with high prestige but rather doubtful power, but to the ability to make real deals involving real resources. (1996: 22)

These resources include national resources such as the revenue from taxation, but also international resources, including official assistance.

Reinforcing sovereignty: the role and function of international assistance, 1945–70 Official development assistance formed part of this rubric of sovereignty and Cold War realpolitik. Jackson (1990) contends that an important motivation for the establishment of development assistance after the Second World War was to buttress the empirical sovereignty of newly independent states – in other words, to enable them to develop their capacity to achieve the idealised model of sovereignty assumed by Western powers.

Such an analysis provides a political correlate to the economic theory of modernisation that dominated the emerging development theory of the 1950s. Modernisation theorists drew on Darwinian theories of biological evolution to propose a version of social evolutionism. This asserted that all societies change according to a pre-established pattern, the logic and direction of which are known, unidirectional and linear (Nederveen Pieterse 1991). Rostow (1971), a leading advocate of modernisation theory, proposed two fundamental variations on the evolutionist theme, however. First, he suggested that social change is neither inevitable nor necessarily progressive. Second, in contrast to the more deterministic stance of evolutionism, he believed that external intervention could influence the outcome of social development (Nederveen Pieterse 1991).

Modernisation theorists acknowledged that the process of development was inherently turbulent, carrying with it a risk of conflict (Larrain 1989). They argued that such conflict arose because change is asynchronic, with not all members of a particular society benefiting equally or simultaneously from the fruits of development. However, modernisation theorists assumed that the final stage of modernisation, the achievement of full democracy – or, in Jackson's terms, empirical statehood – would yield structures capable of conflict resolution. In the meantime, according to Rostow (1971), the victims of modernisation needed to be compensated if they were not to be seduced by the appeal of communism and revolution.

In the context of a deepening Cold War, the work of Rostow and others provided the beginnings of a conceptual basis that would be used to justify the transfer of public resources from the rich countries of Western Europe and North America to the Third World. It presented a political rationale to what had previously remained an economic argument. In the immediate post-war years, the USA had resisted calls from those who had called for such assistance. It had argued that, while loans on 'soft' terms might overcome the problem of scarce capital seen as a primary obstacle to modernisation, international transfers would distort these emerging economies and block the development of sustainable and equitable trade networks (Angelli and Murphy 1988).

However, in a context of worrying geopolitical trends, US policy-makers reconsidered their positions. The creation of the People's Republic of China (1949), the outbreak of the Korean War (1950) and the establishment of a Soviet foreign aid programme (1953) forced a re-examination of isolationist policies in the USA (Angelli and Murphy 1988). Direct conflict between the two superpowers was no longer seen as the primary threat to the West. Rather the priority was to secure spheres of influence, in other words to create strategic alliances with other states. Thus, in the early 1950s, the USA was persuaded to support demands from the Third World that they should be entitled to receive grants and loans from the newly established International Bank for Reconstruction and Development, later more commonly known as the World Bank (Ruttan 1996).

International assistance provided a tangible means of building links with allied regimes. It also provided a direct means of enabling fragile, new states to reinforce their sovereign claims – in part by contributing to their internal legitimacy, for example through the provision of basic services, in part by enabling those identified with juridical sovereignty – typically those in possession of the capital cities – with the means to enforce control (Angelli and Murphy 1988; Clapham 1996; Ruttan 1996).

During the early years of development assistance the link between aid and security was overt, therefore, in both the founding traditions of the international aid regime. On the one hand, liberal internationalists pointed to the economic factors that had contributed to the Second World War. Underdevelopment, inequality and economic instability were seen as important causes of conflict. The rationale for the creation of the United Nations and its development agencies and the Bretton Woods institutions was to address these factors through international cooperation (Ruttan 1996). At the same time, political realists saw such investments as a means of controlling the expansion of communism. In other words, there was a marriage of convenience between the liberal internationalists and the realists, both of whom claimed that aid could and would serve a role in the prevention of conflict in the Third World, and ultimately beyond. As discussed in Chapter 3, a similar convergence of interest is becoming apparent in relation to the contemporary version of 'aid as peace-maker' proposed since the 1990s.

Importantly, such an alliance could be sustained because, despite their apparent political differences, disparate groups of development theorists and practitioners, and indeed their successors, shared a common paradigm: developmentalism. Nederveen Pieterse (1991) notes that the apparently conflicting theories of modernisation, with their roots in political realism, and the Marxist and neo-Marxist theories of dependency and internationalism that grew up through the 1960s and 1970s, share the same umbrella. He argues that all these approaches remained grounded in an assumption that the path and the outcome of development were known, and that it resembled closely the experience of Western, developed states.

A further important point of common reference for these apparently divergent schools was their shared commitment to the state as the vehicle for development. While differing in their preference for the political hue of regimes, both modernisationists and Marxists shared the assumption, that, at least in the medium term, the mechanism for modernisation was that of sovereign governments.

Developmentalism and the Economic Crisis of the 1970s

The upheavals in the international political economy of the 1970s did much to discredit the version of modernisation promoted by Rostow. Struggling to finance the Vietnam War, the USA devalued the dollar in 1971, a measure that increased US competitiveness in world markets, but had a corresponding recessionary effect in other Western countries, and indeed in the Third World (Angelli and Murphy 1988). Efforts to address internal structural imbalances in the American economy coincided with a series of external shocks to the world economy. Between 1971 and 1974 the price of oil increased approximately tenfold (Spero 1977). These price increases were felt most acutely in the oil-importing countries of the Third World, which were forced to devote an ever larger share of scarce hard currency to buying oil and oil-related products.[1]

The decade also saw a mounting crisis of world food supply, and in particular growing dependence of many countries of the Third World on the West to meet the gaps in food supply. Between 1949 and 1951 twelve million tonnes of grain were imported by the South. In 1972, 36 million tonnes were imported. This also placed considerable strain on the balance of payments in developing countries, and further increased the political leverage of the West over developing countries.

During the 1970s, the political function of aid, confidently asserted in previous decades, became hidden behind what Cox (1992) describes as functionalism, reframing aid debates in the apparently technical language of economics rather than appealing directly to a political rationale (Griffin 1991). In the midst of economic crisis, the emphasis of development theory and practice was on adjusting the mechanisms by which aid was delivered and on defining a new, technical language for its achievement. In moves that were to prefigure the advent of structural adjustment programmes in the 1980s, the USA in particular began to place the emphasis on creating an enabling environment for economic growth through a series of economic policy reforms (Angelli and Murphy 1988). Variously known as 'redistribution with growth' and 'basic needs approach', this generation of development theory sought to encourage governments to switch expenditure away from its former focus on basic infrastructure to one concentrating on human capital (Chenery et al. 1974; Streeten 1981).

A driving force behind such policies was an increasing recognition of the failure of earlier versions of modernisation theory to deliver popular legitimacy for some of those governments to which the West was allied (Angelli and Murphy 1988). In this way, elements of the radical discourse on development emerging from the dependency school, particularly in Latin America, were effectively co-opted into the mainstream development discourse (Adelman 1996). Redistribution of wealth was seen to be necessary not as a means of revolution, but as a means of avoiding it. Thus, while the style of overt political engineering proposed by Rostow became unfashionable, development assistance remained a primarily political project. Adelman (1996) quotes

Robert McNamara, president of the World Bank 1968–81, as saying: 'The World Bank took a leading position in formulating poverty alleviation as central to development activities [but was undertaken in good part] *in order to reduce social turmoil and contribute to political stability'* (emphasis added).

Adjusting to Quasi-states: Aid and the Cold War Thaw

Structural adjustment: the privatisation and internationalisation of development The economic crisis of the 1970s continued into the early 1980s. The introduction of monetarist policies in the UK and the USA in the late 1970s and early 1980s served to deepen further the economic crisis confronting the Third World. The recession of this period spread South as import markets declined in the West. By 1982, the Third World's share of global trade had dropped by 2 per cent, while the terms of trade of low-income African countries fell by nearly 14 per cent between 1979 and 1982 (Angelli and Murphy 1988). While trade revenues were falling, the reduction in international liquidity imposed by monetarist policies resulted in a significant increase in interest rates, increasing the debt burden in the Third World. Interest repayments in the Third World doubled between 1979 and 1982 from US$24 billion to US$50 billion (ibid.).

The parlous state of Third World finances, and the dependence it created on the Western-dominated aid system, provided for what Cox (1992) has described as the internationalisation of national economic policies. He argues that this was achieved not only through the dominance provided by economic dependence, but also through a power structure that could be used to shape a consensus between North and South. The shape of this structure was laid down in the 1960s and allowed the penetration of Western states into Third World economic and social decision-making through the provision of expatriate technical assistance (Spero 1977). At the same time, provision of educational opportunities in the West for senior administrators and decision-makers provided for the development of an international policy elite, comprising 'fragments' of states, located in specialist ministries, particularly ministries of finance, and within international and intergovernmental organisations such as the World Bank and the OECD (Cox 1992). Thus a degree of consensus, alongside the potential for coercion implied by dependence, was achieved regarding the model for development and the means for its implementation. What Clapham (1996) has described as mono-economics had arrived in the Third World. This required aid-receiving states to conform to a tightly defined economic prescription of stabilisation and adjustment.

The process by which international policy-makers encroached into the sphere of national policy-making was hegemonic in that it was achieved through a combination of coercion and consensus (Angelli and Murphy 1988; Cox 1992). The attachment of explicit economic conditionalities to continued aid flows signalled a mounting international consensus that aid actors might legitimately intervene in affairs previously seen as in the sovereign domain (see Clapham 1996, in particular Chapter 7; Adelman 1996).

However, within the continued confines of the Cold War, the emphasis on respect for juridical sovereignty remained, as did the essentially apolitical, technocratic character of aid. This had been sustained and deepened during the 1970s and early 1980s. Any move towards an overtly political analysis of the problem of development, particularly one interpreted as potentially sympathetic to the socialist agenda, had been strongly deterred by the USA. Its withdrawal of membership in UNESCO in 1984, for example, sent a clear signal to multilateral agencies regarding their compliance with the neo-liberal agendas of the Thatcher and Reagan eras (Ghebali 1985).

Three factors enabled aid agencies to play a more active role in national policy-making, while also ensuring that they were able to present such encroachments as apolitical. First, the process of adjustment was portrayed as an essentially technical task for which there was no alternative. In other words it was rooted in the consensus between international and national bureaucrats that this was the way forward (Angelli and Murphy 1988; Clapham 1996).

Second, formation of such consensus relied in part on a degree of coercion, explicit and implicit. The extent of states' dependence on international assistance to maintain themselves was not insignificant and therefore increased the leverage of aid agencies.

Finally, and perhaps most significantly in the context of this study, was the ongoing reappraisal of the place of the Third World in the Cold War. During the 1980s the strategic importance of these 'peripheral' states, particularly in Africa, diminished (Clough 1992). In this context the necessity for adhering strictly to international legal niceties regarding sovereignty was also reduced. In this way, the economic conditionalities of the early 1980s signalled increased confidence by the West to intervene directly in the affairs of Third World states.

Clapham (1996) describes how, despite the coercive character of the economic conditionalities in the 1980s, recipient governments maintained one important advantage – they *were* sovereign states. As such, the international aid system remained dependent on states agreeing to their own reform. This counted not only in juridical terms, but in terms of the ability of Third World governments to determine whether and how to implement the reform packages proposed by the international community.

However, the ability of many Third World governments to exercise their sovereign rights effectively was diminished by the very measures designed to achieve developmental reforms. As Inayatullah and Blaney (1995) argue, a precondition for the effective use of sovereignty is the availability of resources to enable the state to function effectively: customs and border guards must be paid, as must ministers, tax collectors and schoolteachers. Even some of the most ardent advocates of the rollback of the state have now acknowledged that economic adjustment policies had a detrimental impact on the basic ability of the state to function (World Bank 1997). However, the acknowledgement of the continued importance of the state has been primarily in relation to poor and inconsistent implementation of public policy by recipient country governments themselves, rather than a fundamental reappraisal of the neo-liberal model itself (Moore 1998).

A paradoxical situation had thus emerged. The neo-liberal preoccupation with economics of the 1980s came to override the realist, political imperative of former decades whereby the maintenance of state structures in whatever form was the priority in order to preserve global balance of power. Despite the application of the neo-liberal economic prescription, social, economic and political conditions continued to deteriorate in much of the Third World during the decade.

In 1960, 26 developing states that were then independent were under some form of military control; by 1982 this number had risen to 52 and it continued to rise to 61 in 1992. These regimes were associated with significantly greater levels of abuse of human rights than were their civilian counterparts, and with higher levels of military expenditure (Sivard 1993). More generally the number of wars continued to rise, peaking in 1985.

In social and economic terms too, prospects for development varied considerably between different regions of the 'Third World' and for different sections of countries' populations. While the 'Tiger economies' of South-East and East Asia expanded rapidly, with concomitant improvements in social indicators, in Africa and parts of Latin America the picture was much less optimistic. Clapham (1996) reports, for example, that in 25 of the 36 countries in Africa for which data are available, food production declined significantly in the period 1980–92, increasing demand from food aid imports from 1.6 to 4.2 million tonnes annually in same period. These imports contributed significantly to the food needs of some 50 million people, or 9 per cent of the population of sub-Saharan Africa (Clapham 1996: 164). Similarly, the debt burden continued to expand throughout the 1980s. From a total of US$5,244 million, the scale of public debt increased to US$48,793 million in 1980 and to US$151,176 million in 1994.

Seeking to mitigate these reversals, welfare safety-nets were introduced to compensate those seen to be most adversely affected by the process of adjustment (Duffield 1991). The programmes were funded through structural adjustment loans, and their conceptualisation carried sharp echoes of Rostow's theories of the 1950s, which had emphasised the need to prevent disaffection among those adversely affected by 'asynchronic' progress. They maintained the developmentalist assertion that progress was inevitable, and thus that any social instability or poverty engendered by reform was necessarily transitory in nature.

Significantly, these compensatory measures were delivered outside the state, largely through NGOs. By the end of the 1980s, total NGO income stood at around US$6 billion, having doubled in real terms since the early 1970s. In the same period, official aid grew from 1 per cent to 35 per cent of NGO income. In net terms, NGOs in the early 1990s were transferring more resources than the World Bank to the Third World. This trend has been described by Duffield (1991) as the 'internationalization and privatization of public welfare', whereby responsibility for the financing and provision of basic services has shifted from the domain of national state structures to that of international NGOs.

Compensating for crisis: the rise of relief as a strategy for aid engagement A particular form of the compensatory package designed to address the effects of economic and political decline is relief aid (Duffield 1991). Duffield (1994a) argues that, far from being conceptually distinct from development assistance, relief aid is grounded in an essentially developmentalist paradigm. Like compensatory packages designed under the rubric of structural adjustment, relief programmes have been premised on the assumption that disasters – natural and man-made – are essentially transitory phenomena, primarily defined in terms of a crisis of material supplies. The assumption is that once the hazard (for example, an earthquake or war) has passed, normal development can be resumed. International responses to complex, conflict-induced emergencies have been shaped largely by models derived from natural disasters. These focus on the delivery of supplies, primarily food and medical assistance, to enable survival during periods of temporary crisis (Duffield 1994c).

During the 1980s, humanitarian aid became the primary means of international engagement in countries affected by severe political crises. The term 'complex emergency' was coined towards the end of the 1980s in Mozambique, and was first used as a conceptual device by the UN to negotiate for equal access to government- and rebel-held territory. By emphasising the multi-causality of the crisis, the primacy of political factors in the causation of the emergency was deliberately understated in order to neutralise the situation and to facilitate access. However, as Duffield (1994b) concludes in his review of the evolution of this terminology, while it is pragmatic, such a device risks masking the fact that where countries do indeed face multiple environmental, economic and political risks, it is the *political* dimension of conflict-related emergencies that makes them particularly deadly. In these environments, not only are disasters intentionally created, warring parties often block populations' access to any relief (Macrae and Zwi 1994). Complex political emergencies can therefore be seen as indicating a particular type of quasi-statehood – one where a government's control over its territory is challenged fundamentally, sometimes to the point that the very institutions of state are destroyed.

Until the mid-1980s, the scope for the provision of international assistance was determined by considerations of sovereignty (Borton 1993). Populations living in conflict-affected regions could receive assistance only in government-held areas or in a second country in which they had sought refuge (Duffield 1994a). Reflecting this trend, it is notable that in 1976 the European Commission channelled over 90 per cent of its relief budget through national governments in affected countries. By the early 1990s, this had fallen to less than 6 per cent (Borton 1993).

This shift away from channelling relief through state channels, especially in conflict-affected countries, is arguably the first systemic response by the international aid system to the problem of violence within quasi-states. Although there was little that was new in governments and non-state entities actively targeting civilians, by the mid-1980s this was taking place against a backdrop of economic decline, a reduced ability of many countries to meet their food needs and increasingly weak public institutions.

The international relief system was able to work in conflict zones, and specifically to avoid working directly through state structures, because of changes in the geopolitical context. The effective military disengagement of the West (and indeed of the Eastern bloc) from Africa in the mid-1980s provided one of the first indications of the gradual ending of the Cold War, and so the demise of absolute respect for sovereign borders (Clough 1992). This provided new opportunities for humanitarian action. Duffield (1994a) notes that some of these first tentative steps towards humanitarian interventionism by official donors were taken in the Horn of Africa. The cross-border operations into rebel-held areas of Ethiopia and what is now Eritrea were organised by indigenous organisations affiliated to the liberation fronts. The aid convoys that crossed into Ethiopian territory from Sudan were illegal, since they were undertaken without the consent of the Ethiopian authorities. Initially the relief effort relied only on private funds from international NGOs and from the diaspora of people from these regions (Duffield and Prendergast 1994; Hendrie 1989). From the late 1980s, however, these agencies received the majority of their funds from USAID and the European Commission (Duffield and Prendergast 1994).

The trends evident in development policy of privatisation and liberalisation of aid were now being extended into the humanitarian sphere. Countries experiencing complex political emergencies could thus be seen to embrace an analysis whereby far from being part of the solution, the state had become part of the problem. Rather than engage with the state in order to affect its reform, to varying degrees, the trend was to work outside it.

Relief aid represented the culmination of this approach. In countries such as Ethiopia after 1974, Cambodia in 1982 and Sudan after 1989, for example, development assistance was virtually suspended by Western countries in protest against the policies of the respective regimes. Only relief, channelled through international organisations, usually private, remained in place. Relief therefore came to symbolise not simply the existence of massive humanitarian need, but an effective questioning of sovereignty. While development assistance implied legitimacy of regimes, relief did not. Despite its anti-state rhetoric, development assistance still conferred legitimacy upon, and required the authority of, state institutions for its implementation. In contrast, relief aid did not. Thus the rise of relief and the evolution of its strategies were a response to the crisis of governance and of welfare in many developing countries. It was also a political message from powerful donor countries to Third World states regarding expected norms of behaviour and the changing rules of international relations.

Summary and Conclusions

Since its inception in the 1950s, official development assistance has formed part of a wider strategy to promote peace and security. This strategy was informed by an idealist perspective, which argued that underdevelopment, economic instability and violation of human rights were significant causes of conflict. It was also espoused by the tradition of political realism, which identified similar threats, but was particularly concerned that these conditions might encourage the emergence of communism. In the context of the Cold War, where the main threat of conflict was seen to be *between* states, the issue was how to bolster sovereignty, particularly in newly independent countries, both empirically and in terms of their external legitimacy. Official development assistance was therefore *a priori* and *a posteriori* state-centred – the state defined both the purpose of aid and the mechanism by which it was delivered.

Despite, or indeed because of, the ambitions and technical effectiveness of the early years of development assistance, the process of decolonisation during the 1960s was associated with optimism. This was short-lived, however, in a context of worldwide recession. The impact of these sustained economic crises on the political economies of many Third World countries was not inconsiderable. As their ability diminished to feed themselves, procure adequate oil and service their debts, so too did the ability of public institutions to function. Rather than being able to govern by consent, coercion became a primary means of maintaining control of authority, reflected in rising military expenditures and an increasing number of military regimes in the Third World.

This crisis of internal legitimacy and capacity of many Third World states was not of itself a primary concern of the wider system of international relations. The principle of negative sovereignty prevented overt interference in national affairs: the issue for external powers, particularly the superpowers, was the extent to which the sovereign power endorsed or threatened their respective political agendas internationally.

The easing of the Cold War meant that the incentives for respecting sovereignty absolutely were declining. In the face of the hegemonic, mono-economics of structural adjustment, economic policy became increasingly internationalised (Clapham 1996; Cox 1992). However, the ability of international aid actors to use this newly opened policy space was limited by two factors. On the one hand, sovereign authorities were still sovereign: aid agencies had neither the wish nor the capacity to substitute for the juridical and executive role of governments. Thus sovereign governments had the ability to influence the extent to which they conformed to international policy prescriptions, and to determine how aid resources were used. A second factor was that the scope of sovereign power to define and execute public policy was increasingly limited in practice. The emergence of parallel economies, rising insecurity and a declining public resource base all meant that the ability of states to function as states were expected to function was declining (Jackson 1990).

In this context, the effort to separate economics from politics, a process aid bureaucracies had assiduously endorsed (Cox 1992), was proving increasingly problematic to sustain in practice. The reality in many recipient countries was that the political conditions did not exist for the delivery of effective development assistance. In the face of an emerging number of quasi-states, and a changing international political economy whereby tolerance of declining human rights records was diminishing, new instruments for aid engagement were required.

Note

1. Spero (1977) reports, for example, that in 1974 oil and oil-related products accounted for 26 per cent, 24 per cent and 20 per cent of imports in Senegal, India and Ethiopia respectively.

CHAPTER 3

. . . .

Aid Beyond the State: The Emergence of a 'New' Aid Orthodoxy

§ Chapter 2 concluded with the assertion that by the mid-1980s there was a crisis of statehood emerging in many developing countries. This was associated with violent and repressive methods of governance, and the inability of many states to meet the basic obligations usually associated with sovereignty. There was also a rising, albeit selective, intolerance regarding poor governance within donor governments and among their publics (Clapham 1996). However, it was not until the latter part of that decade and in the early 1990s, in particular, that the aid community began to formulate a consistent response to the challenge of problem states, particularly those affected by conflict.

This chapter aims to chart the evolution of this process. It is particularly concerned to analyse the extent to which the policy innovations proposed over the past decade represent a significant shift in the state-centred paradigm of developmentalism, which had dominated aid theory and practice for nearly five decades.

The Need for a New Aid Paradigm

In the early 1990s, three factors forced the problem of conflict onto the aid policy agenda. First was the decline in political and financial support for official development assistance. Second, there was an increasingly robust critique of the increasingly predominant response to conflict – relief assistance. A third related, but distinct, point was greater scrutiny of the existing relationship between different elements of the aid system, and between the aid system and foreign and security policy. These factors driving the 'new' aid paradigm are examined in detail below.

The financial bottom line: reversing the fortunes of aid In the introduction to his *Agenda for Development*, the former secretary-general of
the United Nations argued that:

> During the Cold War, competition for influence had stimulated interest
> in development, but that competition to bring development to the
> poorest has ended. Many donors have grown weary of the task. Many
> of the poor are dispirited. Development is in crisis. (Boutros-Ghali 1994)

Similarly, a background paper prepared by the US Congressional Research Service in 1996 argued:

> As a foreign policy tool predominantly used in the past to support
> strategic objectives – often related to the Cold War – foreign aid and
> its supporters have come under increasing pressure to demonstrate
> the program's relevance to the growing concerns of bolstering a
> stronger economy at home, promoting democracy and free markets,
> stabilizing international crises and deal with transitional problems
> among others. (Congress of the United States 1994)

The trends in official development assistance (oda) flows suggested
that concern regarding declining support for the aid project was
justified. The 1990s witnessed a decline in oda flows from the OECD
countries that was unprecedented since the 1960s. Riddell (1997) reports that in 1989 the volume of oda fell by a marginal 0.5 per cent
relative to previous years. Since that time, annual falls in oda have
been much steeper: 3.9 per cent in 1992, 5.4 per cent in 1993, 1.3 per
cent in 1994 and 5.4 per cent in 1994. These figures signalled an
absolute decline in oda. They also represented a sustained fall in the
value of oda relative to the GNP of donor countries. In mid-1996, aid
provided by member states of the OECD had fallen to an average of
0.27 per cent of GNP, less than half the UN target of 0.7 per cent.

It was against this backcloth that increased attention began to be
paid to the costs of conflict to the development process. Researchers
such as Reginald Green (1984) undertook important work to assess
the economic effect of war on Third World economies. This work
was given prominence in the advocacy work of UNICEF, for example,
which published a series of studies, particularly on the frontline states
of southern Africa, highlighting the complex direct and indirect economic impact of war (UNICEF 1987).

At the same time, the international costs of conflict and its after-math were also being felt. The peace and stability that had been promised by the ending of the Cold War did yield important settle-ments in a number of countries facilitated by superpower intervention and underwritten by the United Nations. This wave of settlements required expensive military input to secure the transition to peace, in addition to the costs of the civil, rehabilitation components. Alongside the promise of peace, however, the international community con-fronted a significant number of new crises in the early post-Cold War years, including those in Iraq (1991), Somalia (1991/2 onwards) and the break-up of the former Yugoslavia. Combined, these processes of war and peace placed new financial demands on the international commun-ity, with the costs of UN peacekeeping operations doubling between 1990 and 1994 from US$2.4 billion to US$5.7 billion. These escalating costs were seen by many as a direct threat to international support for aid which, in contrast to peace-keeping, is financed largely through voluntary contributions (Boutros-Ghali 1992; Netherlands 1993).

Relief: an emerging critique The rising cost of conflict was also reflected in trends in relief expenditure, which increased significantly in absolute and relative terms from the mid-1980s onwards. Figures

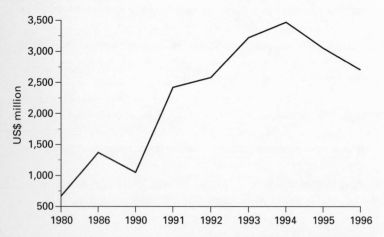

Figure 3.1 Official emergency aid flows (excluding food aid), 1980–96 (*Source*: OECD (various years) *Development Assistance Committee Annual Reports*)

3.1 and 3.2 show emergency aid expenditure from OECD countries between 1989 and 1997 in total and as a proportion of total oda. These data from the Development Assistance Committee (DAC) of the OECD underestimate the total volume of relief expenditure as they exclude emergency food aid. However, they provide an indication of the overall trend.

Importantly, the evidence suggests that much of this increase was accounted for by an increase in the response to conflict-related emergencies. Randel (1994), for example, estimated that in 1993, 97 per cent of relief aid provided by the European Commission (EC) (soon to become the world largest single donor of relief aid) was allocated to complex political emergencies. Similarly in 1994, the World Food Programme (WFP) spent only US$19 million on meeting the primary effects of natural disasters, compared with more than US$1.5 billion in conflict-related emergencies (Webb 1996).

This rise in relief expenditure can be explained not only in terms of a rise in humanitarian need, but in relation to the growing scope for humanitarian intervention from the mid-1980s onwards.

Chapter 2 noted the start of this expansion with the cross-border operation into rebel-held areas of Ethiopia and Eritrea. Scope was expanded still further by the increasing willingness of international

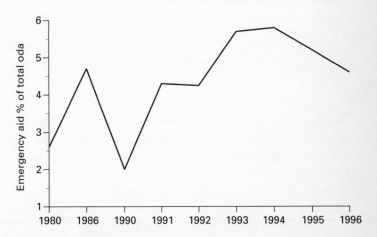

Figure 3.2 Emergency aid as a percentage of total official aid flows (excluding food aid), 1980–96 (*Source*: OECD (various years) *Development Assistance Committee Annual Reports*)

agencies to negotiate their way into conflict zones. During the 1980s NGOs and the United Nations increasingly entered war zones by negotiating access, historically a strategy deployed primarily by the ICRC (Borton 1994; Duffield 1994a). So, for example, in Sudan, a tripartite agreement was reached between the United Nations, the government and rebel forces facilitating humanitarian access on all sides (Karim et al. 1996).

In the early 1990s, precedents were also set for the use of force to secure humanitarian access where negotiation was seen to have failed. In Somalia, Iraqi Kurdistan, Bosnia and Rwanda, for example, armed forces, usually under a UN flag, were deployed to protect humanitarian relief. Importantly, these 'humanitarian interventions' were justified primarily to protect relief agencies, not civilians, from violence (Tomas-evski 1994).

The expansion in humanitarian space was enabled by the softening of the international position regarding sovereignty, particularly that of Western members of the Security Council. It is significant, for example, that following the Kurdish refugee crisis in 1991, the United Nations General Assembly adopted Resolution 46/182, which sought to improve the UN's coordination of relief operations and to sustain the momentum for humanitarian intervention initiated by the formation of safe havens in Iraqi Kurdistan. Importantly, it stated:

> The sovereign, territorial integrity and national unity of states must be fully respected in accordance with the Charter of the United Nations. In this context, humanitarian assistance *should* be provided with the consent of the affected countries, and *in principle* on the basis of an appeal by the affected country. (emphases added)

As a review of the initiative notes, the inclusion of terms 'should' and 'in principle' allowed for the violation of sovereignty if the international community justified intervention on humanitarian grounds (Overseas Development Institute 1993).

The financial and geographical expansion attracted considerable attention from within the aid community and more broadly. No longer associated purely with the logistics of moving emergency food aid to the victims of flood and drought, nor with the secretive workings of the ICRC, humanitarian assistance entered the realm of high politics and media coverage. As relief aid came under increasing scrutiny during the 1990s, so it attracted increasing criticism from an apparently diverse range of sources (Macrae 1998). Two major themes have emerged from nearly a decade of intense evaluation, academic analysis and practice in this field.

First, an important body of work in the early 1990s highlighted the fact that the provision of relief resources may influence significantly the dynamics of conflict. Evidence emerged from a diverse range of conflicts indicating massive manipulation of relief supplies by warring parties and allied commercial and political interest groups. The effect of these manipulations had been to increase further the vulnerability of civilians (see, for example, African Rights 1994; de Waal 1997; Duffield 1994a; Duffield and Prendergast 1994; Keen 1991, 1994). This raised the question of how relief might be better managed to minimise these negative effects. It also raised the tantalising proposition that if aid in wartime could have negative effects, the opposite might also be true. Could aid be used to influence more positively the course of the conflict (Anderson 1996; Keen and Wilson 1994)?

A second strand of criticism regarding relief practice during the past decade has been that while it may provide a temporary palliative, relieving the symptoms of disasters, it does little to reduce people's vulnerability and to enable them to re-establish their lives and livelihoods. There was increasing concern that by focusing on the provision of material supplies, relief was doing little to create the wider conditions for people to resume production, for example, supporting investment in agriculture, marketing, education. In other words, despite the formidable constraints, it was argued, there are opportunities for more developmental approaches that, if adopted, could reduce dependency on international assistance, and empower people to resist future shocks and threats to their livelihoods more effectively. This appeal for more developmental approaches to relief was particularly pertinent in conflict-related emergencies that did not conform to the short time-frame envisaged by conventional disaster relief (Buchanan-Smith and Maxwell 1994).

Aid and politics: a reanalysis of the international division of labour
Adelman (1996) argues that during the 1980s a process was started by which aid and 'politics' were reunited. During the 1960s and 1970s the aid system had sought to protect its operational space from overt

political interference by couching its engagement in technical and particularly economistic language (Griffin 1991). Adelman (1996) argues that during the 1980s there was a new convergence of interests between the aid (economic) domain and that of politics (foreign policy). Specifically, the neo-liberal economic tradition advocated the stripping away of state involvement in production and economic regulation, while also becoming aware of the constraints posed by poor governance to the achievement of economic reform. These interests coincided with the political interests of the foreign policy establishment, particularly in the USA, concerned to protect and pro-mote free trade and ensure stability of states. The mechanism to achieve these changes in Third World policy was no longer seen as only or primarily transfer of resources, but internal political reform (Adelman 1996: 19).

The end of the Cold War added further impetus to this 'reunifica-tion' of aid and politics. There were increasing appeals to utilise the end of superpower confrontation to harness political will to achieve peaceful resolution to conflict. There was thus an assumption that in the post-Cold War era there was sufficient consensus within and between major power blocs, including Europe and the USA, to be able to define coherent foreign policy goals. Further, the importance of coherence between the different facets of international relations – trade, aid and diplomacy – was increasingly emphasised (see, for example, Boutros-Ghali 1992, 1994; Development Assistance Com-mittee 1997; European Commission 1996; United Kingdom 1997).

This reunification was initially conceptual. The firewall between aid and foreign policy, cherished by non-aligned countries in particular (Adelman 1996), was being dismantled in the 'non-aligned' bloc of donor countries such as those of Scandinavia, albeit in terms of a revival of the liberal internationalist ideals of the UN founders. Here it was signalled by a reassertion of the liberal internationalist claim regarding the link between development and peace (Miller 1992; Netherlands 1993; Sida 1999).

In the USA the bid for greater 'coherence' was achieved through institutional innovation. For example, in 1997 change was enacted whereby the administrator of USAID reported no longer directly to the president, but to the secretary of state. In 1992, the Office of Transition Initiatives was formed, which also signalled a new *modus operandi*. Drawing on both relief and development assistance budget lines, it was jointly managed by the State Department and by USAID, thus achieving in institutional terms the coherence between humanitarian and developmental policy, and between aid and politics implied by the new orthodoxy.

In the UK in 1997, the renewed administrative separation of the aid ministry from the department of foreign affairs did not preclude much greater emphasis being placed on ensuring 'coherence' between the aid and political spheres and the newly founded Department for International Development (DFID) claiming an important role in conflict management (United Kingdom 1997, 1999).

These shifts in the analysis of aid and politics reflected those that had taken place in the global political environment. They provided the aid establishment with a mandate not only to claim a role in conflict management, but to define ways of implementing it. In this respect, the paradigm that was to emerge during this decade was a continuation of an earlier trend identified by Ellis. He argues that from the mid-1980s onwards, as the USA and France in particular disengaged from Africa, aid agencies became the primary means for political engagement by the West. In the face of the 'politics of abandonment', he suggests that:

> it is the Bretton Woods institutions, and especially the World Bank, which are left in occupation of the field. It is they which articulate most clearly the policy of the industrialised world toward Africa, based on free trade and liberal policy. (1996: 15)

As outlined above, by the 1990s, however, the essentially economistic and technocratic paradigms of conventional development assistance were proving ineffective in many of the poorest recipient countries, and in securing the political support of donors. Something new was required.

The Evolution of a New Orthodoxy: Relief, Development and War

Aid and war: addressing 'root causes' On 31 January 1992, members of the Security Council met at the heads of state level for the first time in the Council's history. Their final communiqué concluded that:

the absence of war and military states does not itself ensure international peace and security. The non-military sources of instability in the economic, social, humanitarian and ecological fields have become threats to peace and security. The UN membership as a whole needs to give the highest priority to the solution of these matters.

The UN secretary-general was then invited to submit a report outlining the future of the United Nations in conflict management in the post-Cold War era. *An Agenda for Peace*, published in mid-1992, defined responsibility for realising human security as lying first with the Security Council, but also in the General Assembly and in the operational and technical agencies of the UN. Thus, in line with the historic Security Council meeting earlier that year, he proposed a broader vision of security that sought an integrated, cross-sectoral approach. In his *Agendas*, the secretary-general argued that the UN was uniquely placed to provide a focus for 'human security, combining capacity in peace-keeping and development cooperation'. Importantly, he also proposed an expanded role for the United Nations in democratisation:

> There is a new requirement for technical assistance which the United Nations has an obligation to develop and provide when requested: support of the transformation of deficient national structures and capabilities, and for the strengthening of new democratic institutions. The authority of the UN to act in this field would rest on the consensus that social peace is as important as strategic or political peace. (Boutros-Ghali 1992: para 59)

The repeated emphasis placed on technical cooperation and developmental approaches in *An Agenda for Peace* and subsequent deliberations by the Security Council did not, as discussed above, translate into renewed flows of oda. However, this approach did encourage expansion in the concept of the development task from one 'limited to transferring funds and expertise from the haves to the have-nots'. The subsequent *Agenda for Development* (Boutros-Ghali 1994) outlined a much broader task comprising five dimensions: peace, the economy, environmental protection, social justice and democracy. In a note prepared prior to the launch of the report, the secretary-general argued that implementing this new paradigm would require recognising the limitations of conventional development theory and practice in unstable situations, concluding that: 'situations of conflict require a different development strategy from that obtaining under peaceful conditions'.

In March 1996, the European Commission issued a communication to the European Council of Ministers and to the European Parliament. Under the title 'Linking relief, rehabilitation and development' the document advocated the concept of 'structural stability', which would provide a unifying link between European trade, aid and security policy (European Commission 1996). Prepared after the signing of the Maastricht Treaty in 1994, and in the lead up to the Inter-Governmental Conference, it sought to contribute to the development of the European Union's Common Foreign and Security Policy (CFSP). Defined as 'sustainable economic development, democracy, respect for human rights, viable political structures and health social and environmental conditions', the concept of structural stability provided a conceptual umbrella very similar to that of human security proposed by the UN.

The Commission document proposed the establishment of global policy frameworks within which both the different divisions of the European Commission and individual member states could define their work in aid-receiving countries. These would comprise political, social, development and technical aspects which in turn would define 'ways in which conflict prevention as a means of managing the inevitable strains resulting from social, political and economic change can be incorporated into development cooperation strategies'.

At the high-level meeting of the Development Assistance Committee (DAC) of the OECD on 3–4 May 1995, development cooperation ministers and heads of aid agencies examined the implications of conflict for development, and the role of development assistance in its prevention and resolution. This meeting established the Task Force on Conflict, Peace and Development Cooperation to examine further these issues, culminating in the drafting of the *DAC Guidelines on Conflict, Peace and Development Cooperation on the Threshold of the 21st Century* (Development Assistance Committee 1997). At the launch of the *Guidelines*, DAC country ministers issued a statement reiterating the goal of development cooperation as that of achieving 'structural stability'. Again, the importance of achieving coherence between aid and foreign and defence policies was emphasised.

The specific role of development cooperation in conflict management was articulated clearly by the former UK overseas development minister:

> In the long term, it is clear that poverty and deprivation contribute to disorder and conflict. More prosperous countries with better educated and healthier people are better able to cope with the effect of disaster when it does strike. This is one of the reasons why our long-term development strategy to poorer countries of Africa and Asia and elsewhere is so important. It helps people progress out of poverty ... At a time of transition, aid also forms part of our efforts to enable major changes, political and economic, to take place *without disorder*. (Chalker 1996, emphasis added)

This speech is revealing in that, in common with all of the key policy statements emerging from the UN, the EC and the DAC, it combines two strands of analysis. The first is in relation to an analysis of the root causes of conflict. The second is with respect to a model linking relief and development assistance. The idea that aid can be used to address the root causes of migration and war is an old one. Aired first in the mid-1940s, it was revisited in the late 1970s and early 1980s in the context of UN debates regarding measures to address migration, and the potential role of aid in stemming these movements (Suhrke 1994).

In the mid- to late 1970s a series of revolutionary and ethnic liberation struggles extended from Southern Africa and the Horn, into South-East and Central Asia (Cambodia, Vietnam and Afghanistan) and around into Central and Latin America. These upheavals generated major flows of refugees. Between 1979 and 1980 refugee movements from Cuba and Vietnam were generating particular concern within the West. Germany and the USA censured the governments of both these refugee-producing countries. This prompted further debate in the UN's Special Political Committee in 1980 to investigate the root causes of migration. In the context of the continuing Cold War, the debate quickly polarised along familiar political fault lines.

The socialist and non-aligned bloc argued that historical and external factors (including colonialism and continuing inequalities in trade, for example) were the primary causes of poverty, instability and therefore migration. Conversely, the West emphasised the internal causes of conflict, poor governance and ineffective economic policies, and environmental degradation. As Suhrke (1994) reports in her account of this first root-cause debate, discussion throughout the first half of the 1980s remained characterised by division along these ideological lines. The secretary-general's appointment of Sadruddhin Aga Khan as the special rapporteur failed to overcome these divisions. His report emphasised the fact that the issue was less whether the causes of conflicts were internal or external than the importance of understanding the linkages between these two layers of conflict. However, despite some five years of deliberations, the process yielded little in terms of substantive policy change.

The emphasis placed on the internal causes of conflict, familiar from these earlier discussions, has been echoed in more recent policy statements emerging from official aid agencies – bilateral and multilateral – regarding the role of aid in conflict management. As the above extracts highlight, the causes of conflict are located both in the persistent problem of underdevelopment and in the processes of modernisation. As such, aid can assume a dual role in its prevention: first, by promoting development, reducing poverty and improving education; second, by compensating those adversely affected by the development process. Thus, with regard to the latter role, the European Commission comments that:

> the imbalance of political and socio-economic opportunities between different (region, ethnic, religious etc) groups within a given state, and the absence of viable mechanisms for the peaceful conciliation of divergent interests. (European Commission 1996)

heighten the risks of conflict as countries develop. In this context, the end stage of development becomes identified with the achievement of a neo-liberal political economy (Ogata and Wolfensohn 1999).

Thus during the 1990s a consensus has emerged that aid is able to address the problem of conflict. These assertions are based on an analysis of the causes of conflict that focuses largely on internal factors, and assumes that conflict will disappear once modern states have been created. In this sense, the shift in the paradigm has been modest, at best. Rather than presenting a fundamental challenge to development theory, as implied by the UN secretary-general at the beginning of the decade, the European Commission (1996) concludes that: 'Operating with the term structural stability *in no way implies a major departure from the current policies of the European Union*' (emphasis added).

Linking relief, development ... and war   One important modification has been proposed in the existing organisation and conceptualisation of aid in conflict situations – that is the relationship between relief and development assistance. As described in Chapter 2, during the mid-1980s the evolution of the international relief system represented a key adaption by aid actors to deal with violent quasi-states. A feature of this evolution was that it effectively reinforced a political distinction between relief and development assistance. Development assistance remained state-centred in that it remained confined by the principles of juridical sovereignty and assumed empirical sovereignty for its implementation. Relief assistance did not confer legitimacy upon the government of recipient countries: the processes of privatisation and militarisation of relief aid were designed, at least in theory, to ensure that relief could be delivered *despite* national authorities, rather than through them.

During the early 1990s, the emerging orthodoxy sought to collapse the distinction between relief and development aid. Specifically, the defining orthodoxy of assistance in conflict situations became that aid, including relief aid, can and should be developmental. This assertion has derived from the critique of relief aid in chronic political emergencies: namely that it risks creating dependency and does little to address the root or even proximate causes of populations' vulnerability.

In the 1990s the aid community thus faced two key challenges simultaneously. On the one hand, it was asserting a new role in conflict management. On the other hand, it was also seeking to improve the effectiveness of its response to protracted political emergencies. One approach was to link these two issues. The mechanism for this linkage was simple: the revival of another old idea, that of the relief–development continuum. Initially formulated in relation to natural disasters, particularly drought and floods, the continuum concept was based on the idea that well-planned relief could be used to reduce communities' vulnerability to future hazards, for example by using emergency food for work schemes to invest in key infrastructure. Similarly, well-planned development assistance needed to take account of the hazards faced by populations, particularly the poor. Strengthening infrastructure, reducing the financial vulnerability of communities and developing networks for the collection of early warning information could all help to prepare communities better against known hazards, so helping to prevent them from becoming disastrous.

A similar model is now used to explain and justify the role of aid agencies in conflict prevention and resolution. By conceptualising conflict as a hazard that derives primarily from underdevelopment, it becomes possible to see ways in which developmental inputs can be used to reduce conflict. Developmental approaches of capacity-building, for example, become not simply a means of reducing economic dependency on relief assistance, but part of a wider, political project of building the civil institutions necessary to secure a sustainable peace.

Thus the concept of the relief–development continuum and its variants[1] provide a mechanism by which to justify broadening the objectives and responses of aid. By definition, the continuum assumes that it is both feasible and desirable to expand aid from its narrow, palliative and humanitarian purpose. By definition too, the aim is not only to use development assistance to prevent the outbreak of conflict and to contribute to post-conflict rehabilitation, but to apply developmental approaches *during* periods of open conflict.

The orthodoxy taking shape within the aid community comprises two facets: aid can play a role in the prevention, mitigation and resolution of conflict, and that aid should strive to be developmental even during conflict and conflict-induced emergencies. These two basic tenets have become prominant in aid discourse, and have been adopted not only by official donors (Netherlands 1993; Sida 1999; United Kingdom 1997, 1999), and the United Nations (UN Inter-agency Standing Committee on Humanitarian Affairs 1997; UNHCR 1997; United Nations 1994; United Nations Administrative Committee on Coordination 1993), but increasingly by NGOs (see, for example, Pirotte and Husson 1999).

The New Orthodoxy: A Preliminary Critique

The nature of war In making claims regarding the potential role of aid in ameliorating conflict, aid agencies have not been particularly modest. For example, in a paper for its Executive Committee, the UNHCR argued that:

> Given the number of countries involved, the magnitude of the numbers returning and the fact that their successful reintegration is critical to any national reconciliation and reconstruction process, the issues are not simply humanitarian. International security is at stake. (UNHCR 1992: 2)

The dominant interpretation emerging during the 1990s was that the cause of Third World conflict, and thus the threat to international security, lay primarily in internal processes of maldevelopment. This analysis coincided with the re-evaluation of what security meant in the post-Cold War era. For example, in a speech in 1993, the British foreign secretary noted that 'chaos and anarchy are the enemies of commerce' (Hurd 1993). The violence of the collapse of the Somali state in 1991 was seen by many to exemplify the threat to global security and trade. Large-scale migration, particularly from Europe's south Mediterranean fringe and from the Balkans, was now seen as a particular threat (Hathaway 1995; Kemp 1996). In an influential article, Robert Kaplan (1994) presented an apocalyptic vision of Third World decline and the threat that this poses to the developed world in terms of disease, migration and trade.

In seeking to reverse the trend of declining aid flows, aid policy elites have often evoked these perceived threats and appealed directly to the self-interest of donor governments, arguing that aid can play a significant role in preventing them. In doing so, they have conformed to the predominant analysis of the causes of conflict in non-strategic areas described by Kaplan and others. Such an approach means that aid actors can simultaneously claim experience and a legitimate concern, but without confronting the potentially contentious areas of 'external' factors in the causation of conflict (Macrae 1996). Issues of historical and continuing support by donor governments for militarisation of Third World countries, prevailing global trade and aid policies themselves are thus outside the paradigm of change presented by the aid establishment.

Lacking in those documents is a systematic and evidence-based analysis of the actual dynamics of conflict. In portraying conflict as the result of underdevelopment, the implication is that development itself will remove the cause of violence. However, the important work of David Keen (1994) and others portrays a more complex picture of the relationship between poverty, inequality and violence.

First, it suggests that the orchestrators of violence are not only or primarily the poor: they are the political elite. Maintaining power relies upon maintaining control over the means of production and distribution of wealth. Such an analysis suggests that 'development' without power protects neither individuals nor societies from violence. Indeed, the comparative wealth of a group may render it more vulnerable to the threat of violence. Thus it is significant that the centres of violence in Angola, Sierra Leone and Liberia have been associated with wealth. While the frontline in these conflicts may have been occupied by ragged boys, the wars have been fought on behalf of national and international elites seeking to secure lucrative returns from protecting these valuable assets. This suggests that conflict resolution will be a matter not simply of compensating those who have lost out from the process of development, but of confronting some of those who have benefited from it.

By the end of the decade, the propensity to internalise the causes of war had been extended from the domain of economics and sociology to that of psychology. In other words, there has been an increasing emphasis on the impact of personal behaviour on the causation of conflict. In moves reminiscent of the early modernisation theorists, such as Lerner, who emphasised the need for attitudinal change in order to overcome the obstacles to social and economic progress (Larrain 1989), aid actors are taking a renewed interest in the psychology and sociology of violence.

This is evident in the growth of conflict resolution NGOs, many of which base their intervention on the assumption that a major source of conflict is misunderstanding between the different parties. By providing forums to facilitate exchange of ideas, mutual understanding can be achieved, and the source of conflict removed (Duffield 1997a; Pupavac 1997). Similarly, the emergence of large programmes of psycho-social support is often justified with recourse to the idea that conflict-affected populations, particularly children, were more likely to resort to violence to resolve future conflicts. On this basis, early psycho-therapeutic intervention to reassure children and to encourage them to seek peaceful solutions is argued to be important, not only for personal healing but to avert future violence (Summerfield 1999).

As a response to declining aid resources, such accounts are inherently attractive because they reinforce the idea that what is required is less a transfer of resources than a process of internal, even personal, change (Duffield 1997a). The increased emphasis on the developmental goals of self-reliance and sustainability of assistance in conflict-affected countries is indicative of this. There is a continuity between the emphasis on psycho-social dimensions of conflict resolution and the shift in aid programming of the 1980s, from project to programme aid. As Adelman (1996) reports, the advent of structural adjustment signalled the end of the economic orthodoxy that the problem of underdevelopment was primarily associated with the lack of capital and savings. With greater emphasis on institutional change, aid becomes an incentive for such changes, no longer grounded in a process that relies (explicitly or implicitly) on redistribution of wealth (Duffield 1997a; Pupavac 1997). Rather, it is about enabling or persuading recipient countries to become partners in the implementation of the prevailing paradigm (Stiglitz 1998; Wolfensohn 1999).

Interestingly, this emphasis on 'peace from within', drawing on internal resources that need to be managed through improved behaviour, draws on apparently disparate political theories and ideologies. On the one hand it conforms to the isolationist tendencies of realism, which question the rationale of international transfers of public wealth. On the other, it also responds to what might be described as the anti-imperialist critique of aid emerging from within developing countries themselves – hence, for example, the 'new Africanism' espoused by countries such as Ethiopia, Eritrea and Uganda, which has sought to challenge the predominant neo-liberal model of economic interventionism and democratisation.

This sentiment was endorsed by the USA's foreign policy and aid establishments during the mid-1990s, in their strategy of support for 'African solutions to African problems' in approaches to regional security. This approach represents a political variant of the ostensibly socio-economic critique of current humanitarian practice. It has been made forcefully by Alex de Waal (1997), who has argued that the international relief system disempowers not only individuals and households but political and civil institutions. By assuming responsibility for the provision of basic welfare, international agencies absolve national authorities, particularly warring parties, from their responsibilities for forming effective relations with the populations they claim to represent. By seeking to work outside state structures, and structures established by rebel groups, aid undermines the accountability of these bodies, and is itself inherently unaccountable (de Waal 1996, 1997). According to this view, disengagement would not constitute abandonment (Ellis 1996), but is politically responsible.

The tendency to internalise the origins of, and solutions to, conflict is problematic in that it risks idealising both the nature of war and its resolution. While in broad terms the value of liberal, democratic systems of governance and of economic management is specified, lacking is a clearly defined strategy of what to do if and when these conditions are not in place.

This dilemma also emerges from the wider trend in aid policy in the late 1990s, with the emphasis moving away from a punitive regime of conditionality to a strategy of partnership. This emerged not from a rejection of the principle of conditionality, but rather from a recognition that, in practice, conditionality has achieved only limited results (Wolfensohn 1999). In recent speeches, ministers responsible for foreign and aid policy in the UK and the USA have made it clear that their support for Third World governments will be based on such partnerships. What has not been made clear, however, is what options are open to *aid* actors in those cases where partners do not subscribe to the menu of liberal values from which they are invited to choose by the development establishment (Albright 1997; Short 1999). However, while the content of international assistance is increasingly preoccupied with reforming the internal institutions and conditions of violent quasi-states, the design of aid instruments remains premised on the assumptions that such states wish to reform themselves, and indeed that there is a state functioning at all. Neither of these assumptions necessarily applies in those states actively engaged in violent conflict or in its immediate aftermath.

Blurring the boundaries between relief and development Relief – or more properly, humanitarian aid – has traditionally been presented as politically neutral. In contrast, development aid is necessarily partisan, requiring political decisions on behalf of the donor regarding which institutions should or should not be strengthened. During the Cold

War, these decisions were limited to whether or not to support the juridical sovereign government of any particular country. In a context where juridical sovereignty no longer guarantees unconditional development support, but in which humanitarian aid might also be developmental, donor government choices of which authorities will be supported, and when, in what form and under what conditions, necessarily become complex and unpredictable.

By the mid-1990s, the majority of official policy statements had openly rejected what was seen as the formulaic concept of the continuum, with its implication of a clearly demarcated, linear transition from relief to rehabilitation to development (see, for example, Development Assistance Committee 1997; Ogata and Wolfensohn 1999; Sida 1999; United Kingdom 1999). Interestingly, the subsequent models of transition that have been put forward have relied upon an analysis of the nature of the war–peace transition, rather than the political economy of the aid transition itself. For the World Bank, for example, the concept of war–peace transition was important in informing the establishment of the Post-conflict Unit to advise on rehabilitation strategy. The Bank, like others, quickly recognised that the post-conflict concept was also inaccurate in that it implied absolute cessation of violence. However, the term 'post-conflict' remains in place, albeit with the caveat that it does not imply absolute peace. Similarly, the UNHCR, in its guidelines on refugee reintegration, notes:

> As some of these [internal] conflicts subside, states reemerging from the ashes of destruction may still undergo periods of intense if sporadic fighting. It may therefore be inaccurate, even misleading to talk about 'post-conflict situations' as such situations do not pass directly from conflict to post-conflict conditions. *We shall however retain the term 'post-conflict'* to indicate those war-torn societies that are undergoing some form of transition towards a more peaceful and stable situation. (1999: xvii, emphasis added)

In such definitions, the distinction between war and peace is effectively blurred.

The mandates of relief and development agencies are becoming correspondingly blurred as they seek to define new ways of working in chronic political emergencies. Thus, for example, the UNDP, the World Bank and the DAC, usually associated with development assistance, are now actively engaged in the definition and execution of aid policy in relation to conflict-affected countries (Development Assistance Committee 1997; UNDP 1996; World Bank 1998). Conversely, agencies usually associated primarily with relief are increasingly seeking developmental approaches to guide their work in these situations. For example, the UN Office for the Coordination of Humanitarian Affairs (UNOCHA, formerly DHA), the UNHCR and the Inter-Agency Standing Committee on Humanitarian Affairs (IASC) have all undertaken extensive reviews of their programming approaches in chronic emergencies and have advocated developmental approaches (DHA and UNDP 1997; Lautze and Hammock 1996; UNHCR 1999).

Collapsing the distinction between relief and development aid changes their respective political meanings. It implies a willingness and ability to make decisions that humanitarian actors have deliberately sought to avoid making: those regarding the legitimacy and desirability of strengthening institutions, particularly governmental authorities, in conflict situations. Yet the implications of this shift are rarely explicitly acknowledged by advocates of developmental relief. Revealingly, however, the issue of how to translate the global rhetoric into operational strategies is the subject of considerable tension in many countries between different agencies and between aid organisations, governments and non-state entities such as rebel groups. Thus, for example, the issue of whether and how relief assistance should seek to be developmental in content and design has been the subject of considerable political interest in Sudan, particularly since the *de facto* embargo on development assistance was imposed in 1989 (Buchanan-Smith et al. 1999; Karim et al. 1996). Similarly, in Afghanistan, the Taliban, which controls most of the territory, including the capital, Kabul, is not recognised by Western governments in protest against what is perceived to be its discriminatory and fundamentalist Islamic regime. Despite this, agencies actively seek developmental space, and in doing so face dilemmas with regard to which institutions to support and how these can be sustained (Cholmondeley 1997; Wiles et al. 1999).

It is problematic that there are no universal principles according to which the political legitimacy implied by developmental approaches can and should be accorded to belligerent parties. The choice facing aid agencies working in conflict situations is whether to adopt a strict interpretation of neutrality, which does not imply political endorsement or recognition. The other framework currently in place is that of development assistance, which rests upon juridical sovereignty. The latter remains politically 'blind': not only does acceptance of juridical sovereignty remain the primary basis for the legitimacy of the aid project, it is also a highly pragmatic approach. As argued previously, development assistance remains dependent on the state, any state, for its legitimacy and for implementation of policy reform.

Blurring the boundaries between aid and politics A further characteristic of the new aid orthodoxy is that it actively seeks to overcome the boundary between aid and foreign policy that has characterised international relations at least since the 1960s. The blurring of this boundary is indicated by the fact that aid agencies can make increasingly bold claims regarding their political function. The emergence of new budget lines and organisational structures responsible for conflict management within donor government departments is one indication of this trend, as is the emergence of a new generation of 'conflict resolution' NGOs, many of which receive funding from official aid sources (Sorbo et al. 1997).

The new-found confidence of aid actors in the political arena might be seen to result from a greater emphasis on achieving policy coherence between the aid and foreign policy agencies, and to utilise the specific operational skills and financing of assistance in order to reinforce political strategies for peace. Thus, for example, Dame Margaret Anstee, former SRSG in Angola, argued in a major report for the UN:

> The process of peace-building is in fundamental ways different from the kind of activities subsumed under the heading 'development', although these form a highly important component. The main distinction is that while development activities naturally have to operate in a context, this is not their primary purpose, whereas in the case of peace-building political considerations take centre stage. In such situations, developmental and humanitarian programmes *must contribute to the overall political purpose of consolidating peace and preventing renewed conflict* as well as serve their normal function of improving conditions of life and relieving hardship. Thus, the political objectives should always prevail. (Anstee 1996, emphasis added)

In this spirit of coherence, the programme of UN reform, outlined by the new secretary-general in 1997, put in place the Executive Committee on Peace and Security, chaired by the Department for Political Affairs, which was to have responsibility for guiding UN policy, including that of development and relief agencies, in situations of post-conflict transition (United Nations 1997). Similar reforms, or variants of them, are in place in a number of international bodies and donor government countries (Macrae and Leader 2000).

Strikingly absent from many aid policy documents that call for increased coherence between the aid, trade, defence and foreign policy spheres is a definition of the political content and values to underpin this new, holistic approach – in other words, *whose* politics are driving international relations, including those governing aid relations.

This question becomes increasingly pressing in relation to conflict-affected countries when the distinction between relief and development assistance is fudged, as described above. If aid (including relief aid) is subsumed by politics, then it becomes legitimate to utilise humanitarian aid to influence political events. The neutrality of assistance is thus lost.

Summary and Conclusions

What the above analysis suggests is that the context in which aid relations are being conducted has changed significantly over the past decade. This has demanded an increasing sensitivity to political context by aid actors. Aid actors have had to respond to the changing framework for global political relations, signalled by weakening respect for juridical sovereignty. At the same time, aid actors have claimed a renewed role in shaping political conditions in recipient countries, both directly in relation to governments and indirectly by supporting peaceful development through civil society.

However, there is a risk that in entering this territory of conflict management the aid establishment replicates what Leftwich (1994) has described elsewhere as the technicist fallacy, in that: 'there is a managerial fix in the normally difficult affairs of human societies'.

This tendency towards a managerial interpretation of the conflict agenda is evident in the preoccupation with, for example, budget lines, coordination arrangements and the development of additional activities to fulfil a variety of new functions. Thus, for example, the discourse of the UNHCR on the issue of relief–development linkages has been preoccupied with defining appropriate partnerships with developmental agencies and with identifying new budget lines to finance rehabilitation programmes (Macrae 1999). Similarly, for nearly a decade, the UN more broadly has been struggling to define a framework for coordinating its relief, developmental and political responses in conflict situations, particularly those where a legitimate and functioning state is absent.

Thus, rather than a fundamental revision, the paradigm that has governed aid for over five decades has been adjusted only modestly despite marked changes in the international political context. The conceptual, ethical and juridical constraints to applying this 'new' aid paradigm remain enormous. As the case studies presented in subsequent chapters reveal, in the absence of a resolution to the multiple challenges of quasi-statehood, not only is the legitimacy of the aid enterprise compromised, but so too are its technical quality and efficiency.

Cliffe and Luckham (1999) are among the few writers who have acknowledged the crucial importance of resolving the problem of statehood in responding to complex political emergencies. However, in their search for improved international policy and practice in this arena, they underestimate the political economy of aid itself, focusing their analysis more on the environment *within* recipient countries. In particular, they do not acknowledge that a condition of moving from relief to development aid instruments both requires and signifies changes in the claims of incumbent authorities to legitimacy. In other words, unless there is a sovereign government in place, development assistance cannot be resumed, and the resumption of such assistance itself legitimises the new regime.

Moving along the relief–development continuum implies 'scaling up' the aid response. This is in terms of the target of aid (from the individual to the level of society); spatially (from the level of individual projects to trying to ensure national coverage, including, for example, the development of macro-economic policy); and temporally (from the short to the long term). This process of scaling up requires the presence of a unified, central government that both embodies and executes policy. For aid to work developmentally requires not only

that such a central body be in place, but that it is perceived internationally to be legitimate.

In situations where statehood remains contested or weak or its
legitimacy is doubted, the international aid regime faces considerable
problems. The history of development assistance outlined in Chapter
2 concluded that its key rationale has been to reinforce empirical
sovereignty. The concept of developmental relief assumes that the
intention is to move towards a resumption of development assistance,
but does not necessarily make it explicit that such a move implies
legitimation of the recipient state.

Developmental aid faces a major problem in those cases where the
legitimacy of the state is in question. In particular, the question
emerges as to whether the international community can pursue developmental approaches while simultaneously withholding the external
legitimation implied by development aid. This is the dilemma that
faces international actors in situations of 'post'-conflict transition and
is exacerbated by the various weaknesses of this type of quasi-states.
This is the subject of Chapter 5.

A second major dilemma of aid programming in quasi-states relates
to sustainability. A primary tenet of the emerging orthodoxy regarding
developmental relief is that, by adopting new and innovative approaches, dependence on relief aid can be reduced and self-reliance
enhanced. Yet the particular context of transition and the particular
forms of aid deployed in them render sustainability elusive. The
absolute scarcity of resources in these environments of itself questions
the viability of the goal of sustainability. This problem is exacerbated
by particular dilemmas of aid management. If a primary goal of
assistance is that it should be sustainable, then this implies adopting
aid instruments that bolster the empirical capacity of the state-building,
yet it is precisely these types of instrument that the political context
makes so difficult to deploy. These issues are the subject of Chapter 6.

Note

1. These include: linking relief, rehabilitation and development; developmental relief; capacity-building.

CHAPTER 4

The Context of Recovery: An Overview of War and its Impact in Cambodia, Ethiopia and Uganda

§ Chapter 3 concluded by outlining two key dilemmas confronting aid actors involved in health sector rehabilitation – legitimacy and sustainability. The particular attributes of conflict-affected states make these dilemmas inherently difficult to address, challenging the state-centric nature of both developmental aid and health planning models.

While the presence of a unified, functioning state is a necessary condition for the transition from relief to development aid to take place, it is not sufficient. The aid transition is critically determined by international political relations between the affected country and donor governments. In other words, international legitimation is also a necessary condition for 'linking' relief and development aid.

This chapter has three aims. First, it analyses the state of empirical and juridical statehood prior to and during the prolonged conflicts experienced by the three case study countries. This provides the contextual background to the more detailed analysis of the process of transition itself, presented in Chapter 5. Second, it charts the historical ebbs and flows in the countries' international relations and in aid flows, so illustrating the political conditions required to effect the aid transition in the 'post'-conflict period. Third, recognising that the provision of public health services constitutes a core part of empirical statehood, it assesses the implications of a weakening public sector for health provision. In other words, it characterises more precisely the nature of the problems rehabilitation aid needs to tackle. The chapter therefore provides a contextual overview of war, the state and international relations in Cambodia, Ethiopia and Uganda respectively.

It then examines the health needs and health services in the three case study countries at the time of 'transition'.

Two key themes cut across these sections, and these are then linked together in the final section, thus preparing the ground for Chapters 5 and 6. The first theme is that of legitimacy. In reviewing the origins of conflict in all three countries the lack of internal legitimacy in state–society relations is revealed, with the state relying instead largely on coercion to maintain its power. Superimposed upon this internal dynamic of conflict has been an external component, particularly in the cases of Cambodia and Ethiopia. External intervention in these conflicts has been primarily driven not by concern for the internal legitimacy of regimes, but rather by geopolitical considerations. The latter consideration has shaped aid relations and, in particular, defined the scope for developmental aid. In examining the transition from relief to development aid, it is therefore important to scrutinise the conditions according to which external legitimation of the regime has been granted, and the extent to which this has been associated with internal legitimation of the new regime by the populations concerned. The political economy of regime legitimation in situations of 'post'-conflict transition, and the role of aid in it, is a focus of Chapter 5.

The second theme, from a comparative review of the three countries, is that the poverty of the state has created dependence to maintain its financial and political survival. The underdevelopment of these economies is structural, pre-dating the onset of military conflict. The poverty of the state, at least of the public administration, means that in these countries the basic conditions of empirical sovereignty, such as providing for the basic food, health and other needs of the people, have remained unfulfilled, in turn further compromising the legitimacy of the state. This suggests that to re-establish empirical sovereignty, which includes the provision of effective and sustainable public health services, requires a significant investment in public in-stitutions.[1]

Thus, as the remainder of this chapter makes clear, the protracted, multi-dimensional nature of these conflicts needs to be better under-stood, not simply as a *cause* of the breakdown of the state and of public services, but as a *consequence* of the contested internal and external legitimacy of these states. The implication of this is that the cessation of hostility is an insufficient condition for the establishment of sustainable health systems and developmental aid relations: other, structural political and economic factors must also be addressed.

War, the State and International Relations in Cambodia[2]

Cambodia's geography has been a significant determinant of its vulnerability to violent conflict. For many centuries it has been the subject of war and occupation by its two larger neighbours – Thailand and Vietnam. In the twentieth century it became one of the centres of the Cold War.

After Cambodia's independence from France in 1953, Prince Sihanouk, the head of state, navigated a difficult political course in an effort to insulate his country from persistent conflicts in Laos and Vietnam by asserting Cambodia's political neutrality. However, this small and poor country proved unable to secure internally the resources required for its economic and military survival. The country's neutrality quickly collapsed as the government sought external financial support first from the USA and then from the Soviet Union throughout the 1960s. During this period the country faced increasing military threats from leftist and rightist guerrilla groups, which drew variously on external support from the USSR, China and the USA.

In 1970, the USA backed a coup by Lon Nol, leader of one of the rightist groups. The new regime actively supported anti-communist groups based in South Vietnam, so plunging the country into the Vietnam War. The Cambodian communist parties, including the Khmer Rouge, received backing from China, and the Cambodian conflict soon had a clear regional and international dynamic. Curtis (1989) describes the heavy toll resulting from the spillover of fighting from Vietnam, which displaced two million people (one-third of the population) from their homes.[3]

Throughout the early 1970s, the Cambodian state was further weakened economically and in terms of its perceived legitimacy, particularly among the rural population. Agricultural production slumped: rice production fell by half from its 1968/9 level of 2.5 million tonnes to under one million tonnes in 1973/4. Instead of redressing this gap, available public resources were channelled into the military. The country thus became ever more dependent on external aid to sustain itself. Between 1970 and 1975, the Khmer Republic received some

US$1.8 billion in military aid and a further US$503 in 'humanitarian' aid from the USA. By 1974 the only food available in Phnom Penh was provided by US airlift (see Lanjouw et al. 1998). This support, together with that from other bilateral aid programmes, the international financial institutions and the UN agencies, proved crucial to maintaining the government and remaining public services.

Disenchanted by the weakness of the regime and its seeming inability to bring stability to the country, and under pressure from Congress, the USA ceased its support for Lon Nol in January 1975. Without external backing, the government was effectively bankrupt, and unable to finance the continuation of the war. The Khmer Rouge entered Phnom Penh on 17 April 1975, and announced a worker-peasant revolution. Using its own interpretation of Maoism, the Khmer Rouge sought a totalitarian solution to the country's external dependence and the growing disparities between rural and urban society. It expelled the country's three million city-dwellers into rural areas, forcing them to work in the newly established agricultural collectives and industrial work camps. All aspects of life became the subject of state control, from production, to eating, to marriage and the family. Money was rendered obsolete. Relations with all external powers, other than China, were severed, and movement in and out of the country was highly restricted. The numbers who died during this period are widely contested, ranging from one to three million people.[4]

In December 1978, in partial response to incursions by the Khmer Rouge into its territory, Vietnam, with support from Cambodian opposition forces, launched an invasion into Cambodia. By 7 January 1979 these forces had taken control of Phnom Penh. The Vietnamese backed the installation of a new government under the leadership of Heng Sarim, leader of the Kampuchean National United Front of National Salvation (KNUFNS). The Vietnamese intervention was seen variously as an invasion by a foreign power and, as such, an illegal occupation; and as a liberating army acting to restore respect for human rights and overthrow totalitarianism.

Prince Sihanouk, among others, appealed to the United Nations to condemn the invasion. However, the Security Council was unable to reach a consensus on the question of the legality of the new Cambodian government.[5] In June 1982, three anti-Vietnamese resistance groups based in Thailand formed the Coalition Government of

Democratic Kampuchea (CGDK). This comprised the Khmer Rouge, the KPNLF, led by Son Sann, and the party led by Sihanouk, FUN-CINPEC. This alliance of former enemies had one common objective: the removal of what they saw as the occupying force of Vietnam. They shared this objective with the USA and China, in particular, both of whom provided overt and covert support for this unlikely alliance. Importantly, the CGDK was to occupy Cambodia's seat at the UN General Assembly until 1991, so denying Heng Sarim's regime international legitimacy.

The overthrow of the Khmer Rouge revealed a massive humanitarian crisis in the country, prompting one of the largest relief operations in history.[6] Official relief inside Cambodia and for Cambodian refugees in Thailand totalled some US$678.3 million (Kiljunen 1984, cited in Lanjouw et al. 1998). A further US$400 million of assistance was provided in Cambodia between 1979 and 1981 by Vietnam and the Soviet Union, with NGOs providing an additional US$110 million (see Benson 1992; Lanjouw et al. 1998; Shawcross 1984).

By early January 1982, famine had subsided and some refugees were returning spontaneously to the country. The UN declared that the emergency was over. In the context of the Cold War, and the fact that the CGDK was recognised as the sovereign of Cambodia, this declaration signalled a renewed period of isolation for the country. It was subject to an international embargo on trade and development aid, and the resources for rehabilitation and reconstruction had to come from within the country and from its few allies in the Eastern bloc and Vietnam. The process of rehabilitation was further slowed by conscription, which drafted all men between the ages of 18 and 30 into the army, at a time when the ability of the country to feed itself and to produce the most basic goods was extremely limited.

In 1979, the country lacked a currency, functioning markets, tax collection mechanisms, public administration and manufacturing infrastructure. Reversing this legacy was a massive task, one that the government tackled using coercion, while also trying to build political support among the country's population. The reorganisation of agricultural production into *Krom Samaki* (solidarity groups) was intended to increase agricultural production. The new regime also re-established the public administration, initially dominated by Vietnamese officials but gradually assumed by Cambodian cadres. Both these moves offered the government mechanisms through which the newly formed Cambodian Communist Party (CCP) could undertake its programme of political re-education.

Aware of the political legacy of the Khmer Rouge and the distrust this had created, for example regarding collectivisation of agriculture, and suffering too from an absolute scarcity of resources, the new government took a necessarily pragmatic ideological line. *Laisser-faire* approaches to economic production were an inevitable result of the country's inability to meet demand for basic goods. Left unregulated, however, this pragmatic approach to economic management quickly resulted in a strong parallel market.

During the 1980s, Eastern bloc countries and Vietnam remained the primary source of support for the new government. A few Western NGOs and UNICEF remained in the country, but unusually they worked primarily with and through the Cambodian government, largely in and around Phnom Penh (Mysliwiec 1994).

The start of peace negotiations in the late 1980s coincided with a period of economic and political liberalisation, paving the way for a gradual increase in international presence inside Cambodia itself. Between 1988 and 1990, the UN sent more than a dozen fact-finding missions to the country, and in mid-1990, USAID began a dialogue with the Vietnamese government and the state of Cambodia (Lanjouw et al. 1998). This period was thus crucial in laying the ground for the resolution of the ongoing conflict and the normalisation of Cambodia's international relations.

In sum, in the decade 1979–88 Cambodia's sovereignty was questioned juridically. At the same time, the empirical sovereignty remained very weak, and the state lacked internal legitimacy. Like former regimes, the SOC was highly dependent on international aid for its survival.

War, the State and International Relations in Ethiopia 1974–91

Until 1974, Ethiopia was a feudal empire, dominated by the Amhara ethnic group (Zewde 1994). The unity of the empire was maintained by promoting intermarriage between members of the extended imperial family and local dignitaries in 'occupied' territories. Becoming *amharized*, in other words adopting the Amhara language and culture and membership of the Ethiopian Orthodox Church, was a precondition for upward mobility within political and bureaucratic circles (Krylow 1994). The last emperor, Haile Selassie, introduced limited administrative reforms and delegated some political authority to a nominal parliament. However, the economy continued to centre on the extraction by the aristocracy of 50–70 per cent of peasant production (Dessalegn 1994). Under-investment in rural production systems and in the country's infrastructure meant little agricultural surplus and limited access to either markets or services (Krylow 1994).

In 1952, Eritrea, a former Italian colony that had been declared a UN protectorate after the Second World War, was federated against its wishes into Ethiopia. The Eritrean Liberation Front (ELF) was formed, and in 1961 began an armed struggle to overthrow Ethiopian rule that was to last three decades. In March 1974 the imperial regime was finally ousted by a military takeover, which coincided with a period of widespread and intense famine in the country. The new government comprised a committee, or Derg, made up of a group of young officers. In 1975, the government, now led by a young officer, Mengistu Haile Miriam, adopted a revolutionary socialist agenda, initiating an extensive programme of nationalisation across the industrial, financial and agricultural sectors. These reforms nationalised and then redistributed land to the peasantry, a process managed, largely competently, by a newly established network of Peasants' Associations (PAs) (Dessalegn 1994).

Initially, there was optimism that the new government would redress the over-centralisation of the state, and empower non-Amharas to take greater control over their political and economic affairs. Instead, however, it deepened the centralised political and administrative structures that had characterised the empire, albeit under a new umbrella of state socialism. The Derg's failure to respond to calls for the independence of Eritrea stiffened opposition, reflected in a move away from the narrow, conservative and Muslim-dominated ELF to a more broadly based political movement, the Eritrean People's Liberation Front (EPLF).

Elsewhere, new challenges to the internal legitimacy of the state emerged. In 1975, the Tigrayan People's Liberation Front (TPLF) was established, seeking to assert greater regional autonomy.[7] In 1977, President Said Barre of Somalia launched an incursion into Ethiopia, claiming sovereignty over the Ogaden region. The Ogaden war became internationalised as both the USA and the Soviet Union sought to reinforce their respective allies along the strategic Red Sea coast. Following the takeover of the Derg, the USA had switched its political support from Ethiopia to Somalia, prompting a converse exchange of loyalty on the part of the USSR. The war, which last nearly a year, and caused extensive displacement, death and injury, ended with an Ethiopian victory. Meanwhile, the state was turning on itself. The period 1977–82 claimed an estimated 12–15,000 lives in purges that became known as the Red Terror.

Ethiopia's Soviet-backed government remained a worrying anomaly for the US government in the Red Sea region, where the majority of states (Kenya, Somalia and Sudan) were Western allies. The Carter administration, reinforced by a series of Congressional Amendments, decided to invoke human rights conditionalities and thus effectively blocked aid to the country (Duffield and Prendergast 1994). The USA also applied pressure to limit other multilateral and bilateral aid to Ethiopia, opposing loans to the country by the World Bank and the African Development Bank, for example.

The US position was not shared initially by the majority of European donor countries. Sweden, for example, actively welcomed the revolutionary regime, deciding to maintain its development programme in the country despite growing recognition of the Ethiopian government's poor human rights record (interview, diplomat, Addis Ababa, March 1995). The European Commission was particularly supportive of the Mengistu regime. The Lomé Agreement, which governed the EC's aid relations in Africa, stipulated clearly an unconditional respect for the sovereignty of aid-receiving countries. Ethiopia became one of the EC's largest aid programmes, and the Commission actively supported the government's policy, including its programme of resettlement and villagisation initiated in the late 1970s (Duffield and Prendergast 1994; Maxwell et al. 1995).

As famine intensified once again in the mid-1980s, and evidence of food aid diversion and of human rights violations associated with villagisation and the war increased, so European donor opinion began to change.[8] Villagisation and collectivisation of agriculture displaced 400,000 families, or 1.8 million people, from their homes and land (Dessalegn 1993). In parallel to the villagisation programme was a another policy – resettlement. Linked to the prosecution of the war in the north, the government's resettlement schemes were enacted in 1984/5, a year of widespread famine, and sought to remove a potential source of support for the rebels. An estimated 750,000 households, some 3.5 million people, were forcibly relocated in poorly organised moves southwards (Holcomb and Clay 1985). As a result of inadequate logistics and preparations at resettlement sites, some 6–8 per cent of those resettled are estimated to have died (Dessalegn 1993).

The combination of policies of ruthless prosecution of the war and military socialism continued to rely upon extraction from peasant production through taxation, fees and control of markets. Dessalegn (1992) estimated that up to one-third of peasant production was accrued by the state. In order to maintain this level of extraction, the Peasants' Associations (PA), established as an instrument of revolutionary change controlled by the peasantry, soon became an instrument of state control. Entwined with the Ethiopian Socialist Party, which had been officially launched only in 1984, the PAs provided an unparalleled network through which the state could penetrate down to often small and isolated communities. The responsibilities of these organisations and other similar production-linked rural organisations expanded to include tax collection, law and order and even military recruitment (Clapham 1988).

As detailed in Chapter 6, despite, and in part because of, these policies the economic outlook remained bleak during the Mengistu era. The combination of war, economic mismanagement of previous regimes, substantial external debt, and dependence on rain-fed agriculture in a drought-prone region meant that the country remained vulnerable to chronic economic decline and acute economic instability. The military continued to act as a significant drain on the economy, consuming not only valuable human resources, but also the lion's share of public budgets. During the period 1987/88 to 1990/1 per capita agricultural production declined by 2.7 per cent. The country thus became increasingly dependent on food imports, while the decline in the production of exportable goods, and continued high military expenditure, meant that the government lacked the resources to pay for these imports.

Recognising its political weakness, and in need of re-establishing international economic support, in March 1990 the Mengistu regime signalled a major policy about-turn, declaring socialism a failure, dissolving the Ethiopian Socialist Party and collectivised production strategies, and promoting a mixed economy. However, these policy changes were insufficient to prevent military defeat or to persuade official aid agencies to resume their support.[9]

As the government weakened in the late 1980s and early 1990s, so opposition consolidated in the shape of a coalition party known as the Ethiopian People's Democratic Movement, and its military front (EPRDM/F). This was led by the TPLF, but also embraced Oromo and Amhara groups.[10]

Clapham (1996) describes how some insurgent movements operate as quasi-states, demonstrating aspects of empirical statehood, controlling territory and resources and in some cases, such as the TPLF, enjoying popular support (Duffield and Prendergast 1994; Hendrie 1989, 1994). Juridically, however, such movements lack any formal status. The process of achieving external legitimation was an incremental one for the TPLF/EPRDM and was linked intimately with the politics of food and relief aid.

Throughout the early 1980s, food security remained precarious in the northern regions as a result of war and drought (Hendrie 1989), and the government blocked food deliveries as part of its counter-insurgency strategy (Duffield and Prendergast 1994). As famine intensified, the government sought to lure populations out of rebel-held territory by providing food aid. Partially successful, it was this strategy that culminated in the fatal gatherings at the famine camps of Wollo, pictured on televisions worldwide. In order to avoid moving into government-held territory and risk internal deportation under the resettlement scheme, others left the country entirely, seeking refuge in neighbouring Sudan (Hendrie 1989).

The legitimation of the rebel movements became intimately linked with enabling populations to stay in their homes or to return from exile in Sudan. As described in Chapter 2, the cross-border relief operation from Sudan into rebel-held areas of Tigray and Eritrea marked a significant moment in international humanitarian policy (Duffield 1994a), and consolidated the rebel movements as serious political actors internally and internationally (Duffield and Prendergast 1994). Initially funded by private, voluntary contributions from church-based Northern NGOS and indigenous contributions, by the mid-1980s the cross-border operation attracted major official aid contributions from the USA and the European Commission, albeit channelled discreetly through third-party NGOS (Duffield and Prendergast 1994).

The relief operations, and the contacts with civil groups in the USA and Europe they provided, constituted a political bridge that the rebel movements' insurgents could use to prepare the ground for the normalisation of aid relations after the defeat of Mengistu in June 1991. In the weeks leading up to the regime's defeat, a process of 'transferring' sovereignty and international legitimacy to the TPLF-dominated opposition group – the EPRDM – was already under way. The Dutch government, for example, reported meeting at a very senior level a leading EPRDM figure on 1 May 1991; three weeks later the representative was the minister of foreign affairs (interview, diplomat, Addis Ababa, March 1995). Thus, as the Derg became increasingly discredited politically and on the battlefield, so the foundations for the transition from relief to development aid were being laid.

In summary, Ethiopia has experienced sustained problems in establishing itself as a legitimate unified state. While state institutions have proved remarkably efficient in terms of their penetration into remote rural communities, this enormous bureaucratic capacity has been used to enable massive extraction of resources from the peasants and not to deliver effective protection and services (Clapham 1988). The country remained highly dependent on aid, in particular, to feed itself. Aid has been highly politicised in Ethiopia, with tight restrictions on development aid into government-held areas after the revolution, and played an important role in legitimising rebel groups in the lead up to their takeover of power in 1991.

War, the State and International Relations in Uganda

The stage for conflict was set in Uganda during the colonial era. The British had relied upon creating ethnic division in order to rule the territory, setting in train a pattern of differential and inequitable development and of militarisation of power (Ghebali 1985). The colonial state comprised three ethnically and politically fragmented provinces, and a fourth that consisted of an historically and politically coherent unit (Wrigley 1988). It was this latter province, Buganda, that formed the staging-post for the creation of the British Protectorate of Uganda in the nineteenth century, and acted as the political and commercial focus for the building of a colonial state.

The Baganda, the people of Buganda, were allowed to maintain their dominant position in the country and from its peoples an educated and privileged elite emerged (Low 1988). As preparations for independence got under way, in 1953 the *kabaka* (king) of Buganda sought to retain the autonomy of his kingdom by establishing special privileges for it in the constitution. The British authorities responded by deporting him, prompting a fierce reaction from his supporters. The nationalism of the Baganda alienated other ethnic groups who feared continued marginalisation. At the forefront of the opposition to Bagandan supremacy was Milton Obote, leader of the Uganda People's Congress (UPC). The pre-independence elections in 1962 suffered from these divisions, culminating in the first of a series of fragile and unlikely coalitions, lead by Obote, but including the *kabaka*.[11] In 1966, the president suspended the constitution and ordered the army to attack the *kabaka*'s palace and forcibly remove him. The series of alliances on which Obote relied to maintain power became ever more precarious, increasing his dependence on the army.

In the end, even the army proved an unreliable ally, however. In 1971, Idi Amin, a senior army officer, seized power in a coup backed by Britain and Israel. Amin's army was characterised by ethnic division, which had hardened under the factionalised political system of the late 1960s and early 1970s. The new president responded to these threats by mounting vicious campaigns against the Langi and Acholi ethnic groups of northern Uganda, the mainstay of Obote's support. Once again, to compensate for the alienation of one section of the population, Amin sought alliances with others. Again, however, these quickly failed.

A year after seizing power, Amin expelled the country's 80,000 Asians and seized their assets. This policy of supposed 'Africanisation' of Ugandan commercial and economic life failed to yield sustained popular support. Instead, it catalysed a process of economic decline that marked the beginnings of a predatory economy. In order to survive the state relied increasingly upon asset-stripping, bribery for licences and unregulated trade (Green 1981). The violent political economy of Idi Amin's rule is estimated to have claimed some 300,000 lives (Sivard 1993).

Throughout the 1970s, the Amin dictatorship had been a source of concern to the neighbouring Tanzanian government. It had provided a home for Ugandan exiles, encouraging them to organise into opposition and develop an alternative basis for government. As his power base weakened, Amin launched a diversionary attack on Tanzania in December 1978, so prompting a tough military response from that country's president, Julius Nyerere. By April 1979, Tanzanian authorities had effectively overthrown Amin's government, paving the way for a series of precarious transitional governments, each of which managed to further alienate different segments of the country's rich variety of ethnic groups and further divide the ever powerful army.

Elections in 1980 re-established Milton Obote as president, although the results were widely considered fraudulent. However, the new regime signalled the re-establishment of aid relations with Uganda, and the resumption of lending from the World Bank and the IMF. Within months of his 'election', however, Obote faced insurgencies from a number of forces, in particular that of the National Resistance Army (NRA), led by Yoweri Museveni. The successes of this force prompted a new reign of terror by the Obote regime, which many have described as worse even than that of Amin. Within the 'Luwero Triangle', the home area of the NRM, Obote mounted a particularly vicious counter-insurgency campaign, forcibly resettling large populations in order to remove civilian support for the NRA. The fighting during this period led to over 300,000 deaths (Sivard 1993). In Luwero district alone more than 200,000 skulls were found scattered (Luwero District Administration 1988).

By 1984, insecurity and persistent abuse of human rights led to growing tensions between the government and bilateral donors, leading to substantial reductions in aid flows (Economist Intelligence Unit 1992). Divisions within the army weakened Obote's grip on power and paved the way for a coup in July 1985. During the rest of that year, the newly formed government sought a negotiated peace with the NRA, and the two parties signed a truce in December 1985. Despite the agreement, however, the NRA continued to move towards Kampala, seizing power in early 1986, and installing Museveni as Uganda's eighth president.

However, the NRM inherited a country in tatters. The potential that had led Winston Churchill to famously proclaim Uganda as the

Pearl of Africa had remained at best unrealised, at worst squandered. The state remained a precarious institution, unable to garner sufficient legitimacy from all sections of the population either by appeal to national identity, or in return for protection and basic services. The majority of the population survived despite the state, not because of it. In this context of political instability and violence, development aid relations were repeatedly interrupted.

Public Health: Needs and Response in Quasi-states

Health and health services in quasi-states In an important paper, Zwi and Ugalde (1989) map out the conceptual basis of an epidemiology of political violence. Their paper made a significant contribution to a literature that emerged in the late 1980s and sought to count the broader costs of war (see also, for example, Green 1994; Stewart 1994; UNICEF 1987). The paper also contributed to the growing legitimation of the issue of conflict and political violence on the international health policy agenda, and more broadly in development studies.[12] The authors distinguish between the direct and indirect effects of conflict. These are listed in Table 4.1.

Table 4.1 Direct and indirect impacts of political violence on health and health systems

Direct effects of political violence on health and health systems	Indirect effects of political violence on health and health systems
Death	Economic pressures and disruption
Disability	Decreased food production and distribution
Injury	Family destruction (e.g. more orphans and abandoned children)
Destruction of health services	Refugees
Disruption of health programmes	Psychological stress
Psychological stress	Impact on housing, water supply and sewage disposal
	Economic pressures on those caring for war-disabled

Source: Zwi and Ugalde 1989: 633.

Zwi and Ugalde further disaggregate the impacts of conflict on health services (see Table 4.2).

This research confirms the significant direct and indirect effects of conflict on health and health services (the detailed findings of interviews with communities and health workers can be found in the individual country reports). However, it also highlights a potential problem with the approach adopted by Zwi and Ugalde, namely that it risks confusing the particular *consequences* of violence with its causes. It can wrongly associate increased health need and the problems facing health systems in conflict-affected countries with violence *per se*, rather than with the political economy of violent states. In doing so, it risks assuming that once the problem of violence is removed, then a 'normal' process of health development can be resumed. This approach risks sustaining the developmentalist fallacy that conflict is an interruption to the otherwise progressive process of health and health systems development.

In order to counter this fallacy, the analysis presented below adopts a more historical, contextual approach to analysing the problems

Table 4.2 The impact of political violence on health services

---

Disruption of lines of communication and referral
Diminished training and supervision of staff
Physical isolation of services from each other
Increased difficulty of attracting staff to work in peripheral areas
Increased difficulty in gaining access to services, e.g. due to curfews
Disruption of mass campaigns
Disruption of routine monitoring and surveillance measures
Reduced infectious disease control measures, e.g. malaria control
Lack of supplies including drugs and equipment
Emigration of skilled health personnel
Greater dependence on foreign personnel and aid
Diversion of resources to providing acute care for injuries
Long-term demand on health services for providing rehabilitation services
Death, assault and repression of health workers
Destruction of health facilities

Source: Zwi and Ugalde 1989: 635.

facing the public health sector in the three case study countries. This suggests that many of these problems pre-dated the onset of conflict, and were symptomatic of long-standing structural political and economic pressures, not simply of violence.

Health, health systems and 'war': Cambodia Cambodia's health system was inherited from the French colonial administration, and was largely hospital-based. In the post-independence period, this emphasis on curative care, particularly in urban areas, was sustained. Coverage was expanded and more Cambodian health professionals were trained, funded largely by external assistance. Despite considerable investment in disease control and maternal and child health projects, by 1967 only 15 per cent coverage had been achieved (Lanjouw et al. 1998).

The subsuming of Cambodia into the Vietnam War in the early 1970s had a devastating human and economic cost, interrupting production and forcing mass population displacement as well as directly killing over 700,000 people, some 10 per cent of the population (Curtis 1989). The war also severely damaged the health system: of the 29 hospital facilities that were operational in early 1970, 16 were destroyed or damaged (Lanjouw et al. 1998).

The disastrous public health situation was exacerbated during the Khmer Rouge period, which saw not only continuing declines in food production and health conditions, but also the dismantling of the nascent public health system. Lanjouw et al. (1998) describe the devastating impact of conflict on the human resource base. The combination of conflict, out-migration and purges targeting 'intellectuals' saw a reduction in the number of doctors and health officers from an estimated 462 in 1969 to approximately 50 in 1979. In place of the previously existing system, the regime emphasised the promotion of traditional medicine, and the training of community health workers. Many young people were trained, often for very short periods, but without clear guidance on hygiene or diagnosis. Their impact was therefore limited and even negative in terms of health impact.

While some of the hospital infrastructure had been maintained by the Khmer Rouge in order to provide health services to the military and the political elite, even this residual infrastructure was destroyed as they retreated in the face of the Vietnamese invasion. During the international emergency operation (1979–82) some US$13.4 million was allocated to the health sector, predominantly for hospital rehabilitation and the re-establishment of medical supplies. By August 1979, significant progress had been made in the rehabilitation of the health infrastructure, and during the early 1980s there were important developments in terms of the new government's policy, which emphasised decentralisation of health service delivery and free healthcare for all, with an emphasis on maternal and child health.

However, as Lanjouw et al. (1998) report, the withdrawal of international assistance, the imposition of trade and aid sanctions and the persistent poverty of the country combined to limit the extent to which the newly restored infrastructure could provide effective health services. During the early 1980s, there were persistent and fundamental problems in the sector, including a chronic shortage of drugs and health personnel, particularly outside Phnom Penh. The government sought to respond to these problems by adapting the Vietnamese model of health service provision. Under the close scrutiny of Vietnamese political and technical advisers, the physical infrastructure was expanded significantly. In order to meet demand, a new generation of health workers were trained at a remarkable rate given the scarcity of basic financial resources and other inputs. However, the rapid pace at which training took place necessarily meant compromising on quality. Further, as in many countries, the tendency was for trained health workers (particularly doctors) to remain in Phnom Penh, limiting the quality of rural services.

Despite the policy commitment to primary healthcare, the emphasis remained largely curative. Drug supplies had improved, but remained inadequate despite substantial imports from the Soviet bloc of raw materials for local pharmaceutical production and of 'finished' drugs. In addition, UNICEF and ICRC provided inputs estimated at approximately US$10 million per year.[13]

The effects of continued conflict and international isolation, particularly after 1982, meant that the gains in health and health service provision remained threatened. Populations were again displaced from their homes, and the effort to clear forests in the border area as part of the counter-insurgency campaign exacerbated the problem of malaria. Lanjouw et al. (1998) note that, despite these significant constraints and setbacks, the 1980s did yield progress on key indicators. According to UNICEF (1989) statistics, in the period 1980–87 general mortality rates halved from 30/1,000 to 12.4/1,000, as did infant mortality rates, which fell from 212/1,000 to 120/1,000.

Health, health systems and war: Ethiopia   There was no developed health policy in Ethiopia until 1950 when, as part of his modernising strategy for the country, Emperor Haile Selassie sought to establish a public health system. This policy was elaborated further during the 1960s, in collaboration with the WHO. However, by the time of the military takeover by the Derg in 1974, only some 15 per cent of the population was estimated to have access to 'modern' health services (Ethiopia 1978).

The WHO/UNICEF-sponsored Alma Ata Declaration on Health for All of 1978 did not go unrecognised by Ethiopia. The government committed itself to the strategy early, and by 1980 primary healthcare had become official health policy (UNICEF 1982). The principal mechanism for implementation was the training and deployment of community health agents (CHAs) (Ethiopia 1978). Between 1978 and 1981, 2,500 CHAs and traditional birth attendants were trained. During the same period, the hospital network continued to expand, but at a slower rate than in the past.[14] The extent to which health service provision could be decentralised and become rooted in a community-based service was limited, however, by staffing and budgetary short-ages, which limited the supervision and training of staff working at the lower levels of the system (World Bank 1985).[15]

Optimistic forecasts that the strategies of the early 1980s had signifi-cantly increased the population's access to health services were crushed by a World Bank report in 1985. This built on the results of the census conducted a year earlier. This had revealed that the population comprised some 42 million people, some 8 million more than pre-viously estimated. These revised figures implied a significant downward revision in estimates of coverage from 45 per cent to 35 per cent. Yet even this figure was presumed to be an over-estimate because of the extremely low aggregate rates of health services utilisation: 0.6 out-patient visits per head per year, compared with an average of 2 in other countries with large rural populations (ibid.). Despite steady growth in social sector budgets between 1974 and 1982, real growth remained substantially lower and, as described in detail in Chapter 6, actually declined every year after 1985 (UNICEF 1982).[16] Imbalances in secular allocations also emerged during this period, with urban and tertiary facilities capturing a disproportionate share of the government budget (World Bank 1994a). The net effect of these trends was a further reduction in coverage. As in all situations, it is difficult to disentangle the particular effects of conflict from those associated with chronic poverty and vulnerability to drought, for example, and political decline. However, it has been estimated that over one million Ethiopians died during the 30 years of war in northern Ethiopia, excluding Eritrean casualties (Ethiopia 1993). A large number of people were also disabled by the fighting. Kloos (1992) estimated that about one-third of the 300,000 prisoners of war returning home were disabled, while the 1984 census revealed more than 40,000 people who had had limbs amputated.

Health, health systems and war: Uganda   As in Cambodia, the Ugandan health system was shaped during the colonial period. It too was hospital-based and biased in favour of urban areas. Unlike many of its neighbours, which initiated community-based services in the late 1960s and 1970s, the Ugandan expansion of health services into rural areas consisted largely of building district hospitals. However, there was also a slow expansion of lower-level facilities, and by 1970 nearly 60 per cent of the population was living within ten kilometres of a health unit (Dodge 1986).

The political crisis that emerged in the 1970s reversed these gains, however. The 1970s and 1980s were associated with a decline rather than improvement in health status, with infant, child and under-five mortality all rising, particularly during 1978–82.[17] High rates of out-migration from towns to rural areas led to a reduction in the capacity of small farmers to feed extended families and a subsequent increase in malnutrition and related pathologies. The emergence of lucrative smuggling routes was linked to the spread of HIV, as prostitution became widespread along the main roads in and out of the country (Bond and Vincent 1990). Smallman-Raynor and Cliff (1991) argue that patterns of HIV infection in Uganda were also strongly correlated with ethnic patterns of army recruitment after 1979. Their work suggests that rape and other changes in sexual behaviour in the context of war had an important impact on the pattern of STD transmission, including HIV. This observation has been echoed by

Zwi and Cabral (1991) in relation to other conflicts and related 'high-risk' situations.

The ability of the health system to respond to the increased and altered disease burden was also significantly reduced. As in Cambodia and Ethiopia, health facilities suffered from the effects of neglect and the absence of repair for nearly two decades. This, along with the more direct effects of the militarisation of society – for example, the use of health facilities as military barracks and looting – meant that by 1986 the infrastructure was in a very poor state of repair, with many facilities barely useable (Annet and Janovsky 1988).

The human resource base was also shattered. The expulsion of the Asian community in 1972, combined with the general climate of insecurity and violence during the Amin years, prompted a massive 'brain drain', whereby the number of doctors registered in the country fell from 978 in 1967–68 to 564 in 1979, and pharmacists from 116 to 15. Also affected was the capacity in the public administration to formulate and execute health policy. This led one expatriate adviser working in the sector to comment that:

> While the weakness in the public sector is not unique to Uganda, at the central level, there is a particular problem because it was there that the brain drain was most acute during the periods of instability [leaving] a problem in terms of middle and senior level capacity within the country.

A senior Ugandan health planner also blamed the slow pace of health policy development after 1986 on this lack of experienced senior staff. Interviews with health staff in Luwero and Soroti noted that it was typically senior personnel who left the districts first, leaving relatively junior staff in charge of hospitals, health centres and management activities.

As Chapter 6 details, during the 1970s and 1980s there were significant changes in the financing of the sector, further reducing its capacity to function. As access to public health facilities declined in terms of both quantity and quality of service provision, so reliance increased on private provision. In 1988 it was estimated that about 50 per cent of healthcare was provided by the missions (Annet and Janovsky 1988). Private expenditure was estimated to account for four-fifths of total health expenditure in the country (ibid).[18] Interviews conducted during the course of this research confirmed the findings of Whyte's (1990) work that self-management, the most extreme form of privatisation, was often the only option available to people isolated and impoverished. Thus one woman in Semuto, Luwero district, recounted:

> Before the war, the people used to seek healthcare from the health centre seven miles away. While in the bush, people had to rely on traditional herbs and others simply went without any form of treatment ... People returned to their homes in 1985, but at that time the health unit wasn't working, therefore people continued to rely on traditional herbs and those with emergency medical needs sometimes contacted the NRA barracks for assistance.

The interviews in Soroti and Luwero confirmed that the missions proved more resilient to the impacts of conflict since their perceived neutrality meant that their buildings and staff were not targeted by the different factions, external resources remained available to sustain activities and staff tended to share a religious motivation that encouraged them to stay in often extremely difficult situations.

In summary, the war had a devastating impact on health and health services in Uganda. Its effects were superimposed on a health system that, in common with other non-conflict-affected countries, was unlikely to have proved either sustainable or equitable.

Summary and Conclusions

This chapter has described the history of conflict and its impact on national political economies and on health and health systems in the three case study countries. While there are significant differences between the countries in terms of the origins of conflict and impacts, there are also important similarities.

First, the protracted and multi-faceted nature of conflict is evident. Each of the countries has experienced not one, but a series of conflicts, each of which has had its roots in internal political dynamics and regional and international interventions. Cumulatively, these successive conflicts have characterised the political landscape over decades. The complex and protracted nature of these conflicts has both reflected and exacerbated the problem of state formation in these countries.

The inability to form a legitimate basis for governance, and for the state to secure and redistribute the resources required to establish its legitimacy, has constituted the major obstacle to health systems' development.

Violence and contested governance have also shaped the history of aid relations in the three countries, influencing heavily the flow of aid, particularly of development assistance. Ideological factors were important in influencing aid flows, particularly with regard to the USA in Ethiopia and Cambodia. Whatever the political preference of donor countries, operationally their room for manoeuvre has been heavily compromised by persistent and widespread insecurity and the collapse of public institutions.

What is also evident in the three case studies is that the crisis of health and of health systems is structural, not simply infrastructural. Cambodia's dependence on international assistance to sustain its hospital-based system was evident from the 1960s, and in all three countries coverage of public health services remained low and worsened during the decades of conflict. Inequalities between urban and rural areas were apparent since the earliest days of Western medicine being introduced, as were the problems caused by intra-sectoral allocations, leaving primary healthcare policies largely un-implemented in favour of hospital-based care. A further common feature is the particularly weak human resource base at all levels of each health system.

In light of the problems faced in sustaining public health services by other least developed countries that are not directly affected by conflict (see, for example, LaFond 1995), it becomes clear that, while military violence undoubtedly played a major role in creating health crises, it alone was not primarily responsible for the poor functioning of the health systems. Rather, the essential problem was a breakdown in the functioning of the political institutions that governed economic and social life. In addition to threatening life, through the use of widespread torture, military action and failure to protect populations from criminal violence, the state determined the opportunities for production and for access to basic services such as health. Thus, as important as, if not more so than, the military transition from war to peace is the political process of transition associated with regime change. The extent to which successor regimes prove legitimate (nationally and internationally) and competent is thus seen to be a critical determinant of the functioning of aid and of *public* health systems.

Developing a *publicly* financed health system is now widely understood to be a necessary condition for health development, and it is accepted that public health gains will not be adequately secured in the least developed countries primarily through private provision. The World Bank lists three 'economic rationales' for maintaining the involvement of government in the health sector:

- The poor cannot always afford healthcare that would improve their productivity and well-being. Publicly-financed investment in the health of the poor can thus be seen as part of a wider strategy of poverty alleviation and reduction;
- Some actions that promote health, for example control of infectious disease, are pure public goods or create large positive externalities that the private market cannot match;
- Market failures in health care meant that government intervention can raise welfare by improving how these markets function. (World Bank 1993)

In addition to the economic arguments in favour of public provision might be added that the provision of health services serves a political function, legitimating the state in the eyes of the population (Clapham 1996; Moore 1998). The provision of basic public services constitutes part of what it is to be an empirical state. It is thus a working assumption of this study that a key task facing rehabilitation aid planners is to rebuild public capacity for the delivery of health services. This is not only because such capacity is widely accepted to be a *sine qua non* of effective and equitable provision, but because reconstituting such capacity is also a precondition for the development of effective and legitimate statehood. Chapter 5 examines how the context of weak and unstable statehood has affected the organisation and execution of rehabilitation aid programming.

Notes

1. See Inyatullah and Blaney (1995) for a more detailed analysis of the costs of statehood.

2. This contextual section draws extensively on Lanjouw et al. (1998); Curtis (1994).

3. In the early 1970s, as many tonnes of explosive were dropped on Cambodia as had fallen on Germany during the whole of the Second World War.

4. See Lanjouw et al. (1998), particularly Chapter 2, for a detailed analysis of why this was the case and of the different estimates.

5. China and the Soviet Union consistently disagreed on the question of the legitimacy of the new regime, reflecting their own geopolitical interests in South-East Asia. China allied itself with the US and European members of the Council in opposing the Vietnamese-backed government, while the USSR lobbied for its recognition.

6. Shawcross (1984), in one of the earliest and most detailed accounts of any single humanitarian operation, analyses in vivid detail the layers of national and international politics that shaped the relief operations for Cambodia.

7. By 1983, when Meles Zenawi became the chief ideologue of the TPLF, the movement started to move away from a narrow, Tigrayan ideology and towards a state-wide orientation. It was this attempt to establish a broad-based political movement, which rejected the political principles and organisation of the Derg, that provided for the formation of the EPRDF (Krylow 1994).

8. Duffield and Prendergast (1994) provide a fascinating account of the constitutional struggle between the European Commission and Parliament in 1982, as the latter tried to impose political conditions on European Aid, a move rejected by the Commission on the grounds that it reflected undue US political influence (see also Maxwell et al. 1995).

9. For example, in a review of its policy under Mengistu, a World Bank document referred to this period as follows:

> The Bank's activities under the previous administration were limited to a core programme because of the Government's failure to introduce a feasible and convincing programme of reform. With the economy in dire straits the Government announced a dramatic policy shift away from centrally planned economy to open market principles in March of 1990. However, from that point on, the security situation rapidly deteriorated and not enough of the announced programme was implemented to make a fundamental difference to the economic situation before the previous Government fell to rebel forces in May 1991. (World Bank, 1992a)

10. Specifically, the Ethiopian People's Democratic Movement in Wollo and Gojam, a splinter group of the Ethiopian People's Revolutionary Party (EPRP), and the Oromo People's Democratic Organisation, a group formed largely of Oromo soldiers who had been prisoners of war under the Derg, and liberated by the EPRDF.

11. The first election led to the surprise victory of the Catholic-dominated Democratic Party. This led Obote to form an anti-government alliance with the KY party, so forcing a second election that resulted in Obote becoming president.

12. It is significant, for example, that it was not until the mid-1990s that agencies such as the UK's Overseas Development Administration included conflict as an issue on its specialist health research agenda. Equally, until this period there was a virtual absence of courses for health professionals that focused on the particular health needs of conflict-affected populations, and operational demands of conflict. Now there is an abundance of such courses at masters degree level, including those at the London School of Hygiene and Tropical Medicine, Liverpool School of Hygiene and Tulane University.

13. Draper and Watts (1989) *Report of the Kampuchean Needs Assessment Study*, Bangkok, UNDP, cited in Lanjouw et al. (1988).

14. UNICEF (1982) reports that the rate of growth of the hospital sector between 1974 and 1981 was only 2 per cent, while the number of health centres increased by 44 per cent and of health stations by 200 per cent.

15. One of the arguments put forward by the government in favour of the villagisation programmes of the early 1980s was that it would increase the accessibility of health services, a view apparently shared initially by UNICEF (1982).

16. In the period 1985/6 to 1988/9 as a share of total recurrent expenditure, health declined from 2.58 per cent to 2.3 per cent. In the same period, military expenditure continued to escalate from 23.6 per cent to 30.6 per cent (Ethiopia 1994). See Chapter 6 for further details of trends in public sector spending, including health.

17. The following table summarises these trends:

	Infant mortality rate	Child mortality rate	Under-fives mortality rate
1973–77	92	97	180
1978–82	114	97	200
1983–88	101	88	180

Source: UNICEF (1989) *Women and Children: A Situation Analysis*, UNICEF, Kampala.

18. Whyte (1990) provides a fascinating account of the process of privatisation of health provision in Uganda during the 1970s and 1980s.

. . . .

CHAPTER 5

The Legitimacy Dilemma: Aid in a Vacuum

§ Chapter 3 described the emergence of a 'new' aid orthodoxy: namely that in conflict-affected countries aid can and should be more developmental, and that by adopting these objectives and working methods aid could contribute to wider goals of peace-building. This chapter examines the relief to development aid transition in practice in the three case study countries, building upon the conceptual framework presented in Chapters 2 and 3. As these earlier chapters argued, the developmentalist paradigm underpinning the new orthodoxy makes important assumptions regarding the recipient state. In particular, it assumes that a juridical body exists that has the competence to manage aid and that the state is internationally recognised.

Chapter 4 described how, in all three countries, conflict reflected and exacerbated the weakness of empirical sovereignty and the internal legitimacy of successive regimes, and how this had had sustained and negative consequences for the establishment of effective health services. It further highlighted the linkages between access to international assistance and international legitimation, and demonstrated that at the time of transition the legitimacy of the new regimes was far from clear.

This chapter argues that the particular political conditions prevailing at the time of transition critically influenced the form, channels and systems of aid available for rehabilitation aid. *Form* means whether aid is provided as project, programme, loan or grant and as relief or development aid. The term *channels* refers to whether aid is delivered through multilateral, bilateral or NGO mechanisms. *Systems* are the mechanisms in place for making aid policy (Cassels 1998). Clearly these are linked. A particular form of aid will influence the use of particular channels that, in turn, use their own accounting and management systems. These choices determine the objectives, time-frame and content of aid programmes, and their impact on health systems.

It is the contention of this chapter that the choice of the form of aid is shaped profoundly by the political context, and in particular by the peculiar problems of empirical and juridical sovereignty as states undergo political transition. It therefore describes these peculiar conditions of statehood in relation to the case studies. This analysis of empirical and juridical sovereignty is used to examine how aid agencies confronted the particular dilemma of legitimacy identified in Chapter 3. It questions how the international community can seek to buttress the empirical sovereignty of states through the provision of developmental aid, while at the same time limiting development assistance on the grounds that the conditions of empirical and juridical sovereignty are not in place. In other words, how do aid actors engage with states when they are not yet sure that they like them and/or when those states cannot act as states. It concludes that the problem of legitimacy in transitional states, combined with their empirical weakness, confines the forms of aid to those that are least likely to meet developmental goals.

The chapter then describes the specific national and international political dynamics of transition and the way in which this influenced the form and content of aid in Cambodia, Ethiopia and Uganda respectively, and comparatively analyses the trends in the aid transition across the three countries.

In Search of a Constitution for Decision-making: Cambodia

UNTAC and all that: the political framework for transition International efforts to resolve the Cambodian conflict resulted in one of the most complex and expensive mechanisms to provide a legitimate political bridge for decision-making in a situation of post-conflict transition. As described in Chapter 4, during the 1980s there was no effective sovereign Cambodian state: the *de facto* government remained unrecognised by the majority of Western governments, while the body that was accorded the status of juridical sovereign controlled little territory and none of the state institutions. Thus, in the lead-up to the elections in May 1993, it was unclear who was to oversee the process of rehabilitation, monitor the demobilisation and re-formation of a national army, organise elections and maintain basic functions of the public administration. In terms of aid management, the issue was who would determine the allocation of the millions of dollars pledged for rehabilitation assistance.

The Paris Accords established the United Nations Transitional Authority in Cambodia (UNTAC). This body was to provide the framework for political decision-making. It was intended to distinguish and separate territorial from political control during the transition period. Unique in international law, UNTAC drew its legitimacy from a body comprising the four Cambodian factions – the Supreme National Council (SNC).[1] The SNC comprised thirteen members, and was chaired by Prince Sihanouk, the former head of state (1954–70). Importantly, the SNC embodied the juridical entity recognised by the United Nations. The SNC delegated all powers necessary to implement the Paris Accords to the United Nations, the latter represented by the special representative of the secretary-general (SRSG), Yasushi Akashi. UNTAC's mandate, which was to last no more than 18 months, comprised seven components: military, civilian policing, electoral, civil administration, repatriation, human rights, economic affairs and rehabilitation (Curtis 1994).[2]

The Accords also included a Declaration on the Rehabilitation and Reconstruction of Cambodia. This determined that international efforts in support of Cambodia's rehabilitation should focus on urgent humanitarian needs (food and health), resettlement and essential restoration of basic services (Curtis 1994). The Rehabilitation Component of UNTAC, which had its own Directorate, was to coordinate these efforts and to work according to three principles:

- *Sovereignty* – the Cambodian people (during the transitional period embodied in the SNC) and the government to be elected should be primarily responsible for delivering reconstruction assistance.
- *Respect for local capacity* – external assistance should complement and supplement local resources.
- *Balance* – assistance should benefit all areas, especially the most disadvantaged. (CCC 1992)

In June 1992 the Ministerial Conference on Rehabilitation and Reconstruction was held in Tokyo. Attended by 33 countries and 13 international organisations, it provided an opportunity for donor countries to pledge their support for the UN appeal for US$595 million to finance the immediate relief and rehabilitation needs. The appeal was oversubscribed, with pledges exceeding US$800 million, of which US$43 million was targeted to the health sector (Curtis 1994).[3]

In order to realise the principle of sovereignty laid out in the Declaration, the SNC was to scrutinise aid decisions through a special committee, the Technical Advisory Committee (TAC). Including representatives of all factions, the TAC, chaired by the UNTAC director of rehabilitation, was to solicit approval of all proposed project proposals, excluding those implemented by NGOs.

UNTAC in practice From an early stage, the factions signalled that they would not comply fully with the Paris Accords, and UNTAC struggled to establish political control and security.[4] In this context of continued hostility (including military action) and distrust among the factions and their respective backers, delegating responsibility to a third party (the United Nations) for public policy provided a potential means of neutralising decision-making. In Meier's (1993) terms, the UN provided a 'constitution for decision-making', a means of deciding how decisions could be made regarding implementation of the Accords, including its provisions for rehabilitation.

To an extent UNTAC, the SNC and the TAC served this role effectively. By December 1993, the TAC had approved 47 programmes valued at US$370 million (Lanjouw et al. 1998). This agreement was primarily secured for projects that would start *after* the elections, including a three-year programme for UNICEF and a large Asian Development Bank loan.[5] However, its capacity to influence aid expenditures *during* the rehabilitation phase itself was more limited. Neither the SNC nor UNTAC worked as a government, nor were they able to set and enforce public policy. As Lanjouw et al. (1998) report, they did not do so for three main reasons.

First, the UN mission in Cambodia interpreted its mandate differently. Rather than acting as a temporary power, which would then hand over power to a newly elected government (rather as had the colonial powers), the SRSG sought a more consensual and pragmatic approach. The SRSG saw UNTAC's legitimacy as contingent upon achieving consensus in the SNC. In particular his approach was contingent upon the UN treating the State of Cambodia (SOC) as a faction, rather than what it was – the *de facto* government of Cambodia. This interpretation of the UNTAC mandate, and its emphasis on achieving distance from the existing public administration, was to have profound implications for the execution of its mandate (Curtis 1994; Fitzgerald 1994). It also downplayed the right of the SRSG to overrule the SNC (Utting 1994). It assumed that the SNC could achieve consensus; that the SNC itself was seen as legitimate by the various political factions; and, indeed, that the factions could claim to be representative of the Cambodian people. All of these assumptions proved questionable.

A second factor limiting the SNC as a forum for decision-making on rehabilitation was that the factions did not allow it to function as such. The Khmer Rouge initially refused to cooperate in the TAC reviews, so preventing the achievement of consensus. Following the June 1992 United Nations Appeal for Cambodia, the Khmer Rouge adopted a more positive approach and facilitated the functioning of the TAC. However, TAC approval was driven predominantly by the political concerns of the factions, and in particular those of the non-communist groups to ensure that the SOC did not benefit from aid during the transitional period. As Lanjouw et al. (1998) point out, two events are illustrative in this respect.

The first was the inaction of the SNC in the face of the sharp fall in the value of the riel in March 1993 from 2,500 to 4,000 to the US dollar. A report by the UN secretary-general suggested that this sharp drop was due neither to the SOC authorities nor to UNTAC interventions, but to the unwillingness of non-SOC parties to support the riel (United Nations 1993). In so doing, the three other factions were trying to destabilise the SOC.

Similarly, the factions blocked agreement on a US$75 million World Bank Emergency Rehabilitation Project (ERP) and an IMF loan, both of which were planned to start after the elections, and were crucial to maintain the macro-economic stability of the country and of the public administration. The head of UNTAC's Rehabilitation and Economic Affairs is reported as concluding in May 1993 that: 'macro-economic stability could now only be defined in terms of maintaining current nominal levels of expenditure, including those for civil service salaries' (cited in Lanjouw et al. 1998), a minimalist definition by any account. Balance of payments support was critically affected, as were financial resources to ensure the delivery of public services. In effect, 'Cambodia's economy was put on hold for 19 months' (Davies 1993, cited in Lanjouw et al. 1998).

The impacts of this absence of macro-economic policy control are well described by Fitzgerald (1994). He argues that the public administration could not be used as a counterpart for financial and technical cooperation, and that there was no balance of payments support during the transitional period, leaving the state critically weakened. These conclusions are echoed by the Cooperation Committee for Cambodia (CCC 1992), which highlighted the implications of this financial crisis for public services such as health and education.

The inability of UNTAC to exert sufficient pressure upon the factions to agree to protect macro-economic stability is indicative of a third reason why the UNTAC/SNC arrangement did not provide an effective constitution for decision-making, namely that Western donors were at best ambivalent in their attitude to the constitutional machinery set up in Paris. Whether as a result of scepticism regarding the viability of the TAC as a decision-making body, or as a deliberate policy, bilateral donors frequently bypassed the TAC, so undermining efforts to coordinate aid during the transitional period. They did so in two main ways.

First, by sub-contracting NGOs directly, donors bypassed the TAC mechanisms. This strategy led to a mushrooming of international NGOs working in the country. In 1991 there were approximately 60 international NGOs in Cambodia. This rose to 87 in 1992 and to 105 in 1993, with many nearly doubling their number of staff in those years (Lanjouw et al. 1998). Much of the assistance from these agencies was directed towards Phnom Penh and the north-western provinces to which the majority of the refugees sought to return. This expansion in the number and activity of NGOs heightened the coordination challenge, as each organisation came with its own needs assessment, strategy for implementation and, in some cases, its own political agenda.

The US government, in particular, saw the provision of aid through NGOs as part of a strategy to 'level the playing field', by providing indirect, non-military assistance to the non-communist, non-Khmer Rouge factions (Lanjouw et al. 1998; USAID 1994).[6] It went so far as to make its funding conditional upon NGOs *not* working with government institutions. The political factors driving its allocation of rehabilitation resources were particularly evident in its selection of sites for assistance in non-SOC-controlled districts, and the lavish resources allocated to them.[7] Similarly, the European Commission focused its efforts in the north-west of the country, implementing projects exclusively through NGOs and by passing UNTAC–SNC structures (interview, European Commission official, 3 May 1994).[8]

A second strategy was more indirect: donors did not sufficiently support the UNTAC rehabilitation component in its efforts to coordinate aid and to mediate the TAC. The Unit remained underfunded and understaffed. Chopra et al. conclude that:

> The rehabilitation component [of UNTAC] adopted a relaxed approach to the challenge of coordination. Whether reflecting the wishes of donors, the strategies chosen by UNTAC, or the limitations imposed by Phnom Penh with the staff of only seven professionals the component did not harness the external resources adequately in the sense of UNTAC's rehabilitation plan. Activities also suffered from inadequate representation at provincial level, where of several UNTAC components it alone lacked its own staff. (1993: 29)[9]

The lack of staff was particularly significant in relation to UNTAC's ability to fulfil its mandate in the area of the public administration. The Paris Accords had stipulated that all existing ministries and departments would continue to function during the transition period, with UNTAC providing oversight. UNTAC was also to have direct control over ministries of foreign affairs, defence, finance, public security and information. In effect, it was to act as a shadow government.

Its capacity to do so was limited, however, not only by the ratio of UNTAC personnel to Cambodian civil servants (there were 400 of the former and 200,000 of the latter), but by the linguistic obstacles facing international civil servants attempting to shadow and control an essentially hostile bureaucracy, run by one of the factions of the CPP, which had governed the state of Cambodia (Lanjouw et al. 1998). The existing public administration therefore remained under the control of the SOC, so giving credence to donor governments' fears that to work with the public administration would be to reinforce what they saw as an illegitimate regime.

Thus, even had the UN provided a means of impartial decision-making, its capacity to execute these decisions was extremely limited. It did not control the public administration, and therefore public resources. Nor did it control directly international public resources for health, since UNTAC did not function as a funding channel. Instead, aid was provided directly to individual UN agencies and NGOs. The combination of systems to manage aid (UNTAC, SNC), the form of aid – largely short-term 'rehabilitation' funds – and the particular channels used to disburse it (NGOs) all militated against a coherent aid effort.

It was particularly difficult for the UN to ensure adherence to the principle of impartiality enshrined in the declaration. The distribution of aid was highly inequitable. Phnom Penh, with only 7 per cent of the population, received 43 per cent of donor assistance. In contrast, the central lowlands, where two-thirds of the population lived, received only 21 per cent. Reflecting donor interests and the emphasis

---

*Box 5.1 The goals and objectives of health policy
in Cambodia, 1992*

- To provide essential healthcare to people living in remote provinces and districts previously without access to health services
- To provide maximum support to the health of mothers and children, including the promotion of birth spacing
- To pay particular attention to the needs of those who have suffered as a result of recent conflicts, such as widows, orphans, disabled, etc.
- To involve people in decisions regarding their health services
- To coordinate and distribute equitably the significant external resource inputs from international agencies

The mechanisms through which these objectives were to be achieved were to adopt a district health systems approach, improve water and sanitation, develop drug supply systems and promote improved nutrition.

Source: Cambodia 1992.

placed on repatriation, there were also significant inequalities in re-habilitation assistance received by provinces to which large numbers of refugees returned. The World Bank (1994b) estimated, for example, that per capita aid receipts were approximately US$5 in the north-western provinces,[10] more than double the $2 per capita in the central lowlands and remote north-east of the country.[11]

The framework for health policy in transition The weaknesses of policy that characterised the public sector in Cambodia generally in the early 1990s were felt in relation to health policy. In 1992, with the assistance of the WHO, a strategy had been prepared outlining the goals and objectives of health policy in the country (see Box 5.1).

These objectives were articulated by the Ministry of Health, but it had itself relatively little control over the organisation, financing and delivery of health services, which were largely the responsibility of provincial and district authorities. The key central systems of training and accreditation of health staff and the production and distribution of essential drugs had effectively ground to a halt in the early 1990s under the strain of the financing crisis (World Bank 1992b). Prob-lematic too was that while the policy statement outlined broad objectives, it did not clearly indicate how these were to be achieved, particularly given a very low resource base. In this respect, the World Bank (1992b) noted that the lack of a strategic policy framework constituted an important constraint to health policy during the transi-tion period.

Aiding the health sector From 1982 to 1990, UNICEF was the only UN agency operating in Cambodia.[12] The signing of the Paris Accords provided for the beginnings of a normalisation of relations between the UN agencies and Cambodia. The UNDP opened a liaison office in 1990 and then appointed a resident representative in 1991. The signing of the agreements also allowed the WHO and the UNFPA to start to provide technical support to the health sector in 1991, although they lacked fully accredited representation in Phnom Penh (CCC 1992).

Upon arrival, the WHO sought to assist the Cambodian health sector by plugging the gap in policy-making capacity and aid co-ordination. It sought to re-establish in Cambodia its conventional role in providing technical assistance to the government. This normalisation of aid relations was tentative and conditional until there was an elected government in place, a fact that was to have implications for the UN's ability to provide a leadership role in the coordination of health aid. The WHO office was not fully accredited, and was run instead by a special envoy of the director-general.[13] Aid provided by the organisation had to be channelled through a humanitarian assistance programme, and to steer clear of the 'usual WHO development terminology for the time being for political and mandate reasons' (Kreysler 1991, cited in Lanjouw et al. 1998).

The former special envoy to Cambodia described the WHO's role as follows:

> The main mission of WHO was to give a sense of direction to the development of health services in very difficult times ... The difficulty was that [the required] policy review needed to come from government, but at the time before elections took place this posed considerable problems. There were four guerrilla factions. The Vietnamese group [*sic*] controlled the administration and 75 per cent of the country, but were denied validity by the UN. However, WHO decided that it should support them. There was a major problem in that we were dealing with an illegal government. (interview, Geneva, 10 May 1994)

The main mechanism the WHO sought to use to provide such direction was to bolster the CoCom (the Coordinating Committee for Health), a committee first established by the SOC in the late 1980s. From 1992 onwards, the WHO provided extensive support to this committee. The terms of reference and working practices of the CoCom helped to define the relationships between the Transitional National Authority and the range of actors in the health sector. The CoCom's objectives were to monitor and evaluate all health activities by international aid agencies working in the health sector; to provide advice; and to make recommendations to the MOH in order to support the planning, coordination and implementation of health sector activities in Cambodia. It also had responsibility for gathering information on health needs and the activities of different aid agencies in the country.

The CoCom was supported by a Secretariat, which drew heavily on WHO staff. Significantly, the CoCom's Executive Committee was chaired by the SOC director of cabinet and included the director-general of health, the director of policy and planning and the director of international relations. In other words, the CoCom was led by members of what was perceived by Western donors as 'an illegal government'. The WHO's active support for the SOC-dominated public administration attracted considerable criticism: 'Some people in UNTAC and UNDP were furious that such a committee should be formed, effectively legitimating the Vietnamese-backed authorities' (interview, WHO official, Geneva, 10 May 1994). In this respect, the health sector suffered from the wider paradox of UNTAC, namely that it was mandated to define and coordinate public policy, but had no mechanism by which to implement it.

The WHO justified its strategy in terms of the essentially human-itarian nature of its concern for health, and its recognition that if rehabilitation measures were indeed to serve as a basis for long-term sectoral development, then re-establishment of national capacity to manage that assistance was critical, as was a degree of consistency in rehabilitation strategies. However, the WHO's position in the aid system, and within UNTAC, left it with little authority to influence decision-making, since it was not a funding agency, nor was it linked to any process of resource allocation. Similarly, the CoCom did not provide an alternative to a functioning Ministry of Health, able to direct international interventions in terms of coverage and scale. Thus the WHO relied upon the establishment of consensus within CoCom in order to secure influence.

However, there was a lack of consensus between the WHO and other major operational international organisations, particularly UNI-CEF and Médecins Sans Frontières (MSF) regarding the appropriate model for health sector rehabilitation. The WHO started from the premise that the health system should remain in its current form, and in particular advocated the rehabilitation of all facilities down to the level of the commune (*khum*). MSF and UNICEF argued that such a system was unaffordable and unable to provide sufficient quality of care. They therefore recommended the consolidation of facilities into what became known as 'super-*khums*', and the introduction of com-munity financing schemes. The Ministry of Health (MOH) lacked a clear view on the issue. Ultimately it came down on the side of the WHO model, largely on political grounds: the *khum* had constituted the unit for political organisation of Cambodia under the SOC providing a focus for the party (interview, medical coordinator, MSF, Phnom Penh, December 1994).[14]

The establishment of CoCom at national level was followed by a number of provincial coordination committees (ProCoComs), set up to coordinate international assistance at the province and district levels. The ProCoComs were chaired by provincial directors of health, supported by a secretariat (often with inputs from UNICEF's growing network of provincial health advisers[15]) that convened meetings, prepared agendas, and took minutes of meetings between the MOH authorities and international organisations working in the provincial health sector. Support for this process came from both UNICEF and the WHO.[16]

The WHO and UNICEF also supported the establishment of a number of CoCom sub-committees and technical working groups to assist in advising the MOH on the implementation of specific health services. Each sub-committee had its own specific terms of reference, which were reviewed and updated annually. They were intended to meet regularly and feed information to the MOH, through the CoCom, on heath policy and planning issues. Membership reflected the composition of the CoCom, and included one or two NGO representatives with particular experience in the issue concerned, who were identified through MEDICAM, the NGO coordination forum. By 1994 there were eight sub-committees in existence.[17]

In confronting the legitimacy dilemma, the approach adopted by the WHO and by UNICEF prioritised the developmental character of their mandates over the need to remain neutral. They sought to capture rehabilitation resources to invest them in longer-term health development, building capacity at the national and provincial levels for future policy development and implementation. Particularly for the WHO, this entailed compromising a strict interpretation of neutrality. In recognising the inherent contradiction between a developmental approach and not working through public institutions, it inevitably contravened the wider consensus within the UN and much of the donor community regarding relations with the SOC. It sought to assert its neutrality by working as an honest, professional broker and by allocating resources impartially, on the basis of need.[18]

A different response to the legitimacy dilemma might be called the 'humanitarian' approach (Lanjouw et al. 1998), and it was this that was adopted by the ICRC and MSF. While both organisations sought to build the professional capacity of health workers through training programmes, and, in the case of MSF, to develop more appropriate systems of health financing, they deliberately sought to avoid working with either national authorities or with the factions, thus retaining their neutrality. This did not entail the establishment of parallel systems *per se*, since these and other international organisations largely based their interventions in public health facilities. Thus private and international resources, rather than public national resources, become crucial to the maintenance of individual health facilities. The 'humanitarian' model contrasts with the developmental model of the WHO in that the primary objectives are coverage, quality and neutrality, not sustainability. While rehabilitation measures implemented by NGOs and the Red Cross movement were assumed to contribute to the long-term capacity of the public health system, the precise mechanism by which these were to be sustained was (deliberately) not clearly articulated.

A third strategy was inherently more political. In contrast to the ICRC and MSF, which sought to maximise their political distance from all the factions, other NGOs, in particular those working in the north-western provinces and working outside the public health system, were part of a political strategy to boost the opposition parties in the run-up to the elections. This approach was taken primarily by USAID and the EC. Again, here the objective was not primarily the sustainability of health intervention, but rather to boost the legitimacy and capacity of the KPNLF and FUNCINPEC.

It is interesting not only that three such different approaches to the legitimacy dilemma could develop simultaneously, but that they were largely funded by the same donor organisations. Thus the idea of a coherent and principled approach to rehabilitation that respected sovereignty, as laid out in the Declaration on Rehabilitation, quickly dissipated in practice.

The UN agencies alone sought to enhance the capacity of the public administration and thus provide a mechanism for a future government to act as policy-maker and coordinator of aid. Their capacity to do so was limited in the face of the opposing donor strategy of investing directly in NGOs, which, in the absence of central public policy, both privatised and internationalised health policy. While the UN, and in particular the WHO, were in a position to provide technical assistance to the public administration, they could not and did not provide the public sector with a budget.

With SOC administration seen to be illegitimate by international actors, and lacking alternative sources of finance, it ceased to function as a public health actor during the transitional period, exerting little professional influence on the distribution and content of externally financed health programmes (CCC 1992; Fitzgerald 1994; Lanjouw et al. 1998; World Bank and Cambodia 1995). This rehabilitation strategy may have met the requirement of transitional neutrality. However, it undermined any claims that such assistance would serve as the basis for long-term health systems development.

With the exception of projects targeted at refugees, which were funded largely through the UNHCR, aid was not channelled through the bodies that had a coordination mandate. Resources for NGOs were not included in the UN appeal, nor were they subject to review by either the UNTAC/SNC structure or the CoCom. This meant that priority-setting was highly fragmented, precluding systematic identification of needs and limiting the scope for viring resources between different areas. For example, despite the fact that malaria and TB constituted the primary health problem in the country, these received no funding, while the Expanded Programme of Immunisation (EPI) and essential drugs remained underfunded. In contrast, rehabilitation of the physical infrastructure was oversubscribed by US$20 million. As Lanjouw et al. (1998) report, non-disbursement of pledges further threatened the coherence of the rehabilitation effort (see also Peou and Yamada 1998). Of US$43 million pledged to Cambodia's health sector, only US$5 million had been disbursed by the end of 1992. This required agencies to re-analyse constantly their priorities, again largely in an uncoordinated manner.

At a technical level, the performance of bodies designed to achieve a coherent rehabilitation response was patchy. In the absence of a functioning and recognised Ministry of Health, the CoCom and the ProCoComs did not constitute an alternative body for decision-making. These forums lacked both the authority and the ability to influence aid programming. According to Lanjouw et al. (1998), sub-committees met infrequently and their findings were not always reported and relayed through minutes. In some cases NGO agreements were allowed to lapse, while others never signed any agreement at either central or provincial levels.

This scenario, and its negative implications for sustainability, was foreseen by early international missions to Cambodia. Both the World Bank and the UNDP had warned that a highly decentralised and privatised system would emerge and that these would prove unsustainable in the long term (UNDP 1992; World Bank 1992b).

However, in their concern to promote a technically viable development strategy, both these bodies failed to acknowledge the political problem of finding a mechanism for centralised public action during the transition, acceptable to all parties, national and international. Failure to recognise the essential constitutional problem undermined any efforts to make rehabilitation inputs developmental. While the UN sought to provide a supranational body for decision-making, this body was not only weak in itself, but lacked a means to connect with the post-election regime. The UNTAC/SNC structure was an attempt to develop a supranational decision-making body, but in practice it did not work as such.

In sum, in the period 1990–93, the public administration in Cambodia was so weakened (institutionally and financially) that its capacity to provide any continuity of policy following the elections was extremely limited. This meant that after the elections, when the juridical basis of sovereignty was at last established, the new state lacked the capacity to function empirically as a state. There were major discontinuities between the instruments used for of rehabilitation and those of long-term development, which were premised on the existence of a functioning central ministry of health. In short, the aid process during the transition undermined the very institutions upon which it would rely for long-term, developmental strategies.

International Aid for Health Sector Rehabilitation in Ethiopia

The political framework for transition, 1991–94 After three decades of violent conflict, the actual change of government was remarkably peaceful, with the Ethiopian People's Democratic Front (EPRDF) securing Addis Ababa in May 1991 without fighting in the capital.[19] This contrasted not only with previous changes of regime, but also with the almost contemporaneous downfall of Said Barre's government in neighbouring Somalia, which was followed by fighting for control of Mogadishu and the eventual collapse of the Somali state.

In July 1991, the EPRDF convened a meeting with other opposition groups at which it was agreed to form a coalition government, the Transitional Government of Ethiopia (TGE). The new government comprised the offices of the president and the prime minister, and an ethnically mixed council of seventeen ministers, representing seven ethnic groups. The EPRDF dominated the new government, while the Oromo Liberation Front (OLF) formed the second largest bloc (Cohen 1997). This process of coalition-building was backed by the major Western powers, including most significantly the USA, and culminated in the signing of the Transitional Charter, outlining the key principles that were to guide political and economic policy-making (*Negarit Gezata* 1991).

The primary aims of the TGE were to establish a framework for security, uphold respect for human rights, promote liberalisation of the economy, and perhaps most importantly to initiate a process of constitutional reform. For many observers, the TGE was essentially a military regime that operated *de jure* as a civilian government during the period 1991–93 (Brietzke 1995, cited in Cohen 1997). Outside its heartland in Tigray, it had much work to do in terms of generating internal legitimacy. Multi-party elections were held in 1993 to form a Constitutional Assembly in Ethiopia. In the same year, following a referendum, Eritrea declared independence from Ethiopia.

The nature of the political transition in Ethiopia was significant. As the WHO representative at the time explained:

> There was no vacuum here when Mengistu left. That regime existed one day and the next day there was another one. The vice-minister [for health] from the previous regime was still there (although he had been imprisoned for a bit). In the MOH, the old staff stayed in post for 6–12 months after the government took power. (interview, former WHO Representative, Addis Ababa, March 1995)

Thus, in the immediate aftermath of the change of regime, there was continuity rather than collapse of the state, at least at central level. The fact that the bureaucracy continued to function was a significant resource for the new government, and indeed for the international community's rehabilitation efforts. As one former civil servant explained:

The bureaucracy was intact and it was experienced, especially in MOPED [Ministry of Planning and Economic Development], there were people who had a lot of experience over many years. MOPED had the leading role in planning at this time and was involved in supervising the methods and strategies used for needs assessment. There was no resentment between the civil servants and the new government: they were professionals. It was only later on, when the government started to retrench people, and party members were thrown out [that tensions emerged]. (interview, former health liaison officer, Ministry of Planning and Economic Development, Addis Ababa, March 1995)

The continuity and stability at central level were not mirrored in the regions. Cohen (1997) describes how, in the face of opposition by other parties, particularly the OLF, the EPRDF sought to assert itself as the national army, as mandated by the Council of Representatives. Control of the military and definition of which troops comprised the standing army was therefore a major issue. The need to define a framework within which to secure law and order was pressing. Dessalegn (1994), for example, describes how there was considerable looting in May and June 1991 in many rural areas. This violence was neither indiscriminate nor random, but targeted against individuals and institutions associated with the previous regime.[20]

Like the physical infrastructure, the political infrastructure was also vulnerable in rural areas. In many areas, the Peasants' Associations, which had provided the means for the former regime to effect control over vast areas (Krylow 1994), collapsed (Dessalegn 1994). This, together with the problems posed by insecurity, had a significant impact on aid operations, particularly those run by NGOs. The country director of one international NGO reported, for example, that:

There was no civil administration in Hararghe. There were just military groups claiming to represent the government. There was a large degree of instability between mid-1991 and mid-1992. Insecurity was the main constraint to our programme. (interview, March 1995)

Similarly, another explained that the fall of the Mengistu government forced his organisation to rethink its choice of partners in rural areas. Under the Mengistu regime it had worked through the

Peasants' Associations. When these collapsed in 1991, so too did the key counterparts for project implementation (interview, ActionAid official, March 1995). In this case the 'constitution for decision-making' at the local level collapsed, requiring considerable investment by the agency to identify other institutions through which to work. In contrast, in areas of northern Ethiopia, particularly of Tigray, where the TPLF had long acted as the *de facto* government, new local institutions – *baitos* – had emerged as alternative basis for popular participation in political decision-making during the war.

In the spring of 1994, a new constitution was drafted. In June that year elections were held for the Constitutional Assembly to debate the draft, which it then ratified in December (Ethiopia 1994a). This paved the way for multi-party elections in 1995, which reaffirmed the EPRDF's hold on power. The central plank of the constitution was the creation of a Federal Democratic Republic, comprising nine member states, each of which is governed by a State Council.[21] State boundaries are defined on the basis of ethnicity. Underpinning the design of the Ethiopian federal system has been an analysis that the primary causes of conflict and underdevelopment in the country have been over-centralisation of the Ethiopian state, which has marginalised and antagonised the country's many different ethnic groups. By devolving power from the centre to the periphery, it was argued, a climate for economic growth and political freedom could be established (Cohen 1997).

The most controversial element of the constitution is its provision for any of the states to secede from the Federation, subject to a referendum. While in practical terms any attempt at secession would be extremely difficult, subject as it would be to complex financial and electoral conditions, the inclusion of this provision is seen by some conservatives within Ethiopia to threaten the continued existence of a unitary Ethiopian state.

The reformation of the Ethiopian state was always set to be a formidable task. The topography, poor communications and large but poorly educated electorate alone marked significant obstacles. When set against the political history of the country the scale of the challenge is all the more overwhelming. It is no surprise, therefore, that the process of transition has been associated with controversy and instability. Most fundamental, perhaps, are questions regarding the impact of the strategy of ethnic federalism. Many international actors saw the political reforms undertaken by the TGE as radical and potentially destabilising, but also as providing a potential means of resolving an apparently intractable series of conflicts (Cohen 1997).[22]

The political risk of ethnic federalism is that the stability of the Federation is contingent upon the establishment of political structures at the level of individual states that are simultaneously democratic, and also supportive of the federal government. In the early years of the new government this was achieved by a combination of political and financial coercion. Politically, 'puppet' political organisations, known as People's Democratic Organisations, were created in each of the regions. Affiliated to the EPRDF, these parties dominated successive elections (Krylow 1994). Financially, the federal government continues to hold the purse strings and to exercise a major role in the collection and distribution of public revenues. The 1993/4 budget was the first to be prepared in accordance with the new regionalisation policy. Approximately two-thirds of both recurrent and capital budgets remained the responsibility of the federal government (World Bank 1994a). If external assistance is included, the federal authorities control approximately 90 per cent of total revenue (Cohen 1997).

A more immediate set of issues arises with regard to the administrative and financial capacity of the states to take on their new responsibilities. Many of the roles previously the responsibility of central government were delegated to the states. Under the constitution, it is the prerogative of the states to work and legislate in their respective national languages, rather than in Amharic. Middle and senior level management posts in local administrations were formerly dominated by Amhara-speakers, many of whom were not fluent in the local language. As a result of the regionalisation policy, there have been considerable changes in the personnel at state levels and below. At the same time, there have been efforts to devolve power from the centre to the region, by redeploying central ministry staff. These efforts have been plagued by difficulties as civil servants resist the risks associated with moving out of the capital city, including reduced access to health and education opportunities.[23] Inevitably, this has been a turbulent time for state and federal administration alike, and the implications of this were felt in relation to the management of aid and to health policy.

Aid in transition Ethiopia is a rare case of 'post'-conflict transition where a change of regime was enacted by force, but where central state structures did not collapse during the course of the military struggle. However weak the capacity and authority were at the periphery (and even here the military capacity of the EPRDF was formidable), the institutions of the state remained intact. The nature of this transition meant that there was both an authoritative and competent focus for international engagement. Thus, in contrast with Cambodia, the issue was less whether a juridical sovereign government existed than whether the international community sought to endorse it and under what conditions.

As Chapter 4 described, by the time the EPRDF reached Addis Ababa, the ground was laid for the rapid establishment of aid dialogue. Specifically, the prize of international legitimation was the resumption of an aid package channelled through state institutions, rather than outside them, as had been the case during the Mengistu regime. Securing such resources was critical to the survival of the new regime, as the country remained heavily dependent on external aid to meet food needs and to meet the shortfalls in public budgets (UNDP 1995).[24]

The pieces were in place for a transition in the form of aid provided to Ethiopia from one channelled primarily outside the state to one channelled through it. The EPRDF had the political support of key donor countries, in particular that of the USA, which in turn unlocked multilateral resources, most importantly from the World Bank. As one World Bank official commented:

> the Bank has political antennae which have guided its policy in Ethiopia. We used to discuss economic reform with the Mengistu regime and late on it said it wanted reform, but this was because it needed money, there wasn't a genuine commitment. As soon as the new government came in, literally, we looked at the political analysis of stakeholders like the USA, the UK and the Germans who have the resources to do this sort of thing. As major shareholders in the Bank, we have to listen to their views. If they are well disposed towards a country, then we are also likely to be so. (interview, World Bank official, Addis Ababa, March 1995)

This support was not unreserved. In 1994, a senior British aid official noted continued concerns regarding government policy in Ethiopia, in particular regarding the role of the private sector, land reform (interview, Overseas Development Administration official, London, May 1994). The British and others also remained cautious regarding direct support for regionalisation, their memories fresh with the experience of villagisation a decade earlier. Despite these reservations, from May 1991 when the EPRDF took over, to the multi-party elections in August 1995, political support for the new regime was largely unconditional. As a British diplomat put it:

> Donors felt that there was an opportunity for the country and for the region as a whole, and they wanted to go along with the government and we set conditionalities as we went along. Up until now we haven't set many conditionalities. During the transitional period which is going to end in a matter of weeks, donors realised that there was going to be a lot of traffic for the new government to deal with. Now there will be a shift in the mood. If you have a constitutional government which will be recognised by the international community to be so, there is likely to be more conditionality imposed on aid. (interview, British Embassy, Addis Ababa, 31 July 1995)

Despite these reservations, the TGE was unequivocally the juridical sovereign. It also inherited the means to exert its sovereignty empirically and in particular to engage with aid actors. There was a functioning bureaucracy within Ethiopia that could act as the counterpart to aid technicians and provide a credible mechanism for the disbursement of aid through the state. Significant too was the fact that while it was relatively small scale, multilateral actors, including the World Bank, UN and the European Commission, all had ongoing programmes of work in the country, with projects disbursing development assistance funds throughout Mengistu's reign.[25] This was important in terms of the availability of information, and the existence of a knowledge base of aid procedures within the Ethiopian civil service.

This configuration of factors enabled development aid actors, in particular the World Bank and UN agencies, to develop plans relatively rapidly and to access and disburse substantial funds for rehabilitation. Most significant of these plans was the Emergency Recovery and Rehabilitation Programme (ERRP). This alongside the UN's SEPHA (Special Emergency Programme for the Horn of Africa) was to be the centrepiece of aid efforts for health in this period.

SEPHA was developed in mid-1991. Led by a team from the UN Secretariat from New York, it sought to provide a consistent and coherent approach across the UN system. As such, it provided a mechanism to consolidate the appeals of the different UN agencies in response to the multiple disasters in the Horn of Africa in 1991–92. SEPHA also reflected the regional nature of the crisis and the challenge this posed for UN agencies. It therefore challenged the traditional organisation of UN emergency agencies, which had been developed to respond to the needs of specific population groups within the confines of a sovereign state. Instead, SEPHA acknowledged the need for a cross-mandate approach with agencies working across categories such as refugees, internally displaced and those who had stayed in their homes. It also acknowledged the need to think cross-border, for example, to develop strategies for reintegration of returning refugees. Such was the theory. In practice, evaluations of relief operations of the period have questioned the degree to which such ambitious objectives could be achieved (Apthorpe et al. 1995; Netherlands 1994).

Of primary concern here, however, have been the strategies and content of SEPHA programming in the health sector in Ethiopia itself. The Ethiopian component of SEPHA for 1991–92 was budgeted at US$350 million. By July 1992, pledges of some US$209 million had been received (United Nations 1992a). The health component of SEPHA in Ethiopia was budgeted at US$20.68 million, and designed to complement the contributions to the sector made through the ERRP (see below). Specifically, it sought to raise funds for communicable disease control, pharmaceuticals and rehabilitation of health facilities, primarily in the northern regions (United Nations 1991). The health programme sought to build on existing disease control strategies of UNICEF and the WHO, as well as providing additional and specific rehabilitation components. Implementation was to be through governmental channels.

In an update on the 1991 appeal, the WHO/UNICEF reported that, of the US$316 million requested for non-food aid in SEPHA, only US$117 million was allocated (United Nations 1992a). The WHO appealed for US$14.83 million out of the entire requirement of $46.19 million for repair and rehabilitation of health services. By June 1992, it had received only $1.276 million. In a renewed appeal, the WHO called for additional funds of $23.8 million to repair damaged facilities in Assosa, Ogaden and Wollega. Again, these were slow to materialise.

SEPHA was important as a mechanism for an expansion of relief, rather than providing a major vehicle for rehabilitation. Relief items predominated expenditure, managed by the emergencies departments, and its content remained limited largely to the provision of material supplies (United Nations 1991, 1992a, 1992b). The UN lacked a clear mechanism for rehabilitation funding and activities. From an early stage, the TGE indicated that it wished to maximise the flow of resources through governmental channels. For the UN agencies, this implied undertaking protracted negotiations with several ministries at federal and state level. Thus, while the UN, and particularly its specialised food handling agencies, had the capacity to respond to the acute emergency precipitated by the final stages of the conflict and its aftermath, it lacked the flexibility to scale up quickly its developmental programming in the immediate 'post'-conflict period.[26]

By contrast, the World Bank's Emergency Reconstruction and Rehabilitation Programme (ERRP) proved relatively flexible. After the change of government in June 1991, the World Bank sent its first mission to Ethiopia in November. The mission comprised Bank staff, as well as representatives from key bilateral agencies, including the Netherlands (who played a lead role in the health component) and Sweden. As a result of this mission the ERRP was formulated and negotiated very quickly, becoming operational in April 1992.

World Bank documents of this period are worth citing at some length, since they reveal clearly the Bank's conceptualisation of the rehabilitation task, as well as describing its specific strategy in Ethiopia. The first describes the legacy of war:

> Many years of excessive military spending, the diversion of productive enterprises and institutions to support the war effort, extensive war damage and inappropriate economic policies have left the economy and its infrastructure in a devastated condition, matched by a massive social crisis of millions of displaced persons, refugees, demobilised solders, homeless, maimed and unemployed people. The effects of war were worsened by years of famine, mitigated only by large volumes of relief aid. Although the end of the war provides an opportunity to reconstruct Ethiopia's torn economic and social fabric and to begin to shift the emphasis from relief towards economic development and

growth, the extent of social deprivation is such that special measures will need to be taken for the foreseeable future to help mitigate the worst impact of the recently ended war. (World Bank 1992a: 1)

In response, the Bank proposed a two-pronged approach:

The first consists of providing, along with other donors, the emergency assistance needed to begin to overcome the devastating effects of almost two decades of civil war and economic mismanagement, and to recommence economic activity. The proposed ERRP is the center-piece of this phase, providing IDA assistance as part of a larger, co-ordinated program that ensures that the contributions from all donors are complementary … [The ERRP is] designed to ensure that actions necessary for its successful implementation will be sustainable and compatible with the coming reform program. It is not itself a vehicle for policy reform. A policy framework paper is expected in mid-1992 which would provide the basis for the second phase in which the transitional government would embark on implementation of an initial two year program of major economic reforms, aimed at stabilising the economy. An adjustment program is to be introduced in FY93. (ibid.: 3)

The Bank response was premised upon the TGE's need for rapid disbursement of aid in order to stabilise the economy. The memorandum makes clear assumptions about the political conditions under which it is providing aid to the transitional government (TG), stating that: 'the TG, *which is operating through popular consensus,* needs to be able to pursue its program of fundamental economic reform in a climate of restored economic activity and confidence' (ibid.: 7, emphasis added).

Interesting in this statement is the way in which a judgement regarding the political legitimacy of the new government is quickly equated with an analysis of its willingness to undertake a programme of economic reform, backed by the Bank. A condition of development aid actors channelling resources through the new government was their acceptance of its legitimacy, and the granting of this legitimacy lay in the convergence of the political agenda of the new government with what Clapham (1996) calls the 'mono-economics' and 'mono-politics' of a neo-liberal agenda. In conforming with these conditions, the TGE unlocked support for the state.[27]

The Bank's ERRP provided a multilateral mechanism through which key bilateral donors could contribute to a rapidly disbursing fund, designed to maintain cash flow and a minimum level of public expenditure. The ERRP was multi-sectoral and drew upon needs assessments and plans prepared by sectoral ministries and agencies. These had assessed recovery and reconstruction needs of some US$1.4 billion, but their proposals were reviewed and revised downwards by donors to provide a package of some US$657 million of urgent requirements.[28] In addition to meeting urgent needs, the ERRP was also seen as a means of establishing 'good faith' between the donor community and the government, and as paving the way for discussions regarding substantive economic policy reform. In this sense, it was free of conditions – one Bank official reported that:

> Although we had concerns about implementation, we had no concerns about the government's intentions. We tried to simplify things as much as possible and to spread money across sectors to increase absorptive capacity. Right after the ERRP, I worked with a joint IMF–World Bank mission on the country framework … we started to negotiate conditions re: sustainability and growth, it was a very interactive process. The deal was: 'here is $640 million credit for the ERRP, now let's talk'. But it was very positive, we were not imposing very heavy conditionalities. (interview, World Bank official, Addis Ababa, March 1995)

In terms of the health sector, the ERRP aimed to restore a normal supply of pharmaceuticals and supplies and essential equipment of health amenities. It financed imports of nine to twelve months' supply of 60 essential pharmaceuticals and supplies, prioritising health stations. Importantly, the supplies were delivered through the public health system, using the regular distribution channels of the Ministry of Health.

The initial inputs provided by the ERRP were followed by the renegotiation of the Family Health Project (FHP). This also had a rehabilitative component. The FHP had started in 1988, but had been slow to develop and to disburse. Some $10–11 million of the FHP funds were allocated to the ERRP, leaving US$21 million by September 1993. In 1992, the Bank started to discuss restructuring of the FHP, away from its focus on one area in Ethiopia, and to conform with the new government's priorities. Following extensive negotiations throughout 1992 and 1993, the FHP was relaunched. The revamped project sought to target poorer, more remote areas, a reduction in civil works component to 50 per cent of total project costs and a corresponding increase in 'software', such as training and pharmaceuticals. In line with the regionalisation process, decisions regarding which facilities were to be rehabilitated were to be made by the regions.[29]

Significantly, the relaunch of the FHP was agreed *before* the World Bank-led Public Expenditure Review was finalised in 1995 (World Bank 1994a). As described in Chapter 6, the latter report warned of the recurrent cost implications of any significant expansion in the number of health facilities due to rehabilitation and new construction (see, in particular, pp. 118–19). The reason for this sequencing was explained by one official in the following terms:

> The reason why such analysis [of recurrent cost implications] was not done before is that until now [1995] there were barriers between the government and the Bank. We needed a new project to demonstrate commitment through the restructured FHP and we needed some action. This project has helped demonstrate trust and capacity. The government has moved from rehabilitation in its strategy, but we still need to rehabilitate and consolidate. (interview, World Bank official, Addis Ababa, 20 March 1995)

This statement implies that the government was able to present clearly and quickly a viable framework for rehabilitation policy, and that there was consensus between major agencies and donors on key elements of this policy. The extent to which these statements were justified is assessed below. It also makes clear that what was at issue was less the technical or financial viability of the restructured programme than the restoration of an aid process, itself driven by a political desire to provide financial support for the new government.

Health policy in transition   During the transitional period, the framework for health policy was based on the Charter, with particular emphasis on the restoration and expansion of services to areas particularly affected by the war and areas previously under-served (*Negarit Gazeta* 1991). As Chapter 6 details, the health sector benefited from the peace dividend early in the new regime, as the TGE sought to shift expenditure from the military to the social sector. The increase in the resource base was accompanied by a second major change – that of regionalisation. Individual states became responsible for the organisation of health services, using funds devolved from the federal government.

These changes in the financing and organisation of the system did not signal major changes in the *content* of health policy in the immediate 'post'-conflict period, however. In 1993, a Health Policy Task Force published a report, articulating the main problems of the health system (Ethiopia 1993). It acknowledged the strength of previous governments' policy statements, but argued that these had never been fully implemented because of a lack of specificity and of appropriate political and administrative institutions. It concluded by reasserting the principles of PHC, emphasising in particular the need for genuine community participation and devolution of decision-making. Specifically, it proposed that the responsibilities of the central MOH should be confined to the formulation and regulation of national policy guidelines, including those affecting the training and accreditation in addition to the coordination of aid for the health sector. Otherwise, responsibility for service delivery should be placed firmly at regional level.

On finance, the Task Force stated that:

> individuals, families and communities should primarily be responsible for their own health and pay for it on a fee-for-service basis, although free medical services shall be made available for those who do not have the means to cover the cost. In order to implement these concepts, the government should provide an efficient and comprehensive health service and revise the current health financing system. (Ethiopia 1993)

While useful as a statement of general policy direction, the Task Force's report did not (and was not designed to) constitute a binding health policy, or a detailed programme. It was not until 1994 that the Health Policy of the TGE was published, followed by the Health Sector Strategy in 1995 (Ethiopia 1995). These disappointed many observers, particularly within the donor community, who complained of the lack of clarity in government health policy, and in particular a realistic prioritisation of investment.[30] As one UN official put it:

It is not quite clear yet what the main issues are and what strategies should be developed to confront them. Nothing is quite decided – there is a lack of clarity of programming because of the transition, which slows planning with respect to things like the Bamako Initiative. Neither donors nor governments have taken definitive measures. There is a lack of willingness to resolve issues. Donors can't move. (interview, Health Section official, UNICEF, Addis Ababa, March 1995)

Particularly problematic was the fact that while the strategy for policy implementation was apparently in place (regionalisation), the content of policy was not clearly defined, nor were mechanisms for the coordination of national policy. Thus, one MOH planner argued:

There is no means of coordination. Everyone comes along and says what they want to do – hospitals, AIDS – [but] there is no way of looking at the interdependence of donors and ensuring the fair distribution of resources unless there is a central body. The donor group doesn't have an operational role, it is not effective in terms of coordination. Sometimes [the head of the MOH planning unit] joins these meetings. Unless you join this type of group with a body which has influence over resources then it is just a physical meeting of people which doesn't have any operational impact ... The other change is that donors are now dealing direct with the regions – this may be justified by the new policy but the regions are not in a position to manipulate the donors – now whatever the donors want, the regions agree. Donors come in with their own agenda ... In the absence of a counterbalance donors will use their own possibilities – the whole regionalisation process means that there is less questioning of the donor system. From the legal point of view all external assistance must be coordinated by the centre, but you have a loophole where donors can work directly with the regions. (interview, Project Preparation and Monitoring Team official, Ministry of Health, Addis Ababa, March 1995)

Similarly, one bilateral donor official reported that:

When it comes to donor coordination, Ethiopia is in a mess: line ministries never invite more than one donor in at a time to discuss something. Initiatives like the Health Population and Nutrition group have no status in terms of coordination ... people just use the group to endorse what they are doing. While there are higher levels of coordination at the aid and political levels there are no vertical structures to link these with the technical level. There is an EU proposal to enhance coordination, but the people who are attending it haven't attended the other HPN meetings, they are very bureaucratic people. Regionalisation is a big failure because it was done on an ethnic basis – the donors love it, they are neo-colonialists, rushing in to regions 1, 3 and the southern people's but there are big question marks relating to regions 2, 5 and 12 and 4 – who is going to work there? It is a pretty serious situation – the government can't direct donors where to work, they don't dare. This is a big failure on the part of the government, which professes to have a commitment to equitable resource allocation. Aid has to correspond with government policy, but the government doesn't guide donors as to distributions – donors are doing needs assessments rather than the government – this means that whereas donors can prove their priorities, the government has no information to challenge them with. At the moment the government doesn't dare to be seen to be taking money away from one region by proposing donors put it in another region. Donors don't want to work in regions 2 [Afar] and 5 [Somali] because there is nothing there to work with – it is too expensive to start up work there. (interview, Addis Ababa, July 1995)

Despite an increase in the proportion of technical cooperation at the regional level, many agency personnel working at national and regional levels emphasised the difficulties of working effectively at the regional level. Institutional bottlenecks were seen as the key constraint to increasing absorptive capacity in the country. One UN official described the situation as follows:

The mood in [the international community] is that implementation is too slow – a lot of us were hoping that decentralisation would help, we were all hoping that we could work directly with the regions. To date all the facets of decentralisation have not been worked out. Politically it is all fairly clear-cut, but in other ways it isn't. There has been a lot of redeployment of staff from the MOH, which has decongested the central level, but some people just didn't show up in their regional posts, they effectively disappeared from the system. Others went to the region and just waited to hear what they should do. Others who don't speak the language of the region were thrown out. While there has been a reduction at the centre, there hasn't been a corresponding increase in the numbers of staff at regional level – now there is a double shortage and everyone is stretched. (interview, Addis Ababa, July 1995)

Aid agencies, particularly the United Nations agencies that worked through government structures, were thus facing particular problems disbursing funds.[31]

For NGOs, whose mandates did not tie them to working with and through government institutions, the problem of navigating the complex bureaucracies of the centre and the regions was seen to be less problematic. One NGO director said that '[NGOs] come with resources and generally the region just rubber-stamps things' (interview, Addis Ababa, March 1995). Thus, in the context of complex political and bureaucratic change and lack of clarity regarding sectoral policy, NGOs could secure greater room for manoeuvre.

However, NGOs have not played as significant a role in health systems development in Ethiopia as in the other two countries included in this study, since the government actively resisted the privatisation of the aid effort. During the Mengistu regime, the primary role of NGOs was to handle the massive volumes of food aid pledged by the international community. In rebel-held territory, it was the indigenous relief agencies, REST and ERA, not international NGOs, that distributed relief. On assuming power the EPRDF, whose membership had included those rebel groups to which REST was affiliated, sought to maintain national control over aid resources. The government saw international NGOs as a threat to national sovereignty and as diverting resources away from the state.[32] It therefore sought to control NGOs and to deploy them to meet gaps in government provision, in other words to include them within the framework of the state, not outside it.[33]

Thus, in a context of rapid political change and weakened state capacity amidst regionalisation, a policy impasse quickly developed in relation to aid to the health sector. While the international aid support for the health sector had significantly increased in value, it was provided in a climate of considerable political uncertainty, reflected in the turbulence of the newly established regional structures and tighter governmental controls over non-governmental channels. The international aid community made a clear decision to respect and support the juridical sovereignty of the new Ethiopian government, releasing the bulk of its support through balance of payment and programme aid, and switching food aid flows from the NGO to the government sector. In its turn the Ethiopian government was sufficiently confident and robust in its dealings with the international aid community to define clearly the rules under which it would receive aid.[34] However, there was no clear sectoral policy to guide health interventions in this period, nor was there a mechanism to monitor and coordinate the increasing number of projects emerging at a regional level.

Thus in the period 1991–94 donors opted to respect governmental decision-making procedures and to channel resources through the state. However, government was unable to set clear policy priorities or to implement them; government policy precluded widespread use of NGOs to enhance implementing capacity where governmental capacity was weak, a strategy evident in Uganda and Cambodia. In this context, while the volume of aid funds to the health sector increased, this increase was not linked to a medium-term strategy for sectoral development.

Thus, in the case of Ethiopia, political conditions dictated that in the transition period more developmental forms of aid were possible (including balance of payments support, loans and bilateral grants, channelled largely through the Ethiopian state and managed by it). This was possible because the donor community 'bought into' the new regime, quickly legitimating it. This is in stark contrast to Cambodia, where a pattern of state avoidance, and the imposed timeframe of UNTAC, led to the use of forms of aid that were more akin to relief, channelled largely through NGOs, and managed by *ad hoc* and often weak coordination arrangements only loosely linked to the public authorities. In Ethiopia the problem was, however, that once the state had secured aid resources, it lacked a clear policy framework and implementing capacity to use them sustainably.

International Aid for Health Sector Rehabilitation in Uganda

The political context of transition Like many guerrilla movements that achieve power after prolonged insurgency, the National Resistance Movement (NRM) brought with it idealism, enthusiasm and hope.

Outside of a small area, however, it lacked a solid basis of popular support and a corps of cadres able to mobilise the population (Burkey 1991). When the NRM took power, it sought to implement what became known as 'the ten-point plan', which it had developed during the course of its insurgency struggle.[35] The NRM sought to achieve its political and economic objectives of democracy and development by building consensus across sectarian lines and, in particular, replicating throughout the country a system of popular institutions – the Resistance Committees and Councils.[36]

Members of the National Resistance Council (NRC) were drawn from a wide range of political and ethnic backgrounds, making it less a political party than a political movement. Uganda remains a one-party state. The re-establishment of multi-party democracy called for by some donor governments has been debated repeatedly, but has been resisted on the grounds that it would reignite the sectarian politics of the post-independence period.

In addition to the apparently overwhelming task of rebuilding the country, as the NRM transformed itself from a guerrilla movement into a government, it was quickly faced with the development of an armed opposition in the north of the country. By August 1986, two insurgency groups had emerged in the northern districts of Gulu and Kitgum – the Uganda People's Democratic Army (UPDA) and the messianic sect of Alice Lakwena. Lakwena's forces were defeated in late 1987 and a peace agreement made with a substantial part of the UPDA. However, other smaller messianic sects formed and rebel activity persisted. In 1991, a major military operation was mounted against northern rebels, which entailed forcible resettlement of civilians and led to a significant, although often under-reported, humanitarian crisis (Macrae and Bradbury 1998). Museveni's control was also threatened early in the north-east of the country in the districts of Soroti and Kumi, home to the Iteso.[37] After more than four years of insurgency and counter-insurgency, the NRM mounted a major offensive designed to put a halt to the war in the Iteso regions and finally secured a military victory.

Aid in transition   The NRM's takeover of power paved the way for the resumption of aid relations with Western countries. An agreement was signed with the IMF in 1987, committing the country to a programme of stabilisation. This was swiftly followed by the negotiation of a Structural Adjustment Facility (SAF) with the World Bank. The launching of the first Rehabilitation and Development Plan in 1987 was preceded by a package of measures, including currency reform, tight budgeting and cost-cutting, which gained support from both the Bretton Woods institutions (Economist Intelligence Unit 1992). The SAF was replaced in April 1988 by an Enhanced Structural Adjustment Facility, following the government's decision to deepen and hasten the pace of reform (Lateef 1990).

The Rehabilitation and Development Plan called for funding (largely from external aid) of more than US$1 billion over four years. Donor response to this appeal was slow, however, reflecting in part the cautious efforts of the international community to understand the NRM's political agenda. Initially, they were wary of supporting a regime perceived as being inclined towards socialism.

Health 'policy' As described in Chapter 4, by 1986 public institutions throughout Uganda had been severely weakened by the political events of the previous decades and the parlous state of the economy. This included public health institutions, where there was a vacuum in the capacity to execute a clear rehabilitation strategy. The government's primary concern was to consolidate its political power and stabilise the country, leaving little time for health policy. Health issues did yield some political capital, however. Members of the National Resistance Council and local politicians were reported to have lobbied for the reconstruction of local health facilities, particularly hospitals,[38] and high-profile vertical programmes were also politically useful. One NGO representative informant suggested that:

> EPI was perceived politically to be part of the demonstration of how they [the NRM] could reach various parts of the country. By encouraging UNICEF and SCF to inject monies into it, the government was able to show that it was doing something to 'save the children' in all corners of the country. (interview, Kampala, March 1993)

In other words, health interventions were seen as contributing to the internal legitimation of the government.

Overall, however, health did not occupy a prominent position on the political agenda during 1986–90.[39] The government had to be cautious in challenging the status quo in any area of the public sector. Dependent upon the civil service functioning to implement the government programme of political and economic reform, it had to work through a bureaucracy perceived to be resistant to political change and subject to widespread corruption (Burkey 1991).[40]

Yet the bureaucratic machinery itself lacked the capacity for effective and efficient planning and analysis. It was only in the 1992 Rehabilitation Plan, some six years after the NRM took power, that a clear mechanism for priority-setting and rationalisation of sectoral development was set out (Uganda 1992). In 1986 there were no central review and control mechanisms in place. The budget submission from the MOH was reportedly particularly weak, failing to conform to budgeting guidelines, a problem that continued to haunt the MOH at least until 1993 (Save the Children Fund 1993; Uganda 1987).

In the absence of active leadership by the new regime, the civil service was left in charge of policy. The problem was, what policy? A

Box 5.2 Main tenets of Ugandan Ten-year Health Plan, 1991

- Restatement of commitment to comprehensive PHC policy
- Priority accorded to community participation through a network of health committees at different levels of the RC system and the promotion of Community Health Workers
- Decentralisation of the healthcare administration to district level
- Promotion of inter-sectoral collaboration and coordination particularly between ministries, NGOs and donors
- Promotion of private practice and its regulation and control
- Encouragement and partial integration of traditional medicine into the formal health system
- Reorganisation of healthcare into four levels (health centre; rural / district hospital; regional and specialist hospitals; national referral and teaching hospital)
- Promotion of alternative methods of health financing starting with user fees and community financing

Source: Uganda 1991

Health Policy Review Commission was established in 1987 to advise on policy direction. A member of this Commission commented that: 'No one knew what health policy was, over the years it had become an *ad hoc* series of declarations' (interview, former member of the Health Policy Review Commission, Entebbe, April 1993). The investigations of the Commission itself confirmed the uncertainty surrounding health policy and warned that: 'even senior officers are not clear as to the Ministry's policy on specific issues. The absence of clear policies in turn leads to inadequate determination of priorities for the Ministry as a whole' (Uganda 1987: 52).

The Commission published its wide-ranging report late in 1987. It reported that the country had seen a succession of policy reviews, conferences and workshops since independence in 1962, but that few recommendations had ever been wholly implemented because of political uncertainty and lack of commitment and resources. It called for many of the recommendations made in previous reports to be adopted, in particular the findings of a 1980 committee that had advocated the adoption of a Primary Health Care strategy (Uganda 1987).

The formation of the Commission provided an important opportunity for a reappraisal of policy. However, its terms of reference focused primarily on a review of existing policy documents, and did not link the policy and planning tasks. While the report provided a valuable overview of the health system, it lacked a comprehensive, quantified analysis of health needs, financial resources or available levels of human resources. Perhaps more importantly, while it had a policy *advisory* function, the Commission was not empowered to *make* or *enact* policy. In other words, it could not substitute for a functioning Ministry of Health – the juridical and empirical body responsible for health policy-making and implementation.

It was not until 1991 that the government published its National Health Plan (see Box 5.2). The publication of the plan prompted a major outcry among donors. The primary point of contention was that the budget for the plan exceeded the available resources fourfold. Since inadequate resources were available from the public sector, it was argued, a much more minimal package of services should be made available (Okounzi and Macrae 1995).

Aiding recovery: rehabilitation in policy a vacuum The donor response to the 1991 plan can be seen as symptomatic of the poor communication and coordination between different donors and national policy actors after 1986.[41] The absence of a clear national health policy between 1986 and 1991 meant that donors could neither conform with nor fail to conform with government goals:

> donors could do whatever they wanted in the immediate post-conflict period. The government said 'yes' to EPI, 'yes' to the rehabilitation of hospitals, 'yes' to the rehabilitation of Mulago [the main teaching hospital], 'yes' to CDD. There was no attempt to redirect programmes, because there was no central health policy. (interview, NGO representative, Entebbe, March 1993)[42]

Policy during this period might be described as in free-fall. This was not primarily because of a lack of information about and analysis of the healthcare system. Indeed, during 1986–87 a series of studies were commissioned and published by agencies such as UNICEF (Dodge and Weibe 1985), and as part of a project preparation facility for the World Bank (see, for example, Annet and Janovsky 1988; Lee et al. 1987).

However, the technical concerns put forward by some professional planners were swept aside by both national politicians and aid managers, including some who had commissioned the technical reports. For example, the World Bank's country manager reportedly rejected the projects prepared under the Project Preparation Facility and ignored several key recommendations, particularly those concerning the need to rebuild district-level capacity and ensure sustainability of infrastructure redevelopment (interviews, Entebbe, April 1993).

Part of the difficulty for those responsible for technical analysis was that the credit agreement for the First Health Project was completed *before* all the planned appraisal exercises had been implemented, exposing project staff to pressure to implement activities, without confirmation that this policy direction was appropriate (interview, World Bank official, Addis Ababa, April 1995; interview, World Bank official, Entebbe, 1993). Such evidence that was available, as well as additional material collected by the Bank, did raise profound questions regarding the likely efficacy of a strategy that sought to restore the pre-conflict health system (Dodge and Weibe 1985). However, these were largely ignored. As the acting director of the First Health Project explained:

> The World Bank commissioned a series of studies ... the results of these studies were not used completely. When you commission a study, it may not yield the results you require. [Some] studies were done in 1986, but by the time they came to prepare the project in 1987/88, the report findings were already out of date, the situation had changed dramatically. The MOH never used the studies, rather they went straight to what the government wanted – the rehabilitation of hospitals. (interview, 4 May 1993, Entebbe)

The above comments indicate a sleight of hand, whereby the responsibility for the poor design of the rehabilitation strategy is conveniently placed into the domain of the Ugandan government, rather than within the World Bank.

As described above, the government's willingness and ability to direct policy was limited. Nor did donors and international bodies seek to make their support for the sector conditional upon the government's clarifying key areas of policy. Indeed, one World Bank economist commented:

> in the immediate post-conflict period the government was in need of a great deal of money very quickly ... there were vast needs for reconstruction of the physical infrastructure to provide basic services such as education and health. Under these conditions, the Bank did not seek to demand difficult conditions, rather it sought to be extremely helpful. (interview, Kampala, 22 May 1993)

In the absence of an over-arching health strategy (and a functioning mechanism for its enforcement) there was a proliferation of different, project-based interventions funded by different donors and implemented by a variety of NGOs. Nor did donors seek to establish a forum to coordinate their aid to the health sector, either among themselves, or between themselves and the government. Instead, donors and implementing agencies sought niches for their own activities. For example, UNICEF implemented the Expanded Programme of Immunisation (EPI), DANIDA continued to support essential drugs, while a host of other NGOs carved out projects across the country. While several donors and implementing agencies (e.g. the World Bank, SCF,

UNICEF and AMREF) had representatives within the MOH during this period, they were largely concerned with the management of specific projects rather than the development of an overall health policy (Howard and Kiragu 1992).

A number of quasi-autonomous bodies also emerged, such as the Project Implementation Unit of the World Bank, which was to implement the FHP outside ministerial structures. This approach of working outside, or at least alongside, the state was encouraged by concerns regarding the weak capacity of the public health sector. The effects of these management systems, however, was to create a series of unintegrated, 'micro-policy' environments, in other words policies whose extent was limited to that of particular project-type interventions or associated with particular donor agencies, rather than an integrated, national policy framework.

These micro-policies were defined vertically in terms of type of intervention (e.g. immunisation), and geographically within the confines of particular project areas (Glennie 1993a, 1993b). But there was little integration with any national policy (for such did not exist): these micro-policies were linked to the internal policies of the international agencies that supported them. Thus, in the context of a weakened quasi-state, health policy became internationalised, while national capacity and ownership of the public health system further diminished.

Different Folks, Same Strokes: Issues and Implications

The introduction to this chapter proposed that the form of rehabilitation aid, the channels through which it is disbursed and the systems for its management are critically determined by the particular political conditions of 'post'-conflict transition. What emerges from a review of the three countries' experience is that, despite significant differences in the nature of the transition process, there are considerable similarities in terms of the type of aid instrument deployed. A comparative analysis of the case studies suggests that, before the form, channels and systems of relief aid give way to those of development aid three conditions must be satisfied. First the question of juridical sovereignty must be resolved. Second, that juridical sovereignty must be recognised internationally and seen to be legitimate, particularly by Western donor countries. Third, the recipient state must be able to function as a state, in other words be able to demonstrate its empirical sovereignty by making and executing public policy. Table 5.1 summarises these different conditions in the case study countries at the time of transition.

What the evidence from these cases suggests is that, where all three conditions are satisfied, as was the case in Ethiopia, there is the greatest scope for the relatively rapid resumption of developmental forms of aid. Donor governments, most importantly the USA, wished to legitimise the new regime, and within Ethiopia both the expertise and the institutions existed for an effective donor–government dialogue to design programmes to respond rapidly to the new political context, and in particular to switch aid channels to direct more resources through state channels. In the case of the health sector, this meant that aid could play a significant role in stabilising the *public* health system, since it contributed towards maintaining staff salaries and most significantly maintained drug supplies. This is in stark contrast

Table 5.1 Conditions of sovereignty and legitimation in the immediate 'post'-conflict period in Cambodia, Ethiopia and Uganda

	Juridical sovereignty	International legitimation	Empirical sovereignty
Cambodia 1991–93	Suspended, entrusted temporarily to UN	Awaiting election results	Very weak, not least because SOC administration marginalised; significant security threats
Ethiopia 1991	Clearly established	Yes, immediate	State institutions did not collapse, but were weakened by regionalisation; some threats to security
Uganda 1986	Clearly established	Cautious endorsement	Very weak, significant security threats, particularly in north

to both Cambodia and Uganda. In Cambodia, juridical sovereignty was in effect suspended, pending the results of the elections. Although the SNC, and ultimately UNTAC, did have the authority to make decisions regarding rehabilitation aid, the analysis presented above demonstrates that this was undermined by in-fighting between the factions and by donor countries working outside these constitutive bodies. In Uganda, juridical sovereignty was assumed by the NRM on seizing control of Kampala, and the new government recognised internationally, for example by the UN. However, international legitimation was more tentative and incremental – the government having first to prove its international credentials by, for example, signing up to Structural Adjustment Programmes. Once this had been achieved, then new forms of aid became available, in particular loans from the World Bank and significant grants from the EC that were used for health sector rehabilitation.

Unless and until the issues of juridical sovereignty and international legitimation have been resolved, those forms of aid that rely upon state institutions and imply legitimation of the state are withheld. This means maintaining relief and relief-type aid instruments, channelled through NGOs and those multilateral organisations such as the ICRC, UNICEF and the UNHCR that have a humanitarian mandate. Cambodia exemplifies the reliance of the international system on these channels in conditions of uncertain statehood. In Uganda too there was heavy reliance on NGOs to sustain services, particularly in those areas where statehood remained contested after the NRM took power. These areas, such as Soroti in the north, were excluded from the wave of development aid programmes established in the late 1980s.

Even once the issues of juridical sovereignty and legitimation were resolved, however, there were significant constraints to resuming developmental forms of aid and re-establishing systems for its management. For donors, there were procedural obstacles to rapid resumption of bilateral aid programmes, which meant that they relied heavily on multilateral channels, particularly the UN and the World Bank, to act as conduits for their assistance. The delay in re-establishing bilateral relations may have been beneficial in terms of enhancing coordination and coherence, since there were fewer key actors. However, such delays necessarily placed a ceiling on the rate at which the *volume* of assistance could be increased, so in part accounting for the relatively slow rate of increase in aid funds in Ethiopia, for example.

In both Ethiopia and Uganda the World Bank was a key actor for health sector rehabilitation.[43] Interestingly, in both cases in the immediate aftermath of the conflict its assistance was unconditional, and linked largely to the supply of goods (drugs) and the re-establishment of the physical infrastructure. The unconditional character of this aid was seen to be necessary in order to facilitate rapid disbursement of funds, and indeed to foster internal legitimation of the respective governments. Thus the form of aid at this time, and the systems for its management, emphasised the maximisation of aid flows *per se* rather than their technical effectiveness. Thus it was the legitimising function of aid, not the sustainability of aid interventions, that was prioritised.

In all three countries, the scope for adopting developmental approaches to health sector rehabilitation was constrained by the empirical weakness of the state. As Chapter 4 made clear, the problems facing the health sector in all three countries pre-dated their respective conflicts. While peace was a necessary condition for the re-establishment of effective health services, it was not sufficient: more profound reforms were required to address the structural problems of health financing and of inequality of health provision.

However, the scope for addressing these key policy issues was extremely limited in all three countries. The design and implementation of effective health sector reforms requires not only money but political and institutional resources, and these were extremely scarce. The over-riding similarities between these very different contexts are the policy vacuum that prevailed at the time of transition, and the weakness of health institutions at national and local levels. This lack of capacity for policy formulation and implementation meant that there was little scope to examine carefully policy priorities and to establish corresponding mechanisms for resource allocation.[44]

In this context, aid became a means of increasing overall resources flows to the sector either directly through the government or delivered through private NGO channels direct to health centre level. These resources were much needed, as Chapter 6 makes clear, but they were not directed in a *developmental* manner. Rather, because there was no strategy, and because of the form of aid (unconditional assistance delivered largely through NGOs and multilaterals for a limited period of time) donors and aid agencies opted to allocate their resources against health hardware (such as drugs and infrastructure), which allowed for rapid, visible but not necessarily sustainable results.

As the political context determined the form of aid, so the form of aid determined its *content*. In the case of assistance in these 'post'-conflict settings, the forms, channels and systems of aid could deliver projects, but not *policy*. What becomes evident are the differences in the principles that guide relief and development aid interventions. While relief aid is targeted at the level of the individual, is politically unconditional and implemented largely by international agencies working at the level of particular programmes, the 'scaling-up' of this response to embrace the goals of national health systems requires, in current approaches to development aid, the presence of a central, unified state that is seen to be legitimate internationally.

As Chapter 6 makes clear, the choices of strategy that follow from this political context and the dilemmas of the aid transition present major problems in terms of the sustainability of rehabilitation investment. Indeed, rather than contributing to the development of health systems in the three case study countries, the assistance provided during the transitional period can be seen to have undermined it.

Notes

1. In this way, the creation of the UN Trusteeship reflected concern that it might be seen as replicating an essentially colonial approach to sovereignty: the constitution of UNTAC made it clear that it was the political parties of Cambodia that had invited the UN to undertake its role in mediating the political transition.

2. To prepare for UNTAC, the UN fielded UNAMIC – the United Nations Advanced Mission in Cambodia – on 16 October 1991. On 28 February 1992 the Security Council enacted a Resolution 745(1992) to establish UNTAC. However, it was not until May 1992, six months after the SNC moved its headquarters to Phnom Penh, that the SRSG took up his post as head of UNTAC, signalling the start of its implementation. The late deployment of the full UN mission is seen by some to have compromised the operation at an early stage in terms of its ability to achieve security, protect human rights and maintain public scrutiny of the liberalisation process (see CCC 1992).

3. Despite the apparent generosity of this support, these funds were largely for projects to come on stream *after* the elections had taken place. This left much of the rehabilitation effort underfinanced (Peou and Yamada 1998).

4. Chopra et al. (1993) provide an insightful analysis of the limitations of the UN operation in the political and security spheres.

5. It is difficult to estimate the precise proportion of total oda that was processed through the TAC. As later sections make clear, there are no reconciled figures that show total disbursements of oda during the transitional period. However, taking the lower figures produced by the UNDP database, which estimate total disbursements of US$582 million in 1992 and 1993, the total number of disbursing projects approved by the TAC account for approximately US$200 million, less than 34 per cent of the total amount disbursed. Thus, at a conservative estimate, over 60 per cent of aid disbursed during this period was *not* approved by the TAC (see Lanjouw et al. 1998).

6. Indeed, Cambodia was seen by the USA as a pilot country for experimenting with aid in situations of 'post'-conflict rehabilitation worldwide (USAID 1994).

7. Interview, former WHO special envoy to Cambodia, 10 May 1994. In this respect, the author was struck by a visit to a hospital near the Thailand–Cambodia border that had received extensive support from the USA during the early 1990s. It had been equipped with colour televisions, air conditioning and had well-equipped operating theatres, serving both military and civilians. By the time of the visit in December 1994, the hospital was a virtual shell, with very low utilisation and no publicly funded supplies. MSF-Holland was maintaining a minimal presence there, but security remained poor and many of the former inhabitants had left the area.

8. Importantly, the reliance on NGOs as an aid channel was not quickly altered after the elections. The World Bank (1994b) noted that in 1994 only two donors were set to route their assistance through the MOH, accounting for less than 10 per cent of total aid to the sector.

9. At its peak, UNTAC comprised 20,000 international personnel. These included 16,000 military personnel and 3,500 civilian police. This left relatively few staff to coordinate and implement the political (preparation and monitoring of the elections) and the social (rehabilitation) component of the Agreement.

10. These were Battambang, Banteay Meachey and Kandal.

11. The former WHO special envoy to Cambodia (interview, Geneva, May 1994) suggested that, in addition to the political imperative of investing in repatriation, the particular focus of aid agencies on this group stemmed from their awareness that refugees returning home would bring a reduction in their standard of living compared with the Thai refugee camps.

12. At least until the 1990s, UNICEF was in a unique position within the UN family in its ability to work with non-state entities and states such as Cambodia, which were not internationally recognised (Richardson 1995).

13. Interview, 10 May 1994 in Geneva with former special envoy, WHO.

14. The battle to control the policy paradigm guiding health sector reform in Cambodia continued after the elections. A World Bank official commented that: 'UNFPA, UNICEF and USAID are all going [to the Ministry] with their

visions. The MOH will select one of these models ... the problem is that there is nothing left to reform' (interview, World Bank official, June 1994).

15. Interview, provincial health adviser, UNICEF, Battambang, December 1994.

16. Four ProCoComs were established in 1992, and two in 1993. By 1994 there were eight ProCoComs in the 21 provinces/cities throughout the country. The overall objective of the ProCoComs was to facilitate the implementation of national health programmes and policies via provincial health plans through the coordination of NGOs, international organisations and provincial health resources to avoid duplication and maximise health impact. The ProCoCom mechanisms also sought to disseminate information from the CoCom level to the provinces, but do not appear to have functioned well as information-collecting institutions that fed insights and material up to the national level (see Lanjouw et al. 1998).

17. These were: Maternal and Child Health; Mental Health; Health Information Systems; Pharmacy; Hospital Planning and Management; Primary Health Care; Prevention of Blindness; and District Health Strengthening. The establishment of sub-committees was influenced by the enthusiasm of particular actors (individuals and organisations) and in some cases reflected the interests of particular NGOs (for example, MSF in relation to Health Information Systems) in promoting nationally models they had developed at local level. It is not clear, however, whether all key areas of activity – for example, communicable disease control – received the attention they deserved at this point in time. It was notable, for example, that control of tuberculosis in the early days of transition suffered greatly given the unavailability of drugs and lack of further training and support for pre-existing systems of diagnosis, treatment and care (see Lanjouw et al. 1995).

18. Indeed, testament to this was the ability of the WHO to overcome political divisions by asserting that the essentially humanitarian nature of its health mandate was demonstrated by its efforts to unify the health professionals who had been working with the political faction (Hun Chun 1993). These activities were concentrated in the north-west provinces of the country and, as bilateral donor support for the former factions' (FUNCIPEC and KPNLF) health services ended in October 1993, this undertaking was to coordinate and pave the way for the emergence of a civilian health system. It was proposed that this would take place through the integration of factional health staff and health programmes into the national district and provincial health management system. It was supported by a technical planning and working group that considered policy recommendations regarding the strengthening of provincial and district level management capabilities, issues regarding the private sector health services and health facilities, and human resources development. Through this mechanism, the *Health Worker Qualification Equivalencies Paper* was produced in February 1993 and agreed by the SNC factions, collapsing the number of different health worker diplomas nationwide from 59 to 23. However, even by 1995 many health workers who had qualified outside Cambodia remained unrecognised by the new government (Lanjouw et al. 1998).

19. The role of the USA in hastening the capitulation of the Mengistu regime and thus avoiding a pitched battle for control of the capital has been widely cited as important (Duffield and Prendergast 1994; interview, UN official, July 1995). The discipline of the rebel troops was also clearly a major factor in securing a relatively peaceful transition in Addis (interview, UN official, Addis Ababa, March 1995).

20. Interviews conducted during the course of the research in East Hararghe confirmed this analysis. There, throughout 1991 and 1992, intermittent violence caused widespread destruction of government infrastructure, including health centres. This was seen as an expression of defiance of the previous regime which had coerced communities into contributing cash and labour to develop public facilities.

21. These nine states include the three city-states of Addis Ababa, Dire Dawa and Harar, together with the confederation of states that collectively form the Southern People's Administration.

22. Interviews with Western diplomats, as well as confidential interviews with many Ethiopians.

23. For example, interview, UN officials, Addis Ababa, July 1995, and interviews with health staff in East Hararghe.

24. For example, by 1993, of a total capital budget of birr 3.85 billion, 42.9 per cent (1.65 billion birr) was financed from external sources (UNDP 1995: 10). Programme aid and balance of payments support declined from 7.1 per cent of external assistance in 1989 to just 0.1 per cent in 1991, reflecting donor dissatisfaction with the Mengistu regime. On the TGE assuming power, this rose rapidly to 11.4 per cent in 1993, enabling the new government to use resources in line with its own priorities (UNDP 1995: 11).

25. With the exception of the EC, development assistance was limited. As described in Chapter 4, the EC continued with a sizeable programme of development aid throughout the Mengistu government.

26. SEPHA sought to do this through its cross-mandate, cross-border approach. However, the Ethiopian government was equivocal regarding SEPHA as a mechanism for fund-raising, concerned that in channelling funds through the UN it reduced flows through the government administration (interview, Ethiopian Emergencies Unit official, 7 March 1995). Furthermore, SEPHA was really the prelude to the consolidated appeal process that would become routinised following the establishment of the DHA in late 1991. It was thus a collection of appeals by different UN agencies, by definition those responsible for relief. Unlike the later attempts of the strategic framework in Afghanistan (Cholmondeley 1997) it was not a mechanism for strategic linking of relief and development assistance programming.

27. Interviews in Addis Ababa: USAID official, March 1995; British Embassy official, July 1995; Netherlands Embassy official, March 1995; UNDP official, July 1995.

28. Of this requirement, 23 per cent ($150 million) was to be financed from a new World Bank credit, with the remainder coming from reallocation

of existing IDA loans (12 per cent), 19 per cent from the African Development Bank, 18 per cent from the European Commission, and additional funds coming from Japan, Germany, Sweden and the Netherlands.

29. Interview, World Bank Health and Population Division official, Addis Ababa, 19 March 1995.

30. For example, interviews, Netherlands Embassy official; SIDA official, March and July 1995.

31. Interviews, UNICEF Health Section official; Netherlands Embassy official; UN Emergency Unit for Ethiopia official, all in Addis Ababa, March and July 1995.

32. Interviews, USAID official, Addis Ababa, July 1995; World Bank country representative, March 1995; CRDA official, July 1995).

33. Thus NGOs reported that many of the restrictions that had been in place under the Mengistu regime, for example regarding recruitment procedures, had been lifted. They complained, however, that they remained constrained by the state. One NGO official described the new environment as follows: 'the operating environment for NGOs is more fraught with conditions [than in the past]. NGOs were controlled by force under Mengistu, now they are controlled by directives and guidelines which are chipping away at our independence' (interview, Addis Ababa, March 1995).

34. The example set by Eritrea in its dealings with NGOs and the European Commission was potentially sobering for international aid officials based in Ethiopia. The Eritrean government had refused aid that it felt unable to adequately control: sanctions in reverse. As Clapham (1996) points out, aid dependence is a two-way street: without a government willing to expend aid, individual bureaucrats as well as the system more generally lose credibility.

35. The programme set out a range of objectives, including the achievement of democracy and security; the elimination of all forms of sectarianism; the defence of national boundaries from external aggression; the achievement of an integrated and self-sustaining economy; the rehabilitation of social services, particularly in war-ravaged areas; the ending of corruption; improving living conditions for those who had suffered disproportionately from previous government policies; the defence of human rights throughout Africa.

36. This pyramidal structure linked village-level committees (RC1) and parish level to the National Resistance Council (NRC) through a series of sub-county (RC3), county (RC4) and district (RC5) committees.

37. In 1986, one of the first actions of the NRA had been to disarm militia groups formed by the populations in these two districts to protect themselves from violent cattle-raiding from the neighbouring district of Karamoja. This caused widespread resentment among the Iteso, particularly since the NRA proved neither willing nor able to protect them from such raids, and indeed was sometimes implicated in them. The rebel group the Ugandan People's Army (UPA) moved to take advantage of this resentment and the vulnerability felt by this population to insecurity in light of their historical allegiance to Milton Obote, the NRM's foe.

38. Interviews, Ministry of Health Health Planning Unit official, March 1993, Entebbe; World Bank First Health Project official, Entebbe, April 1993.

39. The NRM had executive secretaries for functions such as defence and education, but there was no such representative concerned with health. Similarly, neither health nor education was identified in the president's address at the state opening of the first session of the expanded NRC in April 1989 as being among the eight priority areas of the economic recovery programme (personal communication, health planner, London, April 1994).

40. Also interviews with adviser to the Ministry of Local Government, Kampala, April 1993; editor, *Uganda Confidential*, April 1993.

41. It is telling, for example, that neither the Health Policy Review Commission nor the World Bank acknowledged each other's work during the late 1980s, and the chair of the former was not aware of the extensive project preparation work done by the latter, despite the fact that this contained new and important data.

42. See also the findings of the Health Policy Review Commission, which argued: 'External donors take advantage of this policy vacuum to lobby high level politicians and civil servants, thus prejudicing policy decisions in their favour, but not necessarily in the national interest' (Uganda 1997: 52).

43. In Cambodia, the World Bank conducted some important analyses of the health sector during the UNTAC period, but was not able to operationalise its plan until after the elections because of the problem of juridical sovereignty. Interestingly, despite the complex analysis presented by the Bank, which outlined the need for extensive health sector reforms, the backbone of the Bank's health sector intervention was physical rehabilitation of the infrastructure.

44. As noted earlier, efforts to increase policy capacity in Uganda (UNICEF) and Cambodia (WHO and UNICEF) were significant, but their impact was limited by the fact that the bulk of aid was designed and implemented outside the public health system.

CHAPTER 6

The Sustainability Dilemma

§ Inayatullah and Blaney (1995) have provided an important critique of Jackson's (1990) analysis of the origins of quasi-statehood. They argue that the very poverty of many Third World countries has been an obstacle to effective state formation – fulfilling the conditions of empirical statehood costs money. Jackson notes that a key role of aid has been to buttress empirical sovereignty by providing much-needed resources. He goes on to question the unconditional provision of aid to states that have been unable to satisfy conditions of empirical sovereignty. Inayatullah and Blaney argue that problematic in Jackson's analysis of quasi-statehood (and by implication its conclusions regarding international engagement with these states) is that it presumes that states have failed to meet the conditions of empirical statehood because of internal failures, and that he ignores the features of the global political economy that sustain Third World poverty and dependency.

Two important points follow from these authors' analyses of the determinants of empirical statehood and the function of aid in reinforcing it. First, poverty of itself contributes to the weakness of states. The availability of resources is important in order to generate internal legitimacy. As argued previously, the provision of basic public services, such as health, is an important part of what constitutes empirical statehood. Thus the legitimacy of regimes is in part determined by the willingness and ability of states to provide such services. There is, however, a vicious cycle, whereby the political and economic weaknesses of states themselves act as obstacles to achieving such legitimacy and thus empirical statehood.

Second, as argued in Chapters 2 and 3, if a key function of aid (specifically development aid) is to reinforce empirical sovereignty, then this assumes that donors wish to legitimise the recipient state. Yet Chapter 5 showed that in at least two of the case studies (Cambodia and Uganda) the empirical or juridical sovereignty of the recipient state was questioned, and donors were equivocal in their relationships with these states. This type of situation in turn forces aid agencies to adopt strategies that are the precise opposite of those traditionally associated with development aid: in other words, strategies that do *not* seek to reinforce state structures.

Both these observations challenge the claim that rehabilitation aid (and, more generally, developmental approaches to relief), unlike relief, provides the basis for sustainable development. Analysis of the relationship between sovereignty, legitimacy and aid suggests that claims that rehabilitation aid is sustainable or developmental are problematic on two grounds. First, the very weakness of public financing and institutions (empirical sovereignty) means that, without either very large increases in resources and/or extensive reform of existing healthcare systems, the goal of sustainability is unlikely to be realistic. Second, if the international community withholds international legitimacy this affects the form of aid deployed, as shown in Chapter 5. Resultant forms of aid are deliberately designed to avoid building state capacity. Yet the assumption underpinning rehabilitation assistance is that it will ultimately contribute to the development of a public health system, financed and managed by the state. Because of problems of international legitimation, the particular form of rehabilitation aid is likely to weaken rather than strengthen state institutions, including public health institutions. As such they are not developmental, and in the medium term may make it more difficult to implement sectoral reform and to re-establish effective development aid relations.

The remainder of this chapter analyses these two different challenges to rehabilitation aid. It defines sustainability and its determinants and then examines the implications of the poverty of state institutions for the goal of sustainable health systems development, and the corresponding role of aid in financing public health systems in the three case study countries. It examines how the particular forms of aid and systems of aid management provided in the three countries affected sustainability, and aims to account for the continued prioritisation of sustainability as a policy goal, despite its elusiveness. The chapter concludes by outlining its key issues and implications.

Defining Sustainability and its Determinants

LaFond (1995) defines sustainability as 'the capacity of the health system to function effectively over time with minimum external input'. This definition, like Olsen's (1998) acknowledges both the financial and the organisational determinants of sustainability.[1]

Smithson (1995) identifies three key factors that determine the financial sustainability of public health systems: total GNP, total government expenditure as a proportion of GDP, and the share of this expenditure allocated to the health sector. The financial sustainability of aid interventions is determined by the extent to which governments are able and willing to allocate resources to maintain services, once external actors have withdrawn. In addition to the availability of financing, the ability of national governments to assume responsibility for aid-financed health services is also influenced by the patterns of aid investment. Important determinants of the non-financial, organisational sustainability of rehabilitation aid are choices of project content, the mechanisms used to disburse this assistance and the systems used for its management.

Public Finance and International Aid: The Determinants of Financial Sustainability of the Health Sector in Cambodia, Ethiopia and Uganda

Economic determinants of health sector sustainability The negative effects of conflict on developing economies have been well documented elsewhere (Green 1994; Stewart 1994; UNICEF 1987). The particular dynamics of war economies are complex, and preclude detailed analysis here (see Le Billon 2000 for a full review of this literature). Most important to note here is that these economies are associated with a particularly steep and rapid reduction in public finance, as a result of declining production and the ability of the state to collect and redistribute public wealth.

In each of the three case studies, at the time of regime changes, GDP per capita was low not only in absolute terms, but also compared with regional averages. In Uganda, for example, the fall in incomes per capita between 1973 and 1980 of 6.2 per cent per annum was ten times the regional average (Uganda 1989). In 1991, in Ethiopia the

GDP per capita was US$350, less than half the average for least developed countries (US$720) (UNDP 1991). With a GDP per capita income of US$200 in 1991, Cambodia also ranked among the poorest countries in the world, and certainly in relation to the Asian average (US$683)[2] (World Bank 1993).

In two of the three countries (Cambodia and Ethiopia), the process of military and political transition that took place in the early 1990s coincided with a transition from centrally planned economies to economic liberalisation. In the case of Cambodia, the pace of this economic transition outstripped the capacity of existing public institutions to regulate and tax it (Fitzgerald 1994). This weak institutional base for revenue collection coincided with the rise of the sometimes violent parallel economy in these countries (Green 1981). As internal markets declined and physical insecurity intensified, Ugandan families began to intensify subsistence production (Edmonds 1988).[3] This dynamic combination of factors not only lowered the tax base,[4] but also diminished the capacity of the state to collect tax revenue. For example, by 1991 in Cambodia, tax revenue accounted for only 3 per cent of GDP in 1991 (Fitzgerald 1994). In 1990, public revenue accounted for only 6 per cent of Ugandan GDP, this compared with a regional average of 11 per cent (Lateef 1990). In summary, looking at all the determinants of financial sustainability of health services in these countries shows a bleak picture of absolute scarcity of resources.

An important assumption of much rehabilitation planning is that peace will yield significant financial benefits, as resources are reallocated from defence to the social sector, such as health. In Ethiopia, such benefits were indeed realised. The army under Mengistu was probably the largest in Africa, comprising an estimated 800,000 troops in the late 1980s. Following the EPRDF takeover in 1991, demobilisation of this force resulted in substantial reductions in military spending from 25 per cent of total government expenditures to 8 per cent in 1992–93 (Ethiopia 1994b). This in part explained the new government's ability to double the proportion of public expenditure allocated to the health sector in the period 1991, from under 2 per cent to nearly 4 per cent.

In contrast, in Uganda and Cambodia defence expenditures remained high, reflecting the continued security problems in those countries. In Uganda, for example, official figures suggested that

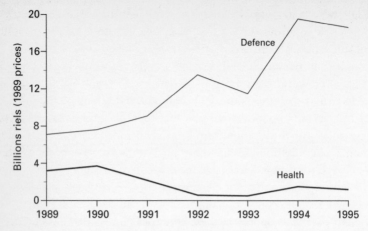

Figure 6.1 Military and public health expenditure in Cambodia, 1989–95
(*Source*: Data presented in Lanjouw et al. 1998, extracted from
Cambodia and World Bank 1995)

defence continued to account for more than one-third of public expenditure in 1988/9 (Uganda 1989), with even this high figure widely seen to be an underestimate.[5] Figure 6.1 shows military and health expenditure in Cambodia during the period 1988–95. The graph shows the relative vulnerability of public health expenditures to increases in military expenditure, particularly in the period 1990–92: as military expenditure rose, so health expenditures fell.

Buying into sovereignty? Trends in aid flows in the three countries
Chapter 5 highlighted the political determinants of aid flows to the three case study countries. At the time of transition there were significant fluctuations in the volume and form of aid flows to the three countries. Figure 6.2 shows aid flows to Cambodia in the period 1970–95. It shows significant peaks and troughs in Western aid flows to the country. The first peak is accounted for by the large emergency operation that followed the defeat of the Khmer Rouge in 1979. This ended abruptly when the UN declared the emergency 'over' in 1982. The Soviet bloc and Vietnam then became significant sources of support until 1989, when their own political and economic difficulties meant that aid was stopped abruptly. The sharp reduction in this assistance was not fully compensated for until 1992, when Western aid flows

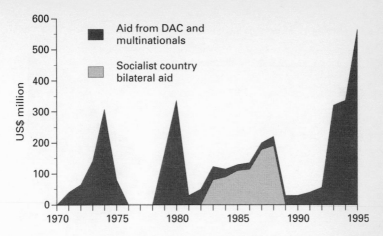

Figure 6.2 Aid to Cambodia from socialist bloc and OECD countries, 1970–95 (*Source*: Development Assistance Committee, OECD, various years; data on socialist countries cited in Lanjouw et al. 1998)

increased significantly. During the period 1989–92/3, which included the UNTAC administration, international support for the Cambodian economy was very limited.

As well as a rapid increase in the *volume* of assistance in the early 1990s, there was also a significant shift in the *form* of that assistance and the *channels* through which it was delivered. While aid from the Soviet bloc was channelled through the Cambodian state during the 1980s, in the transition period it was channelled largely through multilateral organisations and NGOs. Thus the capacity of state institutions to function was doubly jeopardised by an absolute reduction in the resources available nationally and the removal of a direct international subsidy to them.

In Uganda too aid flows fluctuated in line with political conditions (Figure 6.3). After the ousting of Idi Amin in 1979, aid flows increased, falling back again as the war against Obote intensified, rising again after the NRM victory in 1986, and rising more steeply after 1988 once the structural adjustment framework had been cemented in place.

The importance of multilateral and NGO channels is clear during the major periods of instability and in their immediate aftermath. For example, from 1982 to 1988, multilateral and NGO channels provided

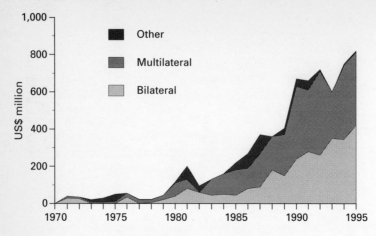

Figure 6.3 Total receipts of official development assistance to Uganda, 1971–95 (*Source*: OECD, various years)

the major mechanism for expanding aid, with a significant delay in reactivating bilateral channels.

As Figure 6.4 shows, in Ethiopia the trend in total oda flows was somewhat different, fluctuating more as a result of dramatic famines (1984/5, 1988 and 1992) associated with drought and war than because of major shifts in the country's international relations.

Indeed, what is revealing here is how *small* the increase in total aid disbursements was after the EPRDF takeover. In 1994 total aid receipts were lower than they had been in 1991.[6] However, significant in the Ethiopia case are changes in the form and channels of assistance. After 1991, bilateral donors returned to Ethiopia with the aim of establishing development assistance programmes. In addition, the scale of World Bank lending increased markedly, providing much more substantial support for balance of payments and programme aid. Furthermore, after 1991 more aid, including relief aid, was channelled through the public sector. From this period the volume of food aid channelled through the RRC rose from nil to 50–60 per cent (interview, UN Emergencies Unit official in Ethiopia, March 1995).

Financing empirical sovereignty: trends in government financing for the health sector As Smithson notes (1995), an important determinant

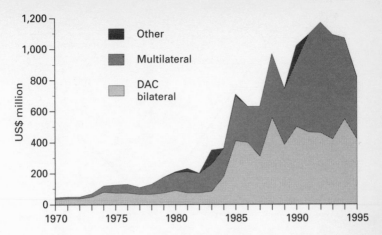

Figure 6.4 Total net receipts of official development assistance to
Ethiopia, 1971–94 (*Source*: OECD, various years)

of the sustainability of the health sector is the proportion of the
public sector budget allocated to it. In all the case study countries
during the periods of conflict and in their immediate aftermath public
sector health expenditures had been relatively low relative to their
pre-conflict levels, and in absolute terms. For example, in Uganda in

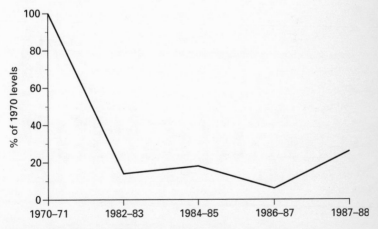

Figure 6.5 Ugandan Ministry of Health expenditure for selected years as
a proportion of the 1979 budget (*Source*: UNICEF 1989: *Children and
Women in Uganda: A Situation Analysis*, UNICEF, Kampala)

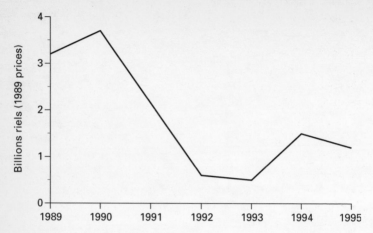

Figure 6.6 Cambodian government expenditure on health, 1989–95
(*Source*: World Bank and Cambodia 1995. A World Bank report for
the 1995 ICORC Conference. Report no. 139565-KH)

1986/7, when the NRM came to power, health accounted for only 4
per cent of public expenditure, roughly one-quarter of the average in
other low-income countries at that time (Lee et al. 1987). In Cambodia,
the health budget had declined from a reported 18 per cent in 1989 to

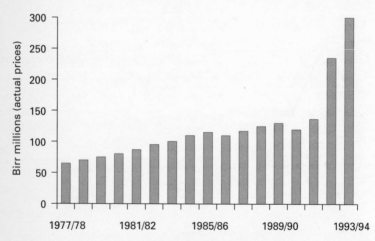

Figure 6.7 Government of Ethiopia total recurrent expenditure on health
(*Source*: World Bank 1994: *Ethiopia: Public Expenditure Policy for Transition*, 3
volumes, Report no. 12992-ET, Country Operations Division, Eastern
Africa Department, Africa Region, IBRD, Washington, DC)

just over 2 per cent in 1992 (see also Figure 6.1). In Ethiopia, recurrent health expenditure constituted less than 3 per cent of government recurrent budgets throughout the period 1977–92, rising to only near 4 per cent in 1993/4 (World Bank 1994a).[7]

Figure 6.5 shows the Ministry of Health expenditures in Uganda for selected years in constant 1979 prices. Similarly, Figure 6.6 shows a sharp decline in the value of Cambodian government health expenditure in the early 1990s. Figure 6.7 shows the trend in government health financing in Ethiopia 1977/8–1993/4.

In all three case study countries, the low GDP per capita, the low real value of public budgets and in particular their health sector components resulted in an absolute scarcity of resources. The extent of this scarcity is summarised in Table 6.1.

In the cases of Cambodia and Uganda, not only were levels of

Table 6.1 Summary of key factors determining the availability of national health resources in Cambodia, Ethiopia and Uganda compared with average least developed country

Indicators (1991)	Cambodia	Ethiopia	Uganda	Average LDC
Percentage of public expenditure allocated to health sector	2 (1992)[1]	3.8[2]	3.4[3]	4.5[3]
GNP per capita (US$)	200[4]	120[2]	170[3]	350[3]
Percentage of GNP allocated to public expenditure	3[4]	n/a	6 (1990)[3]	n/a
Total per capita health expenditure (US$) (1990)	2.45[5]	4[2]	6[3]	24 (sub-Saharan Africa)[3]

Notes: 1. World Bank 1994b.   2. World Bank 1994a.   3. World Bank (1993): *World Development Report*, Oxford University Press, Oxford and New York; 4. Curtis, G. (1994): 'Transition to what?: Cambodia, UNTAC and the peace process', in P. Utting (ed.), *From Hope to Insecurity: The Social Aspects of the Cambodia Peace Process*, UNRISD, Geneva.   5. Figure calculated from estimate of total health expenditure in 1992 (US$19.5 million) (World Bank 1992b, 1994b), divided by estimated population 8 million (World Bank 1993).

public health expenditure low at the time of political transition, but the fact that levels had been much higher in the past meant that there was less money available to maintain the level of staff and infrastructure of a decade earlier. At the same time, needs had increased as a result of population growth and conflict itself. In the case of Uganda, it was calculated that in order to regain their pre-conflict levels, government health budgets would have had to be increased between 5.84 and 12.45 times (Scheyer and Dunlop 1985).[8] In Ethiopia, Bekele et al. (1993) calculated in 1993 that, despite the significant increases in national health budget, the sector remained under-financed by some 75 per cent if it were to restore 45 per cent functional coverage and to implement fully the pay increases agreed for health sector staff.

Exacerbating the problems of absolute scarcity of recurrent funds was the particular impact of conflict on the physical infrastructure. As described in Chapter 4, this derived from both the direct and indirect effects of war. In 1991, UNICEF and the Ministry of Health estimated that 7.5 million people had lost access to health services as a direct result of war and displacement and called for extensive rehabilitation of the infrastructure (United Nations 1991).[9] In Uganda, the country's rehabilitation plan identified 44 government hospitals in need of substantial repair (Uganda 1989). In Cambodia, the UN appealed for US$9 million for infrastructure rehabilitation in 1992, double the national health budget.

Thus, in terms of health financing, the picture was extremely difficult. On the one hand, there was a need for extensive capital investment in order to restore the health infrastructure to its previous levels, as well as to expand it for an increased population and to improve low rates of coverage. On the other hand, recurrent finances remained extremely low.

Financing empirical sovereignty: the role of international aid in financing health sector rehabilitation In a context of absolute and relative scarcity of resources, the expansion in the volume of international assistance represented a significant resource for the health sector in the case study countries. Figures 6.8 and 6.9 show the total expenditure on health by governments and international assistance in Cambodia and Ethiopia. These data show that, while total health expenditures remained extremely low, and aid flows remained low relative to

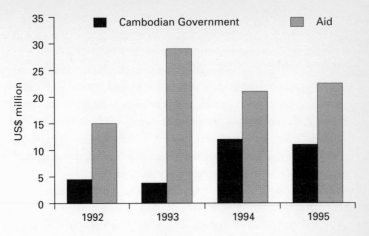

Figure 6.8 Government and aid expenditure on health in Cambodia, 1992–95 (*Source*: World Bank and Cambodia 1995: *Cambodia Rehabilitation Programme: Implementation and Outlook*. A World Bank report for the 1995 ICORC Conference. Report no.: 139565-KH)

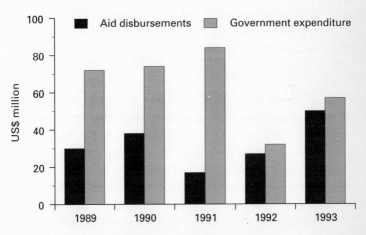

Figure 6.9 Government and aid expenditure on health in Ethiopia, 1989–93

(*Notes*: These figure are converted from data presented by Bekele et al. (1993) and UNDP (1995) for government total expenditure in birr. In order to show the impact of the devaluation on the relative contribution of national and international aid sources, these data were converted into US dollars. The exchange rate used before 1992 is: 2.07 birr=1US$; 1992 onwards figures use the rate of 4.75 birr=1US$.)

regional averages, aid was a very important source of financing for the sector in the 'post'-conflict period. In Ethiopia, the role of aid in health financing increased from 29 per cent in 1989 to 46 per cent in 1992. In Cambodia, international aid accounted for an average of 75 per cent of total health expenditures in the period 1992–95. In Uganda, aid accounted for 62 per cent of health resources in 1990–91 (Save the Children Fund 1993), and by 1998 this figure remained unchanged,[10] demonstrating that aid dependence was far from transitory. In all cases, the pace at which international aid for health increased exceeded that at which national public health expenditure increased. In this way, the sector became rapidly and substantially dependent on external resources.

The developmentalist analysis of relief–development aid linkage (outlined in Chapter 2) would argue that such an expansion in international finance is a necessary, one-off investment to offset the costs of conflict and resume health systems development. In other words, assumptions are made regarding the origins and duration of such dependency. In order to test these assumptions, it is necessary to look at whether the forms of aid and programme content did actually provide the basis for long-term systems development. This is the focus of the following section.

Investing in Development?

Patterns of rehabilitation investment Chapter 5 argued that the particular conditions of 'post'-conflict transition narrowed the options regarding the forms of aid that could be used and the channels for its disbursement. In particular, they resulted in an emphasis on multilateral and NGO channels to enable rapid disbursement of funds outside state channels, over a relatively short period of time (18 to 24 months). These choices, in turn, influenced the *content* of rehabilitation programming, leading to a relatively unbalanced pattern of investment. In particular, it was characterised by a focus on the rehabilitation of the physical infrastructure and the provision of equipment and supplies, with much less investment in the human resource base.

In each of the three countries, a substantial proportion of rehabilitation aid was spent on infrastructure repair. These investments are clearly particularly important given the widespread destruction. What is more difficult is to decide what is both feasible and desirable to rebuild. In Uganda in the mid-1980s, the World Bank commissioned a series of studies to analyse the priorities for rehabilitation assistance and the feasibility of the Bank's assuming a role in the sector. One report noted that to address the health financing crisis facing the country 'a major restructuring of the health services' was required (Lee et al. 1987). However, it continued that:

> Investment is not starting from scratch – enormous investment has gone in to the sector, much of this could be salvaged. A new cost-effective system must be sought and it is likely that this will be in the form of Primary Health Care, provided by health workers close to the villages. However, the village level component will not necessarily be cost-effective without proper support, it can absorb great amounts of money without yielding results and may be rejected by consumers. [However] … immediate investment now will mobilise previous investment in buildings, infrastructure and manpower, which presently work to little effect. (Lee, Hull and Hoare 1987)

The report concluded by advocating that priority be placed on rebuilding the previously existing health infrastructure, on the grounds that not to do so would under-utilise past investment. Alternatively, such historical investments can be seen as 'sunk' costs – in other words, it can be argued that previous investment is not relevant other than indirectly in that it influences future recurrent expenditure (Anne Mills, personal communication, March 1994).

In line with the government's own stated priorities,[11] the World Bank's rehabilitation programme followed the advice to concentrate on the restoration of existing infrastructure. The magnitude of the problem was too large for a single donor, so the rehabilitation tasks were divided among several donors geographically and by type of facility,[12] complicating coordination of planning and the compilation of consolidated figures showing the extent of rehabilitation aid.

In Cambodia, a similar emphasis was placed on the rehabilitation of the physical infrastructure. As in Uganda, quantifying the scale of this investment is made difficult by the lack of consolidated data and the diversity and number of actors engaged in this area. However, an indication of expenditure is that physical rehabilitation was the only item over-subscribed in the health component of the 1992 appeal, totalling US$9 million. In the wake of the elections, this emphasis on physical rehabilitation was maintained, in particular by the World Bank and the Asian Development Bank (Lanjouw et al. 1998).

In Ethiopia, the pattern was similar and if anything emphasised the physical side of the rehabilitation component even more heavily than elsewhere. Here the distinction between rehabilitation and infrastructure development became blurred as the new government sought to address the dual legacies of direct damage to the health infrastructure, and years of under-investment and very low coverage of basic heatlh services in the sector (UNICEF and Transitional Government of Ethiopia 1993).[13] Thus, for example, in 1994 the government budgeted for the rehabilitation of three hundred health facilities and the construction of an additional one hundred. In this case the government itself was the primary source of rehabilitation funding,[14] providing some 55 per cent of the costs of rehabilitating rural facilities and 100 per cent of those for rural hospitals. It was anticipated that donors would provide the remaining share of resources, and indeed the core of the World Bank's Family Health Project in Ethiopia focused on physical infrastructure.

The implications of these substantial investments in the physical infrastructure are of obvious significance for the effectiveness of health sector rehabilitation, and specifically for its sustainability in financial and in organisational terms. Such significant capital investment presumes that there will be sufficient funding available in the future to cover the recurrent costs of staff costs, drugs and other supplies and basic repairs. In the case of Ethiopia, to accommodate the planned rehabilitation and expansion of the health infrastructure is estimated to require an increase of at least 30 per cent over the already much higher 1994 levels of government recurrent expenditure. This is to maintain the existing degree of under-financing described above (World Bank 1994a).

A further similarity between the pattern of rehabilitation expenditure in the three countries is that it emphasised rehabilitation of urban, curative services, particularly in the capital cities. This is not surprising since the aim of rehabilitation strategies was largely to restore what had previously existed, not to challenge the efficiency or equity of the pre-conflict distribution of health services. In Uganda, rehabilitation of Mulago hospital, the national teaching and referral centre, accounted for an estimated 70 per cent of the development budget in 1986/7 (Annet and Janovsky 1988). While Mulago consumed 'only' 13 per cent (some $28.2 million) of total aid requested for the health sector in 1986/7, hospitals in total accounted for over one-quarter of the total appeal (Uganda 1989). Thus, to an extent, international aid served to reinforce and even underwrite the hospital-based approach of the Ugandan health system, committing the government to sustaining this investment.

At the same time, a significant division of labour has emerged between the government sector and external aid in financing the recurrent costs of primary and secondary/tertiary care in the case study countries. In Ethiopia, for example, the aid community was investing more heavily in PHC than in the other sectors. The World Bank calculated that without donor support for PHC the government's recurrent budget would have had to increase by 12 per cent (World Bank 1994a). Similarly in Uganda, the donor investment was particularly high for PHC. Thus in 1987–88, 83 per cent of donor aid went to primary healthcare compared with 33 per cent of government funds (LaFond 1995). In 1991, 77 per cent of recurrent financing on primary healthcare was financed by aid, while the government funded 80 per cent of hospital recurrent costs (Smithson 1995). Thus the pattern of capital expenditure during the rehabilitation period assumed that the government would sustain the recurrent spending associated with these investments, so in effect 'diverting' its resources from the primary sector.

Dependence on donor funding for all aspects of recurrent PHC costs is obviously high, but it is particularly the case in terms of non-salary costs. By 1991, in Uganda, for example, some 95 per cent of non-salary costs – essential drugs, equipment and vaccines – were aid-financed (Smithson 1995). In Ethiopia, the vital role played by donor support for non-salary recurrent costs was demonstrated particularly during the period 1992–93. From a review of trade figures, the World Bank concluded that without the support of the multi-donor ERRP it was unlikely that any drugs would have been imported and distributed to public health facilities in this period (World Bank 1994a). The importance of these drugs in enabling public health facilities to function was confirmed by visits to health facilities undertaken by this study. Interviews with hospital managers and with health assistants in seven facilities in East Hararghe in April 1995 all confirmed that the ERRP had been the major source of drugs during this period.

In Uganda, interviews with health workers in Soroti district highlighted that during the rehabilitation phase, which in the north of the country lasted roughly from 1991 to 1992, health facilities had received drugs from international agencies, in particular MSF-Holland. These donations, together with improved security, had increased utilisation of services. In this case, however, the scaling down of the rehabilitation response had been accompanied by a reduction in the allocation of free drugs from external agencies to these facilities. While drugs became available at cost, many in these communities were unable to afford them. In addition to the historical structural poverty of the area, these communities were now burdened with the additional costs of rebuilding their homes, and key assets such as cattle and agricultural inputs. This meant that cash for health services was very scarce.[15] This and the low salaries for health workers (which led to staff shortages) were seen as the primary reasons for the dramatic fall in the utilisation of the newly rehabilitated facilities. Similarly in Luwero, the limited availability of drugs and the introduction of fees for service were blamed by health workers and community representatives alike for the low utilisation of the public services.

In Cambodia, international support for essential drugs was more limited than was the case in Ethiopia. While in the latter case this formed the core of the initial response to the rehabilitation task, in the former, the provision of essential drugs was noticeably below the amount for which the United Nations had appealed (US$5.14 million as opposed to US$10.43 million). The lack of drugs in public health facilities was identified by the World Bank as a major cause of the decline in utilisation of these facilities and for the rise in private spending on drugs. Lanjouw et al. (1998) report that in 1993 private per capita spending on drugs was estimated at $4.3 per annum. By December 1996, this was estimated to have increased by a factor of nearly 450 per cent (to $18 per capita). This level of private expenditure on drugs exceeded the 1996 budget of the Ministry of Health sevenfold.

While aid allocations for essential drugs in Cambodia were limited, this did not mean that individual health facilities were not dependent on international support for non-salary support. In contrast to Ethiopia, where most ERRP resources were distributed through the public administration of the MOH, in Cambodia the highly projectised pattern of aid disbursement meant that dependency was created at the micro-level, with individual facilities relying on individual NGOs to maintain the flow of basic inputs. For example, the provincial hospital in Kampong Cham spent approximately $20,000 on salaries and patients' food. MSF spent about ten times this amount in the same year on essential drugs, repairs and upkeep (Hirshhorn 1991). Such patterns where NGOs picked up the drugs bills were not uncommon. Data collected by Lanjouw et al. (1998) demonstrate that the majority of NGO health projects had a supplies and provisions component, and that these comprised the largest single type of activity in this sector.

In financing terms in all three countries, the rehabilitation strategies necessarily expanded the health systems relative to their levels in the immediate post-conflict period. This expansion took two main forms. First, rebel-held territory was reintegrated. While governments do not control territory, they may be allocating resources to these facilities on paper, but clearly they are unable to spend money on them. These 'paper funds' may either be reallocated within the sector or elsewhere, or remain unspent. The reincorporation of these facilities into government-controlled territory implies an effective increase in total government expenditure if they are to resume functioning. Second, a similar logic applies in relation to health facilities in government-held areas that cease functioning because of damage to infrastructure or insecurity. As the zone of security expands, so too does the scope for health services to resume functioning, demanding additional resources in terms of material inputs and management support.

In the case of Ethiopia (and Eritrea), from 1989, the EPLF and TPLF controlled territory that was home to approximately five million people (Hendrie, personal communication, 15 March 1999). Similarly, in northern Uganda, as the security situation began to improve in the early 1990s, so there was a need for the government to resume financing health facilities that had been outside its control for several years. The opening up of the north coincided with a period when many donors were experiencing a squeeze in terms of their financing to the country. While they had done much to encourage the process of conflict resolution in the north, they lacked resources to underpin the peace process, including rehabilitation. At the same time, it was politically difficult for the government to reallocate existing national and international funds to the region.[16]

In Cambodia the situation was much more volatile, with populations living in and out of government-controlled areas over time, both as a result of military victories and as populations were displaced across borders and within the country. Here too, however, health services in the border areas, which had been controlled by opposition movements, had received substantial international support. After 1993, it was assumed that these services would be reabsorbed into a unified health system, funded and managed by central government.

The pace of the expansion of the health system in 'post'-conflict situations is set in part by security considerations and in part by the pattern of rehabilitation investment. Ensuring that rehabilitation of the physical infrastructure leads to functional rehabilitation – in other words the re-establishment of effective health services that are used by the population – means making sure that recurrent funds are available in subsequent years. It also requires the presence of effective staffing.

One of the key omissions of rehabilitation planning in all three countries was a human resource strategy. The Ethiopian case demonstrates clearly why such a strategy is important, but also why it can be so difficult to address. Gunneberg (1994) argues powerfully that the success of the ERRP was contingent upon health workers remaining in place, and that they did so largely because they continued to be paid and so could afford to stay in post. This argument was supported by interviews conducted at regional and national levels, which added that there was a particular culture of public service in Ethiopia that also contributed to staff loyalty during the difficult years immediately after the transition. Obviously, if staff had not been in place, then there would have been no one to use the drugs provided through the programme. The fact that the payroll continued to function virtually uninterrupted, and that staff received a small salary rise in the year after the change of government,[17] was not due to any clear international decision to target resources in order to retain staff. Rather, it reflected the nature of the transition itself, which had largely protected public institutions, and the fact that the government was willing and able to increase the public health sector budget.

In contrast, in Uganda and Cambodia public health workers' salaries remained desperately low, when they were paid at all. Despite drastic reductions in the size of the civil services (Lanjouw et al. 1998 report a 25 per cent cut, or some 56,000 employees between 1990 and 1991), the SOC was unable to meet its salary bills, further eroding the already low morale of poorly paid public sector workers. While salaries accounted for a large proportion of health expenditure,[18] in real terms they remained extremely low in all three countries. For example, LaFond (1995) reports that in 1991, the salaries of Ugandan health workers were a mere 2 per cent of their value in the 1970s, providing only 5 to 8 per cent of a living wage. Similarly in Cambodia, public sector wages were also below subsistence levels, averaging US$5–7 per month in 1991.

In this context, health workers took a number of measures to protect and diversify their incomes – finding alternative sources of employment either instead of, or in addition to, their public duties, and charging informal fees for services and for drugs. All of these strategies have an obvious and negative impact on the accessibility and quality of public health provision. The problem of extremely low salaries for public sector workers in these countries was a reflection of the structural problems of public finance, themselves in turn affected by the wider political-economic context.

The problem for aid was twofold. First, to commit significant support for public sector salaries was to acknowledge that the financing crisis facing the sector was not transitory, but rather reflected a long-term problem of poverty of public financing, and of health financing in particular. As one senior Ugandan health official put it: 'staff welfare has never been addressed because donors fear that it is not sustainable. Yet without increasing the motivation of staff, rehabilitation will be impossible' (interview, Ministry of Health official, Entebbe, March 1993).[19]

The second, related, point was that a mechanism was lacking through which such support could be provided. In the context of a highly projectised, emergency-style approach to rehabilitation, policy-based approaches that linked international budgetary support with policy conditionalities were not an option.

Thus what emerged in Uganda and Cambodia was not a parallel system of health service provision with NGOs and public sector providers running different facilities (Duffield 1991). Instead, a complex relationship developed between the national public health system and international finance and management, usually channelled through NGOs. This choice of channel for aid disbursement had significant implications for the coordination and coherence of rehabilitation investment, as described in further detail below.

Channels for disbursement: the impact on organisational sustainability
As Chapter 5 described, in the cases of Cambodia and Uganda, aid was channelled largely outside state institutions during the rehabilitation period, through NGOs, private contractors and quasi-autonomous aid management bodies. In Cambodia, for example, it was estimated that in 1988 NGOs provided approximately US$10 million to the health sector. By 1992 this contribution was estimated at US$28 million (four times the national health budget) (Cambodia 1992).

In Ethiopia, the World Bank-led strategy of channelling drugs through the public sector played an important role in maintaining the functioning and utilisation of public health facilities.[20] While arguably not sustainable in that there was no clear strategy for the government to assume responsibility for financing these expenditures from national resources,[21] this strategy provided a mechanism for equitable allocation of drug supplies between different facilities and different parts of the country. It is testament both to the willingness of a single donor (the Dutch government) to invest in this strategy, and to the efficiency of the Ethiopian public administration at all levels, that the strategy worked.

While the bilateral community sought to use NGOs to provide political distance from the State of Cambodia and the National Resistance Movement in Uganda, their funding was supporting the re-establishment of a network of health facilities, which, it was assumed, would form part of, and be financed by, the public sector. The strategy of investment, which relied on numerous intermediaries in the form of NGOs, lacked a mechanism by which project-based support for individual health facilities could be 'scaled up' (see Chapter 3) to provide a basis for a national health policy framework. There was an assumption that the individual health facilities rehabilitated through micro-projects would be handed over to the state, which would then assume responsibility for their management and financing. However, rehabilitation aid in all three countries made little contribution to the capacity of the state to assume these responsibilities.

In the absence of a strategy to address the national crises in health policy and financing, the steady withdrawal of emergency-style, project-based support for key inputs such as drugs that followed once the rehabilitation period was designated to be over had a major impact on the functioning of individual facilities. Sustainability, or at least continuity of access to services, became critically contingent on NGOs and multilaterals maintaining their drug inputs and, at least informally, some level of salary supplementation.

Where these ceased, as in the Ugandan case, the quality of care rapidly declined, as did utilisation rates. Fieldwork in Luwero and Soroti in Uganda, and in northern Cambodia, revealed pristine health facilities with very few patients as drug supplies and staff inputs had not been sustained. At the level of policy and management, too, the capacity of the public administration to formulate and execute policy and to deliver services was severely limited by low pay and low morale.

In the case of Uganda this meant that the privatisation of health service provision, which had started during the years of war and economic decline, was sustained rather than reversed in the 'post'-conflict period (Macrae et al. 1993; Whyte 1990).[22]

In Cambodia, the decline in public finance meant that the efforts to rebuild a cadre of public health professionals, initiated in the wake of the Khmer Rouge, were not sustained and the human resource base was eroded once again in the early 1990s. This, combined with the effects of unregulated economic liberalisation, meant that the market in private consultations and drug sales expanded rapidly, as indicated by trends in private expenditures identified above.

This pattern of rapid and uncontrolled privatisation, particularly evident in both Cambodia and Uganda, has had significant implications for public health. Not only does it have implications for the equity and efficiency of provision, but it has also accentuated the verticality of some aspects of public health provision, particularly the Expanded Programme on Immunisation (EPI), but also Control of Diarrhoeal Diseases (CDD). As the capacity of the public health system to deliver comprehensive health services declines, so those aspects of the system that can attract special funds come increasingly to define the public health system, as these are the only ones that continue to function. By 1993, the distortions that the vertical programme funding for EPI and CDD activities introduced in Uganda, for example, were well recognised by the aid community by 1993, even by its strongest advocate, UNICEF (Glennie 1993a, 1993b).

In Ethiopia, the problem was somewhat different. Here, aid efforts to maintain the functioning of the public health system were more successful. However, in the context of political upheaval, particularly the process of regionalisation described in Chapter 5, the public administration went through a period of great uncertainty. On the one hand, there was substantial reinvestment in the human resource base as new funds and staff were released by demilitarisation. On the other hand, regionalisation, and in particular its emphasis on recruitment of native speakers of the regional languages, resulted in the loss of personnel at all levels of the health system. These losses occurred from a resource base already below requirements. Kello et al. (1992) report that in the late 1980s, only half of the country's 4,000 nursing posts were filled because of poor pay. The historical legacy of under-investment in training and remuneration of health staff would take time to address.

National and international determinants of sustainability: a summary
The basic determinants of financial sustainability outlined above were known to the key actors working in the sector at the time. Even allowing for the exaggeration of predicted growth in the economy, and in the public share of it, arising from peace (Fitzgerald 1994; Kreimer et al. 1998), the rate of expansion in public budgets required to sustain rehabilitation investment was clearly unlikely to have been achieved. The likely effects of adopting a highly projectised approach to the implementation of rehabilitation planning on managerial systems were also not unpredictable, and indeed were predicted (Annet and Janovsky 1988; World Bank 1992b).

Thus it should have been of little surprise to the international organisations involved that rehabilitation interventions quickly created a dependence on international assistance to maintain basic healthcare that is unlikely to disappear quickly. If it was obvious that such rehabilitation investments made through these particular channels were unlikely to prove sustainable and were known to be so, the question then emerges why millions of dollars were committed to them. It is to exploring this question that we now turn.

Maintaining the Myth: Systems and Strategies of Rehabilitation Planning

Rehabilitation: a relief or development task? In all three countries, an interesting tension emerged between two concepts of rehabilitation. On the one hand were claims that rehabilitation aid provides the starting point for the development of sustainable health systems. On the other, rehabilitation was portrayed as an extension of relief, whereby the objective was to overcome a temporary set of shortages and re-establish the conditions for the resumption of the development process. The new orthodoxy described in Chapter 3 would suggest that these positions are complementary;[23] practice suggests otherwise.

In all three countries, senior international officials engaged in health policy development during the rehabilitation period emphasised that sustainability was *not* a priority concern in the immediate 'post'-conflict period. As Chapter 5 described, in Uganda and Ethiopia no conditions were placed on the rehabilitation loans, and as reported there, concerns for sustainability were seen to be linked with a dialogue about conditionality for which there was neither the time nor inclination. Thus, in Ethiopia, a senior Bank economist responsible for social sector policy commented that: 'During the course of the ERRP we didn't look at the problem of the mix of capital and recurrent funding. An integral part of the [subsequent] policy review is the issue of sustainability' (interview, Addis Ababa, April 1995).

Similarly, national health planners in the countries felt that sustainability was not a primary concern for rehabilitation planning, not least because it was conceptualised as something distinct from health development planning. For example, one senior planner in the Ugandan Ministry of Planning and Economic Development commented that:

> physical rehabilitation is not a plan but a shopping list of essential requirements for the repair of physical structures to put them back to a functional level ... as technicians this is not a very challenging exercise – no planning skills are involved in such a process. It only involves an assessment of the requirements, and this is mainly done by quantity surveyors. A developmental programme is more challenging – this requires technical justification. (interview, 15 April 1993, Kampala)

Similarly, an official of the Ugandan First Health Project argued that:

'With regard to recurrent cost implications, there was an assumption that because the programme was rehabilitating old structures, rather than creating new ones, the future recurrent cost burden would not be increased' (interview, 4 May 1993, Entebbe). Such a view would appear to have been widespread,[24] and indeed has been sustained in the country into the mid-1990s, despite the critical evaluation of rehabilitation efforts in the country undertaken of the World Bank project (Howard and Kiragu 1992). For example, in 1993, the expatriate planner responsible for planning health sector rehabilitation in the northern districts of the country said that:

> The recurrent cost implications of capital investments [in the northern regions] have not been calculated per se, rather there has been an assumption that additional resources can be brought into PHC and the north through rationalisation of provision and improvement in the mechanisms for resource allocation. (interview, senior health economist, Ministry of Health, Entebbe, 14 April 1993)

Striking in many accounts of the omission of sustainability as a central planning objective is the preoccupation with time. In all three cases there was a perceived urgency of response. This was driven not only by the evident scale of need and destruction, but by pressures to re-establish aid relations. Thus, in relation to Uganda, a senior Bank official commented that:

> The pace of the [First Health] project was set by the perception that it was an emergency project. Yet if you want to implement things quickly you forgo meeting a second important objective – that of building institutional capacity nationally … The IDA responded very quickly to the government's request, confirming the credit arrangement even before all the usual bureaucratic process had been completed. The FHP was conceived as an emergency project and the pace of implementation was a primary concern. (interview, World Bank First Health Project official, 4 May 1993)

In addition to the peculiar psychology of rehabilitation planning,[25] rehabilitation instruments themselves also influence the timeframe for planning. In the case of Cambodia, this timeframe was imposed by the Paris Accords, which firmly demarcated the start and the finish of the transition period. In line with the aid/political continuum outlined in Chapter 5, the withdrawal of UNTAC was also taken as the signal for a withdrawal of relief agencies and of the UNHCR's repatriation programme in particular. Similarly, the EC rehabilitation budget line used to finance some health sector rehabilitation aid in Ethiopia specified a time limit of 18 months for project execution. The short time-frame imposed by this conceptualisation of the rehabilitation task further confines the content of rehabilitation programmes to those that yield quick and visible results (i.e. building of structures), and the forms of aid to those that do not necessarily enhance national capacity (the emphasis on NGOs and quasi-autonomous bodies).

Accounting for the myth: the accountability dimension The perception of field staff that sustainability objectives were not primary in the design of rehabilitation projects runs counter to the claims made in key planning documents informing the design of these interventions, and certainly to international policy claims regarding the need to make relief more developmental. Thus, for example, the *Staff Appraisal Report* that formed the basis of the World Bank's First Health Project in Uganda states that the third objective of the programme was: 'to ensure the long-term sustainability and viability of the healthcare delivery system' (World Bank 1988: 1).

It is significant that aid officials responsible for the implementation of rehabilitation aid prioritised the urgency of their intervention over sustainability. However, official documents published by the agencies for which they worked promised that these rehabilitation interventions would constitute the basis for sustainable health systems development. There was thus a dichotomy between the unspoken assumptions according to which aid officials were working, and the official policies against which funds were raised.

When aid investments subsequently proved difficult to sustain, responsibility for this failure was shifted to the governments. In contrast to the days of unconditional investment, in the post-rehabilitation period the continued support of major donors has been made conditional upon governments addressing the sustainability problem that aid agencies themselves had done much to create and deepen.

For example, in 1992 the donor community reacted furiously to the government of Uganda's national health plan, the cost of which exceeded the national health budget fourfold. Following the publication of this report, the donors placed considerable pressure on the government to introduce cost recovery measures, despite lack of evidence at that time regarding their potential impact on the accessibility of services (Macrae et al. 1993; Okounzi and Macrae 1995). Similarly, a senior Bank official made clear that responsibility for sustaining the recurrent costs of rehabilitation investments rested clearly with the government:

> The recurrent cost problem is a difficult one for the Project to answer: nowhere in the project agreement does it state what the Bank's responsibility for this should be ... the *government* has now realised that there is a major threat to the economic sustainability of the health sector. (interview, World Bank First Health Project official, Entebbe, 4 May 1993, emphasis added)

In contrast with the vehemence of the donors' reactions to the perceived mismanagement of health finances by the Ugandan government, the findings of a 1992 evaluation of the World Bank's health sector rehabilitation efforts were relatively understated. Highlighting the imbalance in the response between physical rehabilitation and attention to managerial and planning capacity, it argues that:

> A staff appraisal report of 1988 pointed to [several] main risks: poor implementational capacity of the MOH in view of under-staffing; weak organisation and serious financial, managerial and administrative problems. At mid-term, and with the benefit of hindsight, one can confirm the accuracy of these risks. In retrospect, while the emphasis on physical rehabilitation is understood, the need for planning and management support was underestimated. (Howard and Kiragu 1992)

Commenting on the high level of aid dependence in the social and economic sector in Cambodia, a report published by the World Bank a year after the election argued:

> This situation obviously cannot continue forever. The government is expected to shoulder an increasing share of the cost of rehabilitation and reconstruction and to prepare for the day when the usual cost-sharing arrangements for LDCs are put into effect. (World Bank 1994b)

Sustainability had become an issue, but one for which the government was being made responsible, despite the fact that international aid agencies had themselves contributed millions of dollars to inherently unsustainable investments, and had done little to protect the fragile public institutions that were now expected to manage and finance facilities financed by rehabilitation aid.

Summary

Four key conclusions emerge from this comparative analysis of the sustainability of rehabilitation aid to the health sector.

First, the three case study countries were all very resource-poor, and thus the way in which aid was used exerted a significant influence on the functioning of the health system. In 1993, the World Bank (1993) estimated that least developed countries needed to allocate the equivalent of US$12 per capita to the health sector. Data presented in this chapter, and summarised in Table 6.1, show that actual health expenditures were well below this level, and that the capacity of the public sector to redress this financial gap was extremely limited because of levels of GNP and low proportion of GNP accounted for by the public sector. In such a context, sustaining even minimal coverage is going to be major problem, even if available resources are used in the most optimal fashion. Despite these inherent difficulties, rehabilitation assistance was envisaged to constitute a first important step in the development of sustainable health systems. In particular, it was assumed that the state would assume responsibility for sustaining the recurrent costs associated with extensive rehabilitation of the physical infrastructure.

The evidence suggests not only that the necessary financial resources were unavailable and likely to remain so in the foreseeable future, but that the forms of aid provided actually undermined the institutional capacity of the state to assume these responsibilities. In the cases of Cambodia and Uganda in particular, empirical sovereignty was diminished rather than enhanced by the pattern of rehabilitation investment. There was little investment in public policy-making or in the human resource base, for example. Instead, the supply-driven method, delivered by a large number of different organisations, resulted in a fragmented, highly projectised approach, particularly in Cambodia and Uganda. Where resources were channelled through the state, as was the case in Ethiopia, these were targeted at material supplies, very much as in a large-scale relief effort, and not linked to a strategic process of sectoral reform or support for public sector workers.

A second key finding is that the policy-based approaches that have come to characterise aid to the health sector since the 1990s were not adopted in these environments. Rehabilitation aid was directed at the restoration of the previously existing infrastructure and maintaining the flow of basic supplies instead of at reform. In part, these approaches were adopted because of the reluctance to engage with states, as described in Chapter 5. In addition, however, this approach to rehabilitation reflected a particular set of assumptions regarding the nature of conflict and its impact, and of the scope for a rapid return to conventional development assistance planning. It was assumed that the primary problem facing the sector was infrastructural, not structural: what was required was to restore the *status quo ante*, so allowing the resumption of the path of modernisation, which had been temporarily interrupted.

A third reason for not adopting policy-based approaches was the perception of the urgency of need. This precluded not so much detailed assessment, but rather the process of protracted negotiation with national authorities regarding need and response. Thus priorities were assumed rather than proven, and planning driven by the political and bureaucratic demand for speed rather than technical accuracy.

A fourth point to emerge is that, in contexts of extreme poverty, the trade-off between planning to meet urgent need and planning for sustainability is very real and has direct consequences in terms of communities' access to basic and vital services and supplies. This trade-off is not unique to conflict-affected countries. Smithson states the problem clearly:

> An old adage has it that it is better to give a poor man a fishing net than to give him a fish. While the latter allows temporary succour, the former provides the means for an indefinite supply of fish. A similar sentiment underlies traditional development approaches in the health sector: investment over a limited time span is expected to yield a stream of benefits far into the future. The difficulty arises when the stream of benefits is not forthcoming. (1995: 6)

In other words, what is the fisherman to eat while he is waiting for the fish to bite?

Evidence collected by this study suggests that rehabilitation assistance was effectively increasing access to health services, providing important inputs such as drugs and salary incentives as well as restoring the physical infrastructure. Where approaches to rehabilitation aid were highly projectised, such as in Cambodia and Uganda, the distribution of such resources was sometimes uneven, with different population groups benefiting disproportionately. In the case of Ethiopia, channelling resources through the public health system seems to have countered this problem of equity of distribution. Rehabilitation inputs had the important effect not only of providing health services, but in so doing of re-establishing a sense of normalcy and contributing to the reinforcement of empirical sovereignty, at least at the micro-level. In the absence of a massive increase in resources, the transition from the goal of meeting the urgent need of individuals that characterises relief actions to that of developing sustainable health systems for whole populations necessarily entails a reduction in the quality and quantity of provision for some groups. In Cambodia and Uganda in particular, those who had benefited from rehabilitation aid inputs in the shape of free drugs and subsidised health workers lost these entitlements when the criteria for health planning shifted to an emphasis on sustainability. This finding has been echoed elsewhere (Macrae and Bradbury 1998; Stockton 1996). Thus concern for sustainability may simply mask budget cuts. There is therefore a need to monitor the impact of the aid transition on populations' access to healthcare. In establishing such systems, the most important criterion might be continuity of access, monitored through indicators such as utilisation rates and per capita drug expenditure, rather than sustainability *per se*.

The final point that emerges from the analysis presented in this chapter concerns accountability. In quasi-states, international aid agencies wield significant resources relative to those available nationally for public services. The way in which these resources are deployed has clear political implications for strengthening or weakening the state, but also significant sector-specific impacts that have longer-term effects. The question emerges as to who should be responsible if aid strategies prove to be unsustainable or otherwise ineffective. In the case of Ethiopia, the government sought to maintain its sovereignty and to take responsibility for the deployment of aid, and donors largely agreed to this. In Uganda and Cambodia, however, the government was neither allowed, nor largely able, to take responsibility for rehabilitation planning, which was driven by decisions in donor capitals, not in the recipient countries. Despite this, responsibility for the consequences of decision-making during the rehabilitation period was seen to rest with the respective governments, not with international organisations.

As noted in Chapter 1, there is a scarcity of evaluation of the performance of rehabilitation aid. While this is being redressed slowly, there is much less debate regarding the more fundamental issue regarding accountability for the allocation of funds in aid-dependent quasi-states. The absence of effective mechanisms to coordinate rehabilitation aid and to provide evidence-based decision-making on priorities is not simply a management issue: it is a much more complex issue of how to achieve public accountability in the absence of a benign and competent state.

Notes

1. During the 1980s the sustainability debate was dominated by issues of health economics and financing. This reflected the context of intense financial pressure on health services in developing countries as a combined effect of recession, structural adjustment and declining aid flows. It also reflected the wider dominance of economism in development policy debates during this period (LaFond 1995).

2. Asia here is all countries in Asia excluding India, China and Japan and Taiwan.

3. Edmonds (1988) notes that in 1977 subsistence agriculture accounted for over 30 per cent of agricultural production. Lateef (1990) further estimates that formal exports fell by 9.5 per cent per annum in the years 1973–80.

4. This was confirmed by interviews in northern Uganda in May 1993. Here district chiefs noted that they had had to lower the threshold at which people paid taxes. Using the previous schedules of taxation, so many people would have been exempted from taxation that the district would have had a fraction of the necessary revenue. This indicates the impoverishing effect of conflict in absolute and relative terms, and the acute problems of re-establishing state–society relations in a context of such absolute poverty. On the one hand, imposition of taxes may further alienate from the state people already struggling to survive. On the other, the inability of the state to provided valued services further diminishes its often precarious legitimacy.

5. In an interview, an Oxfam Uganda official reported that in 1986 the NRA was estimated to comprise 15,000 men. By 1991 it was estimated to have 70–100,000 troops as the government incorporated rebel groups into the national army. The collapse in coffee prices worldwide in 1991 had a dramatic

impact on the Ugandan economy, halving its tax revenues. On the expenditure side, military expenditures were protected and were estimated to have consumed 80–90 per cent of government budgets (interview, Kampala, 16 April 1993).

6. US$1,070 in 1994 as opposed to US$1,097 million in 1990.

7. This despite the fact that the money value of health budgets doubled in the period 1991/2 to 1992/3 from just under 2 billion birr to 300 million birr.

8. Scheyer and Dunlop (1985) propose three possible ways to answer this question. First, to identify the actual levels of expenditure in 1968/9, equalise the shilling rate prevailing at the current time and estimate what increase in government expenditure would be required to meet this level. This type of calculation would make no allowance for increases in utilisation rates or population growth. Their calculations, which compare the levels of actual and required expenditure in 1968/9 with that in 1979, suggest that total government expenditure on health would have had to increase 5.84 times. The second method does take account of population growth by comparing per capita government expenditure on health in the two periods. This approach suggests that even in 1979, government would have had to increase expenditure 11.2 times to meet 1968/9 levels of provision. The third option equalises expenditure per visit and the utilisation rate per capita existing in 1969, thus also taking account of population growth. In this case, total 1979 expenditure would need to have been increased 12.45 times. While the authors suggest that this ignores the potential economies of scale, they seek to compensate for this by employing a lower target figure for utilisation rates than that found in 1979.

9. In war-affected regions of the north alone, a total of nine hospitals (100 per cent); 26 health centres (59 per cent) and 177 health stations (40 per cent) were damaged or destroyed.

10. Aid accounted for US$77.5 of a total of US$126.6 million allocated to the sector in 1998/99. Figures from Uganda (1989).

11. The health sector projects listed in the country's 1988/9 Development Plan (Uganda 1989) also emphasised rehabilitation of physical infrastructure, with the largest proportion, nearly 50 per cent (US$91 million), allocated to the physical rehabilitation of hospitals and health centres.

12. The European Development Fund provided rehabilitation funds in south-west Uganda, GTZ in the west, and the Italian government in the northern districts of Arua, Moroto and Gulu, while the World Bank focused on the rehabilitation of nine hospitals, including the national referral hospital, and of 30 rural health centres (World Bank 1988; interview, Ministry of Local Government official, Kampala, 3 April 1993). Additional facilities were also rehabilitated on an *ad hoc* basis by NGOs, such as MSF-Holland in Soroti district, World Vision in Gulu and Save the Children Fund UK in Kumi.

13. Also interview, World Bank Population and Health Division official, March 1995.

14. The degree to which it was able to make these allocations because of increased availability of funds through balance of payments support, programme aid and structural adjustment lending is not clear, of course.

15. This finding was confirmed by Francis Mwesige in his analysis of the impact of the introduction of fees on health services utilisation in Uganda (personal communication, April 1995).

16. Interviews, country representative, Oxfam UK, Kampala, 16 April 1993; British High Commission official, Kampala, 13 April 1993; AMREF official, Entebbe, 17 April 1993.

17. Despite this, Bekele et al. (1993) calculate that restoring Ethiopian health workers' salaries to their 1972 levels would have required a 250 per cent increase in the public health budget.

18. In 1986 salaries accounted for 80 per cent. In an interview, the former WHO special envoy to Cambodia commented that although health workers in Cambodia had always received limited cash payment for their work during the 1980s they benefited from payments in kind of goods such as rice and shoes. This 'barter' arrangement broke down as the economy was liberalised in the late 1980s. In 1986, salaries accounted for 80 per cent of the Ugandan health budget (Smithson, 1985). In 1990, salaries accounted for 64 per cent of the Ethiopian budget (Bekele et al. 1993).

19. LaFond (1995) reports that worldwide donors have been reluctant to commit to subsidising public sector salaries directly, conscious that withdrawing from such a strategy is likely to be difficult if it enables government to substitute public investment elsewhere. Clearly, however, structural aid in the form of balance of payments support and structural adjustment loans, together with tied debt relief, do boost public sector budgets, thus benefiting overall government expenditure, including salaries.

20. It is important to note that while a significant component of international assistance was disbursed through governmental channels in Ethiopia, particularly in terms of pharmaceuticals, here too, the volume of assistance disbursed by NGOs continued to increase even after the demise of the Mengistu regime. So, for example, total NGO disbursements, including food aid, in Ethiopia in 1989 were some US$434 million, increasing to US$633 million in 1993 (UNDP 1995).

21. The ERRP had introduced an element of cost recovery for the drugs it provided, with patients paying a fee for any ERRP drugs consumed. Interviews in East Hararghe suggested that no major problems had been experienced in terms of patients' ability to pay for these drugs. However, as elsewhere, the issue of affordability requires careful investigation. To the author's knowledge in 1994, when the ERRP drugs component was nearly complete, no nationwide study regarding the impact of user fees and charges on health services utilisation had been undertaken. In 1995, major questions were being asked regarding the continuation of drugs supply once the World Bank intervention was complete.

22. The church missions became a particularly important source of health

service provision during the war (interviews at missions in Soroti and Luwero, and interview with Uganda Protestant Medical Bureau official, 21 May 1993; AMREF-Uganda official, 17 April 1993, Entebbe). Interestingly, the sustainability of these was also seen to be threatened by a combination of the decline in funding from religious counterparts in the north and by the demands of providing free health services to patients suffering from chronic diseases such as TB and HIV/AIDS.

23. For example, the heads of the UNHCR and the World Bank have argued that: a common strategy for rehabilitation 'must be dynamic and sequenced so that over time humanitarian type subsidies are replaced by developmental inputs and the economy is moved from a situation of dependence to one where it is self-sustaining and able to engage in the global market. This often requires a difficult process of adjustment, but one agreed with governments, donors and agencies' (Ogata and Wolfensohn 1999).

24. An AMREF-Uganda official commented: 'Part of the lack of attention to issues regarding sustainability was due to the belief that the only difference between Uganda in 1969 and 1986 was the physical damage to the infrastructure. The loss of human and financial capacity was hugely understated' (interview, Entebbe, 17 April 1993).

25. An NGO representative commented with regard to the World Bank's First Health Project: 'The project was an unmitigated disaster and the World Bank has sought to lay the blame for its failure at the feet of the government' (interview, Entebbe, 17 April 1993).

CHAPTER 7
· · · · · · · ·
Conclusion

§   Chapter 3 described and analysed the emergence of a new orthodoxy regarding the role of aid in responding to conflict. This orthodoxy,
developed as part of a wider paradigm of human security, comprises
two key tenets: first, that aid can and should play a role in the management of conflict; second, that it can achieve this by applying more
developmental approaches to the delivery of aid in conflict-affected
areas.

This orthodoxy can be described as hegemonic within the aid
community in that official aid agencies and NGOs have come to
subscribe to it as a result of both coercion and consent. The coercive
element is the significant decline in aid budgets in the aftermath of the
Cold War, so threatening the continuation of the previous form and
volume of aid. In this context, aid agencies have had to justify their
continued relevance. This they have done in an essentially defensive
manner. Rather than reviewing the continued relevance of the developmentalist paradigm, aid actors have largely reasserted it, making
additional claims regarding the ability of aid to manage conflict.

Despite the coercive manner of its inclusion, the placing of the
issue of conflict on the aid policy agenda has not threatened the
fundamental, developmentalist concepts that have underpinned the
organisational structure and culture of aid institutions, and it has thus
not been difficult to secure their consent. By conforming to an analysis
of conflict that focuses primarily on internal economic, social and
psychological causes, aid agencies claim that they can legitimately
play a role in its management. This formulation the role of aid in
conflict management also allows aid institutions to argue that, although some modifications in their approach will be necessary, these
are largely managerial and technocratic concerns.

A review of the aid policy landscape reveals striking consistency in the adoption of this new orthodoxy across the different traditions of development theory and between an apparently diverse range of aid agencies – bilateral, multilateral and non-governmental. The inclusive nature of the orthodoxy reflects its roots in developmentalism, which, as discussed in Chapter 2, has proved almost infinitely flexible in its ability to accommodate apparently disparate political traditions.

The mechanism through which aid actors have sought to assert a role in conflict management has been the relief–development continuum. By making relief assistance more developmental, it has been claimed that aid can play a significant role in reinforcing processes of peace, thereby contributing to the prevention and resolution of conflict. The research reported here suggests that the assumptions underpinning this conceptualisation are highly questionable. Even leaving aside the analyses of the causes of conflict adopted by major aid agencies, the research has highlighted fundamental ethical, technical and institutional issues in the implementation of this new orthodoxy.

War, Peace and Politics: From 'Post'-conflict Transition to Chronic Political Emergencies

Arguably, the three case studies described here are 'old wars'. They took place during the Cold War era and, in the cases of Cambodia and Ethiopia, were profoundly shaped by the ideological stand-off between the superpowers and their respective regional allies. The continued relevance of these case studies derives in part from the fact that experiences gained in these countries have been used to inform the evolution of the new orthodoxy. The interpretation of the successes and failures of aid in these environments has influenced subsequent thinking and practice elsewhere (see, for example, Macrae 1999).

During the early 1990s, it was assumed not only that there was a continuum from relief to rehabilitation to development, but that this continuum paralleled a political transition from war to peace. Figure 7.1 illustrates this idealised model of 'post'-conflict transition, its political and aid components.

This model proved an inadequate guide to aid interventions in all but a few cases of negotiated transition. While internationally mediated settlements did yield a democratically elected government and

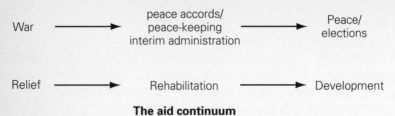

Figure 7.1 The political and aid continua

demobilisation in Mozambique, for example, more common was a pattern of flawed elections, persistent insecurity and recurrent economic crisis. This certainly was the experience of Cambodia. It was also increasingly recognised that the conditions prevailing in the post-Cold War wave of peace settlements were unusual. More common than the framework of peace-keeping and international electoral monitoring was the takeover of power by force (as in Uganda and Ethiopia). Here too, the environment was typically one of persistent insecurity and uncertainty regarding the legitimacy of the new regime.

Thus, by the late 1990s, the problem became less one of how to deal with situations of 'post'-conflict transition, but how to manage *chronic political emergencies* (Macrae et al. 1997) – in other words, how to work in the most vulnerable of quasi-states experiencing protracted crises of legitimacy, security and financing.[1] Each of the case study countries analysed here did experience a process of political transition that provided new opportunities for peace and development, and these should not be understated. However, varying periods of time after the changes in regime and structures of governance that signalled this process of transition, the countries maintained characteristics common to chronic political emergencies. In particular:

- To varying degrees their legitimacy was questioned externally.
- The legitimacy of the new regimes was questioned internally, indicated by persistent insecurity, mixed performance in terms of democratisation and continued abuses of human rights.
- Public institutions were weak.
- There was continued extreme poverty of the population and of the state, and the emergence of strong parallel economies.

The continued relevance of these case studies is thus twofold: experience in these countries has informed the evolution of aid policy; and the context in which aid was delivered is similar to that found in other, chronic political emergencies.

Interestingly, the practical experience of the early 1990s did not engender a radical reform of the idealised model of war–peace transition. Rather than seeing persistent violence and weak statehood as potential threats to development, advocates of the new orthodoxy have effectively accommodated them (Bradbury 1998; Duffield 1996; Macrae et al. 1997). The rhetoric of the new orthodoxy relies upon blurring the distinction between war and peace, with significant implications for the mandate and legitimacy of aid agencies. It is no longer a necessary condition that a legitimate and unified government is in power before developmental strategies are resumed (Duffield 1997b; Macrae 1997a, 1997b). Rather it is currently argued that developmental approaches can and should be adopted during conflict.[2] Developmental approaches are now seen to have a role not simply in peace-building but also in peace-*making*.

The arguments in favour of applying developmental approaches during conflict are seemingly compelling, and this universal appeal has served to create a broad consensus that has underpinned the new orthodoxy. The new orthodoxy is pragmatic in that it recognises that populations are living in, and returning to, these complex environments, and that existing approaches to relief that provide only material supplies are limited in their scope and impact. They are also aspirational, reflecting the desire of aid workers to go beyond their traditional role of providing a palliative, and to address the root causes of vulnerability by engaging in a process of conflict resolution.

The extent to which these aspirations are likely to prove feasible is examined more closely in the remaining sections of the chapter. Specifically, the following section examines the persistent conceptual, legal and ethical problems of applying the new orthodoxy in quasi-states. The subsequent section examines the operational implications for the design of aid instruments, coordination mechanisms and the definition of aid objectives. The penultimate section examines the specific problems of health planning in chronic political emergencies.

'Linking Relief and Development' Aid: Towards a Political Analysis of Aid in Conflict

Proponents of the new orthodoxy assume that the challenge of linking relief and development aid more effectively is essentially a technical and managerial task. By improving the efficiency of these linkages, conflict reduction objectives will be achieved (Macrae 1999). According to this analysis, the distinction between relief and development aid is a bureaucratic anomaly and no longer meaningful.

The empirical evidence presented here challenges this view and suggests that the distinction between humanitarian and developmental strategies is a political one. Preserving this distinction, rather than blurring it, is crucial to maintaining the integrity and technical efficacy of both forms of aid. As earlier chapters demonstrated,[3] the nature of the political distinction between humanitarian and development aid is complex and sometimes deliberately obscured. The distinction reflects both internal conditions within recipient states (their juridical status and their empirical capacity to act as states) and the country's engagement in international relations. Thus, as argued in Chapter 5, the aid system requires that three necessary conditions are fulfilled before the transition from relief to development assistance can be undertaken:

- The question of juridical sovereignty must be resolved, indicated by the presence of a unified, central state recognised internationally.
- The juridical sovereign must be recognised as legitimate by key Western donors, particularly by the USA.
- The recipient state must be able to function as a state, able to make and execute policy and to maintain security.

As described in Chapter 3, the presence of a functioning state, recognised internationally as legitimate, is a necessary condition for the process of 'scaling up' of aid objectives and strategies implied by the relief–development aid transition. This scaling up, from the micro to the macro, from the level of projects to that of policy, signals important shifts in the principles and objectives of aid. It is these differences in principles and objectives that were institutionalised in the bureaucratic procedures that historically separated relief and development aid. This suggests that any modifications to these procedures merit scrutiny of their ethical and legal implications, as well as their likely efficacy.

Of particular interest here are two issues. The first is the tension that emerges between the humanitarian principles of impartiality and neutrality and developmental approaches. The second are the criteria that determine the process of international legitimation required to effect the aid transition. With respect to the first issue, the process of scaling up public policy requires identifying an authoritative and competent body to define policy objectives and to implement them. Further, the provision of development aid of itself legitimises states, since a key function of such aid is to boost empirical sovereignty. In contrast, humanitarian policy does not assume the presence of a unified, central authority that has the legitimacy to determine policy priorities. Highly projectised, and often privatised, the criterion for allocation of resources (at least in theory) is need, and the provision of humanitarian aid by independent humanitarian bodies does not imply recognition or legitimation of the authority controlling the given territory. This brings its own problems, of course, not least because adherence to these principles is very patchy (Leader 1999), and because of the complex accountability trail implied by such a decentralised system of public welfare.

Arguably, the debate regarding the tensions between neutrality and developmental approaches is most pertinent while active conflict persists (Macrae and Leader 2000). Where a settlement is in place, enacted by force or through negotiation, then the priority would seem to lie in reinforcing that settlement, and in particular reinforcing the ability of the new regime to maintain peace and security by buttressing its empirical sovereignty. In practice, however, the idea that developmental principles apply as soon as a situation can be defined as 'post'-conflict is problematic. As indicated above, the idealised political continuum from war to peace is a rare reality. Instead, in many countries the political landscape is characterised by very weak empirical statehood, reflected in persistent insecurity, a breakdown in public services, illegalisation of the economy and widespread human rights violations. As also argued, the distinction between war and peace is becoming increasingly blurred by international agencies. In this context, a crucial question is when, whether and under what conditions international organisations decide to engage with such states developmentally.

A major dilemma appears for official aid agencies in these environments. There is a trend of withholding development aid to regimes that are responsible for widespread violations of basic human rights and demonstrate little inclination to achieve key public policy goals such as poverty alleviation. This selectivity of aid provision has superseded an earlier generation of political conditionality, adopted by donor governments such as the UK and the Netherlands. This approach means that a political analysis is undertaken *as a prelude* to the development of extensive bilateral aid programming, rather than subsequently introducing political conditions. This approach has the advantage of ensuring that aid is targeted at those regimes that provide the most conducive environment for development. As such it has taken account of the critique of aid that emerged during the 1970s and 1980s that aid was uncritical in its support for violent and undemocratic regimes. It has the major disadvantage, however, of excluding those countries where need is arguably the greatest from receiving anything other than relief aid.

There is an urgent need for a fundamental and public debate within and between international aid agencies, particularly among donor governments, regarding how to aid populations in countries experiencing chronic political emergencies. It is in these environments that many of the most vulnerable populations live and where aid is falling.

The first issue in such a debate must be the criteria and mechanisms by which the legitimation accorded by development aid is accorded to new regimes in conflict-affected countries. The World Bank, for example, lacks any formal criteria other than those regarding clearance of debt arrears, which determine when it will resume lending (Kreimer et al. 1998). Informally, as the case studies presented here demonstrate, political support from key Western countries is clearly crucial. Yet donor governments themselves are often incoherent and inconsistent in terms of the criteria they use to encourage the re-establishment of development aid programmes, and are often driven as much by domestic political considerations as by a convincing analysis of need or actually existing development conditions on the ground. This driving of the aid agenda by domestic political considerations has had a clear negative impact on aid effectiveness in the case study countries reviewed here. It has shaped the form of aid and the channels through which it has been disbursed, and this has undermined the sustainability of the investments and equity goals.

A second issue arises where there is a wish to engage with new regimes and to accord them international legitimacy. Such engagement will require the development of new forms of aid that are much more sensitive to the need to support public institutions than is currently the case. Current aid strategies in these environments replicate the paradox noted by Moore (1998) in relation to development aid more broadly, namely, that the application of the neo-liberal paradigm undermines the very public institutions upon which aid agencies rely to continue their engagement and which are central to effective empirical statehood. According to Moore, the re-examination of the role of the state undertaken in the *World Development Report* in 1997 (World Bank 1997) reflected less a review of the question of how aid can contribute to the internal legitimacy of fragile states than a revisiting of colonial pragmatism. The colonial administrations recognised the need for functioning public administrations, including health services, in order to facilitate trade and the collection of taxes (Ellis 1996). Their interest in establishing such regimes was thus to enable more efficient extraction of resources, not to generate legitimate state–society relations.

Currently lacking is a critical analysis of how aid practices influence state–society relations, and how aid agencies assess the legitimacy or otherwise of their partners, whether they be governmental or in civil society. Such a debate is clearly a key precondition for any ethical formulation of developmental relief. It is also necessary to inform a more 'technical' debate regarding the forms and channels of aid to avoid the scenarios that emerged in Uganda and Cambodia, where aid in transition incapacitated the public sector with significant negative long-term effects.

Finally, what the evidence presented here shows is that where aid agencies decide that the conditions do not exist for the re-establishment of development aid relations, this implies that more rigorous analysis of what to do is required. Reasserting the need to adopt developmental principles such as sustainability, at the same time that development aid is withheld, is an untenable and contradictory position. More empirical analysis of the political and economic scope for such strategies is required if such rhetoric is to lead to informed practice. In the absence of such an evidence-based approach, there is a significant risk that the 'principle' of developmental relief will serve to mask budget cuts and the introduction of political conditionality on humanitarian aid (Macrae 1999; Macrae and Leader 2000).

Operational Implications

The inability of the developmental paradigm to accommodate chronic political emergencies is indicated by the restricted range of aid instruments available to respond to them. A noticeable feature of the aid provided in the case study countries is that while they claim developmental objectives, the instruments available are essentially those of relief. The aid community thus relies upon these highly projectised and privatised strategies in the context of contested and weak statehood. This section discusses the operational implications of these approaches.

Projects not policy A striking feature of the experience of health sector rehabilitation aid in the three countries reviewed is that these interventions were not linked to processes of sectoral reform later seen by aid agencies as being necessary for building sustainable public health systems. Rather, rehabilitation measures were seen by national and international policy-makers alike to be distinct from long-term health policy development. Yet in all cases a fundamental premise of sector rehabilitation was that these investments would ultimately provide the basis of national public health systems, and that the respective governments would be willing and able to finance them. There were numerous problems articulating rehabilitation policy with a long-term development strategy for the health sector.

The first was the problem of locating public policy. The juridical institutions, the Ministries of Health and other relevant public bodies (such as district authorities) were clearly the sovereign bodies responsible for policy-making in Ethiopia and Uganda. In Cambodia, the situation was more complex. As Lanjouw et al. (1998) note, those public institutions under SOC control, including what was the Ministry of Health, were essentially relegated to the status of a political faction in the lead-up to the elections. Whatever the configuration of juridical power, in all three countries the ability of public institutions to formulate and execute public policy was critically limited by their institutional weaknesses. These weaknesses, described in Chapters 4, 5 and 6, ranged from the impact of conflict and economic decline on the human resource base, to a lack of political priority dedicated to the sector as governments sought to maintain their political survival.

In the absence of policy, rehabilitation aid became highly project-ised, with a bewildering array of international actors making their own policies around particular projects. This resulted in the familiar problems associated with project-based assistance. Cassels (1998) identi-fies these as including: overloading national administrations, strong emphasis on capital development, distortion of government spending priorities, the establishment of parallel systems of accounting, and procurement and monitoring of capital development. In the case study countries, these negative attributes of project-based assistance were all encountered, and were not counterbalanced by the presence of more programmatic assistance: during the transitional period, projects *were* policy.

Neither the form of aid, nor the channels through which aid was disbursed, were able to provide the basis for subsequent development of a public health sector. Weak public institutions meant there was no mechanism by which project-based assistance (relief) could be scaled up to policy-based assistance (development).

Until the constitutional problem of deciding how decisions would be made is resolved, it is neither feasible nor necessarily desirable to adopt policy-based approaches in these environments. However, there is a need to generate an authoritative and shared analysis of the options for sectoral development in the medium term. This might mean collecting and consolidating basic data on health systems develop-ment, and mapping out key indicators in relation to health financing, coverage and human resources. Public opinion polls and market research to identify priorities for healthcare among the populations and collect information regarding current patterns of health sector utilisation might also be useful.[4] It would be important that such an analysis be perceived as independent of either key donors or the state, and that a process is established to secure ownership of these actors. Such ownership might be achieved both through financial contributions and by using mechanisms to encourage adherence to the findings of such an independent analysis, such as the media, and the use of parliamentary scrutiny and evaluation.

Coordination The difficulties of making the transition from project to policy-based approaches were exacerbated in the three countries by poor inter-agency coordination that itself reflected the juridical and empirical ambiguity of statehood. In Uganda, there was no clear mechanism for aid coordination in the sector. In Ethiopia, there was an aid coordination forum, but in the context of an assertive but operationally powerless recipient state, it lacked any policy content to be coordinated. In Cambodia, the body mandated to coordinate health rehabilitation, the WHO, lacked any influence over the allocation of resources. This latter case exemplified how direct disbursement of official aid to NGOs meant that bilateral donors could circumvent even the most complex coordination arrangements.

The familiar failure to invest in coordination, and in particular to undermine UN structures even where these had a strong legal claim to bolster quasi-states, represented a major threat to the efficiency of aid interventions in the case study countries. In contrast, Pavignani (1998) notes that in Mozambique the efforts made by the Swiss government to foster coherence of bilateral donor rehabilitation aid paid significant dividends. The findings of this study suggest that to be successful responsibility for coordination must be linked to resource allocation mechanisms. This was the case for the ERRP in Ethiopia, but not for the CoCom or the rehabilitation component of UNTAC in Cambodia, for example.

As argued above, it is important that any mechanism that achieves improved coordination and coherence of response is matched by stronger mechanisms to ensure accountability. Robinson (1997) has argued that enhanced coherence and coordination of aid responses may run counter to the interests of recipient countries if they result in a coercive approach to policy change, and, indeed, if they propose consistently inappropriate strategies.

A Healthy Peace? Lessons for Public Health Policy

Many of the issues facing the health sector in the 'post'-conflict case study countries are not unique: they are common to the wider debates on health policy and planning in least developed countries and ways of assisting them (Cassels 1998; Cumper 1993; LaFond 1995). However, as Chapters 4, 5 and 6 have detailed, there are particularities in terms of the needs of populations and health systems, and in terms of the role of aid in conflict-affected countries. This section is therefore concerned to unravel sector-specific lessons arising from the study.

The nature of the crisis: incrementalism and reform In all three countries, rehabilitation aid emphasised physical rather than functional rehabilitation of the health sector. This approach sees conflict as similar to a natural hazard that temporarily disrupts the progressive process of development. In this model, rehabilitation is seen as the link to the resumption of development, providing the physical basis for the resumption of services by restoring infrastructure and plugging a temporary gap in supplies.

This approach to rehabilitation was sustained by the professional culture of international health planning. With important exceptions, both national and international staff responsible for the design of needs assessment emphasised physical damage to the health system. This in turn provided the basis of appeals for aid, which again largely focused on infrastructure and supplies. There was a consistent pattern, most evident in Cambodia and Uganda, of the infrastructure component of rehabilitation dominating funding.

While the need for fundamental review of health policy, and in particular of health financing, was evident in the three countries, the capacity to carry it out was severely limited, as described in Chapter 4. Thus, in common with the findings of LaFond (1995), this research notes the paradox that where the need for sectoral reform is most pressing, the capacity to devise and implement such reforms was most lacking.[5] As the experience of the WHO in Cambodia showed, the process of building up national capacity is painstakingly slow, outstripped by the rapid pace at which aid volumes increase. This initiative was therefore unable to shape significantly the aid response during the critical rehabilitation period.

The research shares a second finding with LaFond (1995), namely that in the context of absolute scarcity of resources, the very goal of sustainability becomes highly problematic. The response to the crisis of sustainability in all three countries has been the adoption of sectoral reforms, including a focus on health financing. However, as discussed below, many of the assumptions about the prospects for health financing have proved highly problematic in the case study countries. Above all, it is not clear whether even the best-planned and best-executed health policy would be able to function effectively. This suggests that a much more realistic timeframe for rehabilitation needs to be adopted, measured in periods of years rather than months.

In the context of weak state capacity for setting overall policy and management, aid actors faced particular difficulties in designing their interventions. However, what is significant is that despite the absence of national capacity to undertake a more fundamental analysis of the health system, international actors made only minimal investment in such analysis themselves. In the few cases where investments were made in such pre-appraisal of rehabilitation strategies, as was the case in Uganda, the findings were largely ignored. What made this neglect so serious was that the pattern of aid investment significantly impacted on the shape of the health system in the short to medium terms, in particular committing national and international actors to a distribution of recurrent finance that was neither equitable nor efficient. This again indicates the need for an independent analysis and monitoring capacity outlined above, and for strengthened accountability mechanisms, as outlined below.

In Uganda and Ethiopia, it was only once the rehabilitation phase was seen to be over that aid actors, in particular the World Bank, began to concern themselves with sustainability issues. The fact that the rehabilitation aid strategies themselves had exacerbated the structural problems facing the health system was largely ignored by aid agencies. Instead, the same actors claimed an expanded role in health policy development in the country (Okounzi and Macrae 1995).

This raises questions regarding the accountability of aid actors working in these environments. In all the case study countries, aid agencies assumed that the respective governments would take responsibility for sustaining rehabilitation interventions, yet the governments themselves were unable or unwilling to exert significant influence over the rehabilitation process. Although there is a trend towards greater evaluation of rehabilitation initiatives (see, for example, Kreimer et al. 1998), there remains a relative absence of independent evaluation of these initiatives. Such evaluation would not only provide a better basis for learning lessons from different national experiences, but would also provide a mechanism for enhancing the accountability of aid actors. The absence of collated data regarding patterns of investment in the health sector is extremely problematic in this regard, and poses a particular threat to effective health planning.

Health financing During the period of transition, the case study countries were relatively low recipients of oda in absolute terms compared with their regional neighbours. The health sector suffered an absolute scarcity of resources, with annual per capita expenditures well below the US$12 recommended by the World Bank (1993). While low in absolute terms, relative to nationally available resources, aid did constitute a very significant resource in all three cases. Thus, in the short term, aid policy-makers can influence significantly populations' access to health services. In addition, because a sizeable percentage of rehabilitation aid is allocated to capital expenditure, this has a significant effect on health systems in the medium term (Macrae et al. 1995).

Aid-supported rehabilitation in the sector tended towards an expansion of the health infrastructure in a climate where resources were contracting in absolute terms (Cambodia and Uganda), and in relative terms as a result of devaluation associated with adjustment (all countries). Ethiopia was unique in yielding a significant peace dividend as a result of demilitarisation. However, the absolute poverty of the country, and the historical neglect of public health, meant that transfers from the military to the social sector were slow to bear fruit.

In Cambodia and Uganda, military expenditure remained high, as the negative effects of conflict in distorting the economy, and in particular public finance, persisted well after the changes of regime. The ability of governments to re-establish effective and equitable taxation systems, and their willingness to shift expenditures from defence to the social sector, is crucial. Closer scrutiny of public finances, and of the political economy of war more generally, by health planners would provide a more robust basis for rehabilitation planning. The work of David Dunlop and associates in Uganda and Ethiopia is a good example of the data that it is possible to collect in these environments (see Sheyer and Dunlop 1985; Bekele et al. 1993). These presented different scenarios indicating in broad terms the implications of different rates of expansion in coverage. While crude, such data quickly indicate the hard choices that need to be made by national and international policy-makers regarding rehabilitation priorities. They also underline the high opportunity costs of inappropriate rehabilitation expenditure.

What the research also suggests is that, without a corresponding policy on the 'software' issues of human resources and institutional issues such as policy-making and planning mechanisms, high levels of expenditure on physical rehabilitation are problematic. While not undervaluing the importance of high-quality referral facilities, these require that a sophisticated system of human and financial resources be in place within an appropriate institutional framework that provides for training, supervision and payment of staff. It is important that the rate of investment in physical infrastructure does not outstrip that in other elements of the health system if functional rehabilitation is to be achieved.

Further research regarding alternative sequencing and prioritisation of rehabilitation aid to the health sector is merited. Of particular interest are likely to be the options for low-cost construction of health infrastructure, such as using temporary or prefabricated structures and mobile health services.

A more modest pace of physical rehabilitation might release re-sources to invest in health-supporting interventions, which do not require the same level of complexity of public institutions as health services. For example, in Cambodia, the water and sanitation compon-ent of the rehabilitation appeal was severely under-funded. Com-parative analysis of the relative sustainability and health gain of different types of intervention would be of particular benefit.

Particularly neglected by international rehabilitation efforts were health staff. As Cassels (1988) argues, it is the effectiveness of this 'software' that exerts the most significant impact on utilisation of health services. The Ethiopian case suggests that where state institu-tions remained relatively strong, and able to pay public employees and to retain them, greater continuity of care was achieved (Gunneberg 1994). Uganda and Cambodia represent the other scenario of decline in public service and rapid privatisation of provision, as health workers sought other strategies to survive.

In these countries, as more generally, aid actors have proved reluc-tant not only to address the problem, but even to acknowledge it. Direct subsidy of the public payroll is seen as highly problematic by aid donors, particularly in the absence of budgetary support programmes. Donors particularly fear that direct subsidy of salary costs is inherently unsustainable, making it impossible to withdraw from a country (LaFond 1995). In those countries where political conditions prohibit direct balance of payments support, indirect subsidy of public budgets is blocked, thereby reducing still further the options for sustaining public sector salaries.

Experiments with community financing schemes to support health workers' salaries, such as the Bamako Initiative, merit further review in conflict and 'post'-conflict settings. These have the potential advantage of enabling communities to use local resources for health promotion, when the state fails to do so. Important to emphasise, however, will be the particular costs facing conflict-affected communities – for example, constant reinvestment in shelter and production due to displacement and damage. Measures to secure more 'sustainable' approaches to health financing will not be successful if the absolute scarcity of resources is not addressed by international and national actors.

Sustainability, standards and accountability As outlined above, the inherent difficulties of achieving sustainable initiatives in these environments reflect important trade-offs between the different objectives of different actors. In particular, if sustainability is to be an important goal of aid programming in these environments, this may suggest compromising another objective, namely coverage.

The sustainability issue is another point where the tensions between the programming approaches of humanitarian and development agencies become apparent. While the former are concerned with maximising the access of individuals, or a particular target group (for example, refugees, children) to particular health services, development agencies focus at the level of populations. Thus two populations could share the same basic indicators of health, nutrition and access to water, but these would prompt different responses from the relief and development communities.

As described above, there are no universal criteria that specify whether and when the transition from relief to development aid should occur: in other words, what constitutes an emergency and when it is over. This raises a question with respect to the 'phasing out' of welfare inputs targeted at the level of individuals and basic standards. In relief operations, while coverage may be limited, the standards and conditions according to which assistance is given are frequently relatively high – for example, allowing populations access to free drugs and food. This emphasis on access switches to a focus on sustainability in developmental programmes.

As the case studies show, this shift in programming objectives often takes place in a way such that the phasing out of relief inputs is not paralleled by a concomitant rise in development aid. In other words, *de facto* there is a reduction in the populations' access to assistance, a finding echoed by others (Karim et al. 1996; Macrae and Bradbury 1998; Stockton 1996). Many aid operations responding to chronic political emergencies have been experiencing sustained declines in their funding over recent years. In this context, there is a need for particular scrutiny of the quantity and quality of coverage of basic services and of standards of nutrition. Health professionals play an important role in monitoring trends in access to health services and health supporting interventions such as food aid.

Conclusion

The experience of delivering aid in the three countries analysed here suggests that the problems of aiding unstable states will not be solved simply by improving aid procedures. A much more fundamental review of aid strategies in chronic political emergencies is required. The uncertain legitimacy and weak capacity of recipient states confined aid responses to the projectised, decentralised and supply-oriented models of relief, which connected poorly to developmental objectives and the resumption of development aid. It is not simply bullishness or an anti-development stance on the part of humanitarian actors that leads some to reject an emphasis on capacity-building and sustainable development: it is a reflection of the particular political and economic context of conflict situations.

As earlier chapters have argued, development agencies are assuming a role in conflict management, but their ability to engage in conflict situations is doubly compromised. Aid remains an instrument of foreign policy, and therefore must conform with the analysis and priorities of individual donor governments, and of the multilateral organisations that play a political role, such as the United Nations. This analysis is necessarily partial, and thus does not constitute a basis for accurate decision-making regarding populations' needs, or the likely technical effectiveness of aid programming. Within the broad parameters of foreign policy, aid has become the primary means of Western political engagement in non-strategic countries, yet the history of development assistance, and of developmentalism more broadly, suggests that aid is peculiarly ill-equipped to play this new political role.

The reunification of aid and politics in the mid-1980s assumed political consensus within the official aid community, and between it and recipient countries regarding the way in which sovereign states managed their internal affairs, and regarding the causes of conflict. Such consensus has been lacking. While juridical sovereignty is no longer automatically protective of states, an alternative basis to guide an increasingly politicised aid agenda is currently lacking. This has left aid agencies in an increasingly uncomfortable space. On the one hand they are at risk of legitimating governments engaged in violating the rights of their citizens, or conversely undermining the formation of legitimate structures. On the other hand, aid agencies risk acting as the relatively cheap, but technically ineffective, instrument of containment.

What this suggests is that aid actors need to develop the capacity to analyse the political impacts of their assistance, and to define explicitly norms of behaviour expected from its partners, and the sanctions likely to be imposed if these norms are violated. This is increasingly being done as donors become more selective in the allocation of development assistance. For such an exercise to be legitimate, it will rest upon aid actors being able to assert convincingly that their primary function is not to serve the foreign policy interests of donor governments, but to alleviate poverty and suffering. This implies an ability to define aid strategy independently of the interests of donor governments. It will also rely on a much clearer statement of what strategies will be pursued where conditions are not seen to be appropriate for development aid. At present, international policy seems to comprise largely the provision of relief. These relief and relief-type instruments, such as rehabilitation, are increasingly expected to deliver on new developmental and conflict-management objectives, but without adequate support from either development or political actors.

The new orthodoxy currently lacks a clearly defined set of principles to guide aid engagement in conflict settings. Defining such principles is not simply a moral nicety, but will be important if aid interventions are to be effective in meeting the needs of conflict-affected populations. They will be important too in maintaining an appropriate and balanced division of international labour in relation to conflict management, and ensuring that aid (both relief and development aid) is not simply a substitute for political action (Eriksson 1996).

Aid agencies have complied willingly as their agenda has expanded almost annually to deliver not just growth, but empowerment of women, environmental protection, good governance and peace, all within a declining resource base. As they contemplate this massive, and often contradictory, list of tasks it is worth reflecting on the advice of one health official. Asked whether he had any advice for others planning rehabilitation interventions in conflict-affected countries, he answered:

'Yes, be modest in your objectives to ensure that priorities are set according to needs.'

Wise words.

Notes

1. Or what Dillon and Reid, in 'Global governance, liberal peace and complex emergency', unpublished mimeo, Lancaster University, 2000, have called 'emerging political complexes'.

2. Thus, for example, in a telling paragraph, recent guidelines produced by UNHCR (1999) note that: 'in countries still in conflict, but where certain areas are safe enough to allow for spontaneous return, the proposed approach [to achieve sustainable return] needs to be adapted for prevailing conditions, but *overall remains valid and applicable*' (emphasis added).

3. See, in particular, Chapters 2, 3, 5 and 6.

4. The feasibility of such methods was recently demonstrated with remarkable results by the ICRC in its study of the views of people living in war-affected and donor countries regarding the laws of war. See ICRC (1999) *People and War*, ICRC, Geneva.

5. Pavignani (1998) in his review of the Mozambican experience of sectoral rehabilitation notes that here national health policy-makers received considerable support from WHO and the World Bank for the 'nationalisation' of health policy in the transition to peace. This investment in planning in the Ministry of Health was seen to have paid important dividends in terms of maintaining national control over public policy and in terms of ensuring its sustainability. However, even here health planners confronted the ultimate impasse of absolute scarcity of resources. This experience is likely to be important to note, particularly where state institutions remain intact and the legitimacy of state institutions is widely accepted.

References

Adelman, H. (1996) 'The dialectic of development theory and practice', unpublished mimeo, York University, Canada.

African Rights (1994) 'Humanitarianism unbound?: Current dilemmas facing multi-mandate relief operations in political emergencies', discussion paper no. 5, African Rights, London.

Albright, M. (1997) 'Remarks at USAID conference on promoting democracy, human rights and reintegration in post-conflict societies', USAID, Washington, DC.

Anderson, M. (1996) 'Do no harm: supporting local capacities for peace through aid', Collaborative for Development Action Local Capacities for Peace Project, Boston, MA.

Angelli, E. and C. Murphy (1988) *America's Quest for Supremacy and the Third World: A Gramscian Analysis*, Pinter, London.

Annet, H. and K. Janovsky (1988) 'Uganda health development proposal: a proposal for funding by the World Bank', Project for the Preparation of the IDA-funded Health and Population Project, Ministry of Health, Entebbe.

Anstee, M. (1996) 'The United Nations' role in post-conflict peace-building: report to the secretary-general', United Nations, New York.

Apthorpe, R., H. Ketel, M. Salih and A. Wood (1995) *What Relief for the Horn? Sida-supported Emergency Operations in Ethiopia, Eritrea, Southern Sudan, Somalia and Djibouti*, SIDA, Stockholm.

Bekele, A., D. Dunlop, L. Forgy, R. Sturgis and V. Barbiero (1993) 'Ethiopia: health financing issues paper for USAID and other donors', USAID, Addis Ababa.

Benson, C. (1992) 'The changing role of NGOs in the provision of relief and rehabilitation assistance. Case study 2: Cambodia and Thailand', ODI working paper no. 75, Overseas Development Institute, London.

Bond, G. and J. Vincent (1990) 'Living on the edge: changing social structures in the context of AIDS', in H. Hansen and M. Twaddle (eds), *Changing Uganda: The Dilemmas of Structural Adjustment and Revolutionary Change*, James Currey, London, pp. 113–29.

Borton, J. (1993) 'Recent trends in the international relief system', *Disasters*, vol. 17, no. 3, pp. 187–201.

— (1994) 'NGOs and relief operations: trends and policy implications', Overseas Development Institute, London.

Boutros-Ghali, B. (1992) *An Agenda for Peace: Preventive Diplomacy, Peacemaking and Peace-keeping. Report of the Secretary-General Pursuant to the Statement Adopted by the Summit Meeting of the Security Council on 31 January 1992*, United Nations, New York.

— (1994) *An Agenda for Development*, United Nations, New York.

Bradbury, M. (1998) 'Normalizing the crisis in Africa', *Disasters*, vol. 22, no. 4, pp. 328–38.

Buchanan-Smith, M. and S. Maxwell (1994a) 'Linking relief and development: an introduction and overview', *IDS Bulletin*, vol. 25, no. 4, pp. 2–16.

Buchanan-Smith, M., S. Collins, C. Dammers, F. Wakesa, and J. Macrae (1999) 'An evaluation of Danish humanitarian assistance to Sudan', Overseas Development Institute, London.

Burkey, I. (1991) 'People's power in theory and practice: the Resistance Council system in Uganda', mimeo, Yale University, New Haven, CT.

Cambodia (1992) *Transitional Health Plan: Part One – Health Situation Analysis: A Framework for Development*, Phnom Penh.

Cassels, A. (1988) *Nepal: Health and Population Sector Review. Report for the Health and Population Division, Overseas Development Administration*, ODA, London.

— (1998) 'Aid instruments and health systems development: an analysis of current practice', *Health Policy and Planning*, vol. 11, no. 4, pp. 354–68.

CCC (1992) *NGOs and the Rehabilitation of Cambodia*, Cooperation Committee for Cambodia, Phnom Penh.

Chalker, L. (1996) 'Can development programmes reduce conflict?', address to the Institute for International Affairs, Stockholm, 1 October.

Chenery, H., M. Ahluwalia, C. Bell, J. Duloy and R. Jolly (1974) *Redistribution with Growth*, Oxford University Press, London.

Cholmondeley, H. (1997) *Mission to Afghanistan and Islamabad 18 June–7 July*, United Nations, New York.

Chopra, J., J. MacKinlay and L. Minear (1993) 'Report on the Cambodian Peace Process', *Research Report* no. 15, Norwegian Institute of International Affairs, Oslo.

Clapham, C. (1988) *Transformation and Continuity in Revolutionary Ethiopia*, Cambridge University Press, Cambridge.

— (1996) *Africa and the International System: The Politics of State Survival*, Cambridge University Press, Cambridge.

Cliffe, L. and R. Luckham (1999) 'Complex political emergencies and the state: failure and the fate of the state', *Third World Quarterly*, vol. 20, no. 1, pp. 27–50.

Clough, M. (1992) *Free at Last? US Policy Towards Africa and the End of the Cold War*, Council on Foreign Relations, Washington, DC.

Cohen, J. (1997) 'Decentralization and ethnic federalism in post-civil war Ethiopia', in K. Kumar (ed.), *Rebuilding Societies After Civil War: Critical*

Roles for International Assistance, Lynne Rienner, Boulder, CO and London, pp. 135–54.

Congress of the United States (1994) *Enhancing US Security Through Foreign Aid*, Congressional Research Office, Washington, DC.

Cox, R. (1992) 'Multilateralism and world order', *Review of International Studies*, vol. 18, pp. 161–80.

Cumper, G. (1993) 'Should we plan for contraction in health services? The Jamaican experience', *Health Policy and Planning*, vol. 8, no. 2, pp. 113–21.

Curtis, G. (1989) *Cambodia: A Country Profile*, Sida, Stockholm.

— (1994) 'Transition to what? Cambodia, UNTAC and the peace process,' in P. Utting (ed.), *Between Hope and Insecurity: The Social Consequences of the Cambodian Peace Process*, UNRISD, Geneva.

Davies, J. (1993) 'Blue berets, green backs: what was the impact?' *Phnom Penh Post*, 22 October.

Dessalegn, R. (1992) *The Dynamics of Rural Poverty: Case Studies from a District in Southern Ethiopia*, Monograph Series 2/92, CODESIRA, Dakar.

— (1993) 'Agrarian change and agrarian crisis: state and peasantry in Ethiopia', in D. Bassett and C. Crummey (eds), *Land in African Agrarian Systems*, University of Wisconsin Press, Madison.

— (1994) 'The unquiet countryside: the collapse of "socialism" and rural agitation 1990 and 1991', in Z. Abebe and S. Pausewang (eds), *Ethiopia in Change: Peasantry, Nationalism and Democracy*, British Academic Press, London and New York, pp. 231–42.

Development Assistance Committee (1997) *DAC Guidelines on Conflict, Peace and Development Cooperation on the Threshold of the 21st Century*, OECD, Paris.

DHA and UNDP (1997) *Building Bridges between Relief and Development. Final Report of a UNDP–DHA workshop, 12–17 April, Turin, UN Staff Training College*, United Nations, Geneva.

Dodge, C. (1986) 'Uganda: rehabilitation or redefinition of health services?', *Social Science and Medicine*, vol. 22, no. 7, pp. 755–61.

Dodge, C. and P. Weibe (1985) *Crisis in Uganda: The Breakdown of Health Services*, Pergamon Press, Oxford.

Duffield, M. (1991) 'The privatization of public welfare, actual adjustment and the replacement of the state in Africa', paper presented at the conference on 'International Privatization: Strategies and Practices', St Andrews, 12–14 September.

— (1994a) 'Complex emergencies and the crisis of developmentalism', *IDS Bulletin*, vol. 25, no. 4, pp. 37–45.

— (1994b) *Complex Political Emergencies with Reference to Angola and Bosnia. An Exploratory Report for UNICEF*, University of Birmingham, Birmingham.

— (1994c) 'The political economy of internal war: asset transfer, complex emergencies and international aid', in J. Macrae and A. Zwi (eds),*War and*

Hunger: Rethinking International Responses to Complex Emergencies, Zed Books, London and New Jersey, pp. 50–69.

— (1996) 'Symphony of the damned: racial discourse, complex political emergencies and humanitarian aid', *Disasters*, vol. 20, no. 3, pp. 173–93.

— (1997a) 'Evaluating conflict resolution: context, models and methodology', background paper prepared as part of evaluation of International Alert, Chr. Michelsen Institute, Bergen.

— (1997b) 'Post-modern conflict, aid policy and humanitarian conditionality', discussion paper prepared for the Emergency Aid Department, Department for International Development, School of Public Policy, University of Birmingham, Birmingham.

Duffield, M. and J. Prendergast (1994) *Without Troops and Tanks: Humanitarian Intervention in Ethiopia and Eritrea*, Red Sea Press, Lawrenceville, GA.

Economist Intelligence Unit (1992) *Uganda Country Profile 1991–1992*, EIU, London.

Edmonds, K. (1988) 'Crisis management: the lessons for Africa from Obote's second term', in H. Hansen and M. Twaddle (eds), *Uganda Now: Between Development and Decay*, James Currey, London, pp. 95–110.

Ellis, S. (1996) 'Africa after the Cold War: new patterns of government and politics', *Development and Change*, vol. 27, no. 1, pp. 1–28.

Eriksson, J. (1996) *The International Response to Conflict and Genocide: Lessons from the Rwanda Experience. Synthesis Report*, Joint Evaluation of Emergency Assistance to Rwanda, Copenhagen.

Ethiopia (1978) *Primary Health Care Status in Revolutionary Ethiopia*, Ministry of Health, Provisional Military Government of Socialist Ethiopia, Addis Ababa.

— (1993) *Report of the National Health Policy Task Force*, Transitional Government of Ethiopia, Council of Ministers, Addis Ababa.

— (1994a) *Survey of Current Economic Conditions in Ethiopia*, Volume II (3), Policy Analysis Unit, Ministry of Planning and Economic Development, Transitional Government of Ethiopia, Addis Ababa.

— (1994b) *The Constitution of the Federal Democratic Republic of Ethiopia*, Government of Ethiopia, Addis Ababa.

— (1995) *Health Sector Strategy*, Transitional Government of Ethiopia, Addis Ababa.

European Commission (1996) *Communication from the Commission to the Council and the European Parliament on Linking Relief, Rehabilitation and Development*, European Commission, Brussels.

Fitzgerald, E. (1994) 'The economic dimension of social development and the peace process in Cambodia', in P. Utting (ed.), *Between Hope and Insecurity: The Social Consequences of the Cambodian Peace Process*, UNRISD, Geneva, pp. 71–94.

Ghebali, V.-Y. (1985) 'The politicisation of UN specialised agencies: a preliminary analysis', *Millennium: Journal of International Studies*, vol. 14, no. 3, pp. 317–34.

Glennie, C. (1993a) 'PHC – long term dream or urgent necessity?', mimeo, UNICEF, Kampala.

— (1993b) 'Towards a basic package of essential health services', Kampala, UNICEF.

Green, R. (1984) 'Magendo in the political economy of Uganda: pathology, parallel system or dominant sub-mode of production?', *IDS Discussion Paper* 164, Institute of Development Studies, Brighton.

— (1994) 'The course of the four horsemen: costs of war and its aftermath in Sub-Saharan Africa', in J. Macrae and A. Zwi (eds), *War and Hunger: Rethinking International Responses to Complex Emergencies*, Zed Books, London and New Jersey, pp. 37–49.

Griffin, K. (1991) 'Foreign aid after the Cold War', *Development and Change*, vol. 22, pp. 645–85.

Gunneberg, C. (1994) *East Hararghe Health Project. Annual Report. 1994*, Save the Children Fund, Harar.

Hathaway, J. (1995) 'New directions to avoid hard problems: the distortion of the palliative role of refugee protection', *Journal of Refugee Studies*, vol. 6, no. 3, pp. 288–94.

Hendrie, B. (1989) 'Cross-border relief operations in Eritrea and Tigray', *Disasters*, vol. 13, no. 4, pp. 351–60.

— (1994) 'Relief behind the lines: the cross-border operation in Tigray,' in J. Macrae and A. Zwi (eds),*War and Hunger: Rethinking International Responses to Complex Emergencies*, Zed Books, London and New Jersey, pp. 125–38.

Hirshhorn, N. (1991) *Critical Needs Assessment in Cambodia: The Humanitarian Issues*, John Snow Inc., Washington, DC.

Holcomb, B. and J. Clay (1985) *Politics and the Ethiopian Famine 1984–1985*, Cultural Survival, Cambridge, MA.

Howard, L. and K. Kiragu (1992) *Mid-term Review: First Health Project*, evaluation report prepared for the Ministry of Health, Government of Uganda, in accordance with the Government of Uganda/IDA Development Credit on the First Health Project, IBRD, Washington, DC and Entebbe.

Hun Chun, Ly (1993) 'Working paper for the unification of Health Services Sub-committee's Planning Team', Ministry of Health, Phnom Penh, November.

Hurd, D. (1993) 'The new disorder', speech by the foreign secretary to the Royal Institute of International Affairs, Chatham House, London, 27 January, Foreign and Commonwealth Office, London.

Inayatullah, N. and D. Blaney (1995) 'Realizing sovereignty', *Review of International Studies*, vol. 21, no. 1, pp. 3–20.

Jackson, R. (1990) *Quasi-states: Sovereignty, International Relations and the Third World*, Cambridge University Press, Cambridge.

Kaplan, R. (1994) 'The coming anarchy', *Atlantic Quarterly*.

Karim, A., M. Duffield, S. Jaspars, A. Benini, J. Macrae, M. Bradbury, D. Johnson, G. Larbi and B. Hendrie (1996) *Operation Lifeline: A Review*, Department of Humanitarian Affairs, Geneva and New York.

Keen, D. (1991) 'A disaster for whom? Local interests and international donors during famine among the Dinka of Sudan',*Disasters*, vol. 15, no. 2, pp. 150–65.

— (1994) *The Benefits of Famine: The Political Economy of Famine in Southwestern Sudan 1985–1988*, Princeton University Press, Princeton, NJ.

Keen, D. and K. Wilson (1994) 'Engaging with violence: a reassessment of relief in wartime', in J. Macrae and A. Zwi (eds), *War and Hunger: Rethinking International Approaches to Complex Emergencies*, Zed Books, London and New Jersey, pp. 209–21.

Kello, A., K. Tesfaye, T. Feyera and M. Selassie (1992) *Health and Health Financing in Ethiopia, A Report for WHO*, WHO, Addis Ababa.

Kemp, A. (1996) 'Migration fears divert EU aid flows', *Observer*, London.

Kiljunen, K. (1984) *Kampuchea: Decade of the Genocide*, Zed Books, London.

Kloos, H. (1992) 'The health impact of war in Ethiopia', *Disasters*, vol. 16, no. 4, pp. 367–54.

Kreimer, A., J. Eriksson, R. Muscat, M. Arnold and C. Scott (1998) *The World Bank's Experience with Post-conflict Reconstruction*, International Bank for Reconstruction and Development, Operations Evaluation Department, Washington, DC.

Kreysler, J. (1991) 'Draft report on Cambodia. Meeting in WHO Western Pacific Regional Office, Manila, November', WHO, Manila.

Krylow, A. (1994) 'Ethnic factors in post-Mengistu Ethiopia', in Z. Abebe and S. Pausewang (eds), *Changing Ethiopia: Peasantry, Nationalism and Democracy*, British Academic Press, London and New York, pp. 231–41.

LaFond, A. (1995) *Sustaining Primary Health Care*, Save the Children/Earthscan, London.

Lanjouw, S., J. Macrae and A. Zwi (1998) *Missing the Point? A Critical Analysis of the Role of International Assistance in Rehabilitation of the Health Sector in Cambodia, 1989–1993*, London School of Hygiene and Tropical Medicine, London.

— (1999) 'Rehabilitating health services in Cambodia: the challenge of co-ordination in chronic political emergencies', *Health Policy and Planning*, vol. 14, no. 3, pp. 229–42.

Larrain, J. (1989) *Theories of Development*, Polity Press, London.

Lateef, K. (1990) 'Structural adjustment in Uganda: the initial experience', in H. Hansen and M. Twaddle (eds), *Changing Uganda: The Dilemmas of Structural Adjustment and Revolutionary Change*, James Currey, London.

Lautze, S. and J. Hammock (1996) 'Coping with crisis: coping with aid. Capacity building, coping mechanisms and dependency, linking relief and development', an analysis prepared for the UN Inter-agency sub-working group on local capacities and coping mechanisms and the linkages between relief and development, International Famine Center, Tufts University.

Le Billon, P. (2000) 'The political economy of war: what relief agencies need to know', *Humanitarian Practice Network*, Overseas Development Institute, London.

Leader, N. (1999) 'Humanitarian principles in practice: a critical review', *Relief and Rehabilitation Network Briefing Paper*, London, Overseas Development Institute, London.

Lee, K., W. Hull and G. Hoare (1987) *The Cost and Financing of Health Services in Uganda*, Ministry of Health and AMREF, Entebbe.

Leftwich, A. (1994) 'Governance, the state and the politics of development', *Development and Change*, vol. 25, pp. 363–86.

Low, D. (1988) 'The dislocated polity,' in H. Hansen and M. Twaddle (eds), *Uganda Now: Between Development and Decay*, James Currey, London, pp. 36–53.

Luwero District Administration (1988) *A Conspectus of Rehabilitation and Development Programmes*, Luwero.

Macrae, J. (1997a) 'Dilemmas of legitimacy, sustainability and coherence: rehabilitating the health sector', in K. Kumar (ed.), *Rebuilding Civil Socieites after Civil War: Critical Roles for International Assistance*, Lynne Rienner, Boulder, CO and London.

— (1997b) 'Aid, geopolitics and principles', paper presented to the DHA-UNDP workshop on linking relief and development, UN Staff Training College, Turin, 14–17 April, Overseas Development Institute, London.

— (1998) 'The death of humanitarianism? an anatomy of the attack', *Disasters*, vol. 22, no. 4, pp. 309–17.

— (1999) *Aiding Peace and War: A Comparative Analysis of Emerging Debates on Reintegration, and Relief Development Aid Linkages in Chronic Political Emergencies*, Overseas Development Institute and UNHCR, London and Geneva.

Macrae, J., M. Bradbury, S. Jaspars, D. Johnson and M. Duffield (1997) 'Conflict, the continuum and chronic emergencies: a critical analysis of the scope for linking relief, rehabilitation and development planning in Sudan', *Disasters*, vol. 21, no. 3, pp. 223–44.

Macrae, J. and M. Bradbury (1998) *Aid in the Twilight Zone: A Critical Analysis of Humanitarian–Development Aid Linkages in Situations of Chronic Instability*, a report for UNICEF, ODI, UNICEF and Brown University, London and New York.

Macrae, J. and N. Leader (2000) 'Shifting sands: the theory and practice of "coherence" between political and humanitarian responses to complex political emergencies', *Humanitarian Policy Group Report* no. 6, Overseas Development Institute, London.

Macrae, J., A. Zwi and H. Birumgi (1993) *A Healthy Peace? Rehabilitation and Development of the Health Sector in a Post-conflict Situation. The Case of Uganda*, London School of Hygiene and Tropical Medicine, London.

Macrae, J. and A. Zwi (1994) 'Famine, complex emergencies and international policy in Africa: an overview,' in J. Macrae and A. Zwi (eds), *War and*

Hunger: Rethinking International Responses to Complex Emergencies, Zed Books, London and New Jersey, pp. 6–36.

Macrae, J., A. Zwi and V. Forsythe (1995) *Post-conflict Rehabilitation: Preliminary Issues for Consideration by the Health Sector*, London School of Hygiene and Tropical Medicine, London.

Maxwell, D. (1999) 'Programmes in chronically vulnerable areas: challenges and lessons learned', *Disasters*, vol. 23, no. 4.

Maxwell, S., A. Kello, D. Belshaw, W. Campbell, Y. Getachew, P. Jenden, M. Teferra and J. Toye (1995) *Evaluation of EC/EU–Ethiopia Cooperation. Main Report*, Institute of Development Studies/Institute of Development Research, Brighton/Addis Ababa.

Meier, G. (1993) 'The new political economy and policy reform', *Journal of International Development*, vol. 5, no. 4, pp. 381–9.

Miller, R. (1992) *Aid as Peacemaker: Canadian Development Assistance and Third World Conflict*, Carelton University Press, Ottawa.

Moore, D. (1998) 'Sail on, O Ship of State: the state in a changing world and Africa', draft manuscript submitted to the *Review of African Political Economy*, Flinders University, Melbourne.

Mysliwiec, E. (1994) 'Cambodia: NGOs in transition', in P. Utting (ed.), *Between Hope and Insecurity: The Social Consequences of the Cambodian Peace Process*, UNRISD, Geneva, pp. 97–142.

Nederveen Pieterse, J. (1991) 'The dilemmas of development discourse: the crisis of developmentalism and the comparative method', *Development and Change*, vol. 22, pp. 5–29.

Negarit Gazeta (1991) *Transitional Period Charter of Ethiopia 1[50]*, Addis Ababa.

Netherlands (1993) *Humanitarian Aid: Between Conflict and Development*, Ministry of Foreign Affairs, The Hague.

— (1994) *Humanitarian Aid to Somalia*, Operations Review Unit, Ministerie van Buitenlande Zaken, The Hague.

OECD (1993) *Annual Report of the Development Assistance Committee 1992*, OECD, Paris.

— (1997) 'Draft DAC policy guidelines on conflict, peace and development cooperation', note by the Secretariat, OECD, Paris.

Ogata, S. and J. Wolfensohn (1999) 'The transition to peace in war-torn societies: some personal observations', paper delivered to a conference at the Brookings Institution, Washington, January, UNHCR/World Bank, Geneva and Washington, DC.

Okounzi, S. and J. Macrae (1995) 'Whose policy is it anyway? International and national influences on health policy development in Uganda', *Health Policy and Planning*, vol. 10, no. 2, pp. 122–32.

Olsen, I. (1998) 'Sustainability of health care: a framework for analysis', *Health Policy and Planning*, vol. 13, no. 3, pp. 287–95.

Overseas Development Administration (1996) 'An approach papaer on conflict handling and the aid programme', Emergency Aid Department, Overseas Development Administration, London.

Overseas Development Institute (1993) 'Recent trends in the international relief system', Briefing Paper Series, Overseas Development Institute, London.

Pavignani, E. (1998) 'The reconstruction process of the health sector in Mozambique', mimeo, Maputo.

Peou, S. and K. Yamada (1998) 'Foreign aid for peace in Cambodia: explaining unfulfilled pledges', draft report, New York, University/International Development Center, New York.

Pirotte, C. and B. G. F. Husson (eds) (1999) *Responding to Emergencies and Fostering Development: The Dilemmas of Humanitarian Aid*, Zed Books, London and New York.

Pupavac, V. (1997) 'Theories of conflict and children's rights', paper presented to the 2nd Convention of the European Association for the Advancement of Social Sciences, Conflict and Cooperation, Nicosia, 19–23 March, University of Nottingham, Nottingham.

Randel, J. (1994) 'Aid, the military and humanitarian assistance: an attempt to identify recent trends', *Journal of International Development*, vol. 6, no. 3, pp. 329–42.

Richardson, J. (1991) *Assessment of UNICEF's Emergency Response: Part Three, Phase 1. The Headquarters Perspective. Issues and Concerns of UNICEF Staff and Results of a Review of Available Literature*, New York: UNICEF.

— (1995) *UNICEF's Emergency Response: Based on Staff Perspectives*, UNICEF, New York.

Riddell, R. (1997) *Aid in the 21st Century*, Office of Development Studies, UNDP, New York.

Robinson, M. (1997) 'Coherence and governance in development cooperation', paper presented at the EADI International Workshop on Policy Coherence in International Cooperation, European Association of Development Researh and Training Institutes, Geneva.

Rostow, W. (1971) *Politics and the Stages of Growth*, Cambridge University Press, Cambridge.

Ruttan, V. (1996) *United States Development Assistance Policy*, Johns Hopkins University Press, Baltimore, MD and London.

Save the Children Fund (1993) *Sustainability in the Health Sector: Uganda Case Study*, Save the Children Fund, London.

Scheyer, S. and D. Dunlop (1985) 'Health services development in Uganda', in C. Dodge and P. Weibe (eds), *Crisis in Uganda: the Breakdown of Health Services*, Pergamon Press, Oxford, pp. 25–42.

Shawcross, W. (1984) *The Quality of Mercy: Cambodia, Holocaust and Modern Conscience*, André Deutsch, London.

Short, C. (1999) 'Security sector reform and the elimination of poverty', a speech by the secretary of state for international development, Centre for Defence Studies, King's College, London, 9 March, Department for International Development, London.

Sida (1999) 'Developmental humanitarian assistance: a concept paper', Swedish International Development Cooperation Agency, Stockholm.

Sivard, R. (1993) *World Military and Social Expenditures 1993*, World Priorities, Washington, DC.

Smallman-Raynor, M. and A. Cliff (1991) 'Civil war and the spread of AIDS in Africa', *Epidemiology of Infectious Disease*, vol. 107, no. 1, pp. 69–80.

Smithson, P. (1995) 'Quarts into pint jugs? The financial viability of health sector investment in low income countries', *Health Policy and Planning*, vol. 10, supplement, pp. 6–16.

Sorbo, G., J. Macrae and L. Wohlgemuth (1997) *NGOs in Conflict: An Evaluation of International Alert*, Chr. Michelsen Institute, Bergen.

Spero, J. (1977) *The Politics of International Economic Relations*, George Allen and Unwin, London.

Stewart, F. (1994) 'War and underdevelopment: can economic analysis help reduce the costs?' mimeo, Queen Elizabeth House, Oxford University, Oxford.

Stiglitz, J. (1998) 'Towards a new paradigm for development: strategies, policies and processes', Prebisch Lecture at UNCTAD, Geneva, October 19, World Bank, Washington, DC.

Stockton, N. (1996) 'Defensive development? The role of the military in relief and development', *Disasters*, vol. 20, no. 3.

Streeten, P. (1981) *First Things First: Meeting Basic Human Needs in Developing Countries*, Oxford University Press, Oxford and New York.

Suhrke, A. (1994) 'Towards a comprehensive refugee policy: conflict and refugees in the post Cold War world', in W. Bohning and M.-L. Schloeter-Paredes (eds), *Aid in place of migration?*, International Labour Office, Geneva, pp. 13–39.

Summerfield, D. (1999) 'A critique of seven assumptions behind psychological trauma programmes in war-affected areas', *Social Science and Medicine*, vol. 48, pp. 1449–62.

Tomasevski, K. (1994) 'Human rights and wars of starvation', in J. Macrae and A. Zwi (eds), *War and Hunger: Rethinking International Responses to Complex Emergencies*, Zed Books, London and New Jersey, pp. 70–91.

Ugalde, A., S. Canas, C. Castillo, C. Paz, E. Selva and O. Solas (1997) *Reconstruction and Development of the Health Sector in a Post-conflict Situation: The Case of El Salvador*, London School of Hygiene and Tropical Medicine/University of Texas, London and Austin.

Uganda (1987) *Report and Recommendations of the Commission of Enquiry into the Medical Services of Uganda*, Ministry of Health, Entebbe.

— (1989) *Rehabilitation and Development Plan 1988/89–1990/1.* 2 Volumes, 2nd edn, Ministry of Planning and Economic Development. Kampala, Ministry of Planning and Economic Development, Kamapla.

— (1991) *National Health Development Plan 1991–2000*, Ministry of Health, Government of Uganda, Entebbe.

— (1992) *Rehabilitation and Development Plan 1991/2–1994/5*, 2 volumes, Ministry of Planning and Economic Development, Kampala.

UNDP (1991) *Human Development Report 1991*, Oxford University Press, New York and Oxford.

— (1992) *Comprehensive Paper on Cambodia*, UNDP New York and Phnom Penh.

— (1995) *Development Cooperation: Ethiopia*, UNDP, Addis Ababa.

— (1996) *Building Bridges Between Relief and Development*, UNDP, New York.

UNHCR (1992) 'Bridging the gap between returnee aid and development: a challenge for the international community', Executive Committee of the High Commissioner's Programme, Sub-committee on Administrative and Financial Matters, 21st Meeting, 20 August, UNHCR, Geneva.

— (1997) 'Policy paper on reintegration in the transition from war to peace, United Nations High Commissioner for Refugees', UNHCR, Geneva.

— (1999) *UNHCR Operational Framework for Repatriation and Reintegration Activities in Post-conflict situations*, Reintegration Section, Division of Operational Support, UNHCR, Geneva.

UNICEF (1982) *Children and Women in Ethiopia: A Situation Analysis*, UNICEF and Ethiopia, Addis Ababa.

— (1987) *Children on the Frontline: The Impact of Apartheid, Destabilization and Warfare on Children in Southern and South Africa*, UNICEF, New York.

— (1989) *Development of Primary Health Care in Kampuchea*, UNICEF, Phnom Penh.

UNICEF and Transitional Government of Ethiopia (1993) *Children and Women in Ethiopia: A Situation Report*, UNICEF/Ethiopia, Addis Ababa.

UN Inter-agency Standing Committee on Humanitarian Affairs (1997) *Preliminary Findings and Recommendations of the Sub-working Group on Local Capacities/Relief and Development*, United Nations, New York.

United Kingdom (1997) *White Paper on International Development*, Department for International Development, London.

— (1999) *Conflict Reduction and Humanitarian Assistance: Policy Statement*, Department for International Development, London.

United Nations (1991) *United Nations Emergency Preparedness Group in Ethiopia. Provisional Assessment of 1992 Emergency Needs*, UN, Addis Ababa.

— (1993) *The United Nations in Cambodia. Fourth Progress Report of the Secretary-General on UNTAC. S/257. 3 May*, UN, New York.

— (1994) *Inter-agency Working Group on the Relief–Development Continuum*, Position Paper, UN, New York.

— (1997) *Renewing the United Nations: A Programme for Reform. Report of the Secretary-General*, UN, New York.

United Nations Administrative Committee on Coordination (1993) *Administrative Committee on Coordination. Summary of Conclusions of its Meeting 19–20 April*, United Nations, Rome.

United Nations Special Emergency Programme for the Horn of Africa (SEPHA) (1992) *Emergency Appeal: Health Sector*, revised document, UN, Addis Ababa.

— (1992b) Updated Consolidated Appeal July–December 1992, UN, Addis Ababa.

USAID (1994) *USAID Assistance Strategy for Cambodia 1994–1997*, USAID, Washington, DC.

Utting, P. (1994) 'Introduction: linking peace and rehabilitation in Cambodia,' in P. Utting (ed.), *Between Hope and Insecurity: The Social Consequences of the Cambodian Peace Process*, UNRISD, Geneva, pp. 1–38.

de Waal, A. (1996) 'Social contract and deterring famine: first thoughts', *Disasters*, vol. 20, no. 3, pp. 194–205.

— (1997) *Famine Crimes: Politics and the Disaster Relief Industry in Africa*, James Currey, Oxford.

Wallensteen, P. and M. Sollenberg (1995) 'After the Cold War: emerging patterns of armed conflict 1989–1994', *Journal of Peace Research*, vol. 32, no. 3, pp. 345–60.

Webb, P. (1996) 'Enabling withdrawal from emergency aid', paper presented to a Workshop of Natural Resources Advisers, Overseas Development Administration, Chichester.

Whyte, S. (1990) 'Medicines and self-help: the privatization of health care in eastern Uganda', in H. Hansen and M. Twaddle (eds), *Changing Uganda: The Dilemmas of Structural Adjustment and Revolutionary Change*, James Currey, London, pp. 130–48.

Wiles, P., N. Leader, L. Chan and C. Horwood (1999) 'Danida's humanitarian assistance to Afghanistan. An evaluation', draft report, Overseas Development Institute, London.

Wolfensohn, J. (1999) *A Proposal for a Comprehensive Development Framework*, World Bank, Washington, DC.

World Bank (1985) *Sector Review Ethiopia: Population, Health and Nutrition*, Population Health and Nutrition Department, Division 1, World Bank, Washington, DC.

— (1988) Staff Appraisal Report: The Republic of Uganda First Health Project World Bank, Washington, DC.

— (1992) *Memorandum and Recommendation of the President of the International Development Association to the Executive Directors on a Proposed Credit of SDR104.9 million to Ethiopia for an Emergency Recovery and Reconstruction Project*, 9 March, report no. P-5702-ET, IBRD, Washington, DC.

— (1992b) *Cambodia: From Rehabilitation to Reconstruction*, IBRD, East Asia and Pacific Region, Country Department 1, Washington, DC.

— (1993) *Investing in Health: World Development Report 1993*, Oxford University Press, New York.

— (1994a) *Ethiopia: Public Expenditure Policy for Transition*, 3 volumes, report no. 12992-ET, Country Operations Division, Eastern Africa Department, Africa Region, IBRD, Washington, DC.

— (1994b) *Cambodia: An Agenda for Rehabilitation*, IBRD, Washington, DC.

— (1997) *World Development Report 1997: The State in a Changing World*, Oxford University Press, New York.

— (1998) *Post-conflict Reconstruction: The Role of the World Bank*, IBRD, Washington, DC.

World Bank and Cambodia (1995) *Cambodia Rehabilitation Programme: Implementation and Outlook*, a World Bank report for the 1995 ICORC Conference, report no. 139565-KH, World Bank, Washington, DC.

Wrigley, C. (1988) 'Four steps towards disaster', in H. Hansen and M. Twaddle (eds), *Uganda Now: Between Development and Decay*, James Currey, London, pp. 27–35.

Zewde, B. (1994) 'Hayla-Selassie: from progressive to reactionary', in Z. Abebe and S. Pausewang (eds), *Ethiopia in Change: Peasantry, Nationalism and Democracy*, British Academic Press, London and New York.

Zwi, A. and J. Cabral (1991) 'Identifying "high risk" situations', *British Medical Journal*, vol. 303, pp. 1527–9.

Zwi, A. and A. Ugalde (1989) 'Towards an epidemiology of political violence in the Third World', *Social Science and Medicine*, vol. 28, no. 7, pp. 633–42.

Index

abandonment, politics of, 31
accountability, 145–7, 149, 169–70
Adelman, H., 14, 30, 40
Afghanistan, 34
Africa, food production in, 18
African Development Bank, 55
aid: agendas of donors, 100; and
    legitimacy dilemma, 73–119; and
    management of conflict, 13; and
    war, 31–6; anti-imperialist critique
    of, 40; as instrument of foreign
    policy, 170–1; as strategy of
    partnership, 41; blurred boundaries
    with politics, 44–5; changing
    context of, 45; channels for, 73, 96,
    140–2; conditionality of, 16, 17, 41,
    160; incapacitates public sector,
    161; dependence on, 29, 47 (in
    Cambodia, 146); development role
    of, 3; developmental *see*
    developmental aid; emergence of
    new orthodoxy, 24–47; forms of, 73
    (shaped by political context, 74);
    humanitarian, 19; influenced by
    ideological factors, 69; invention of,
    9–13; link with security, 12; new
    orthodoxy of, 37–45, 154, 157;
    political economy of, 46;
    politicization of, 58; regionalization
    of, 101; reunified with politics, 30;
    role in conflict management, 3, 7,
    38, 73; search for new paradigm of,
    1, 2, 24–31; systems of, 73;
    unconditional, 113
aid community, policy statements of, 7
AIDS, 100
Alice Lakwena sect, 104
Alma Ata Declaration on Health for
    All, 65

Amhara ethnic group, 53, 91
AMREF agency, 110
Angola, 39
Anstee, Dame Margaret, 44
armed conflict, prevention of, 2
Asian Development Bank, 76, 134

Baganda ethnic group, 59
balance in distribution of aid, 75
Bamako Initiative, 100, 169
basic needs approach, 14
Blaney, D., 17
Bosnia, 28; peace enforcement in, 2
Boutros-Ghali, Boutros: *Agenda for
    Development*, 25, 32; *An Agenda for
    Peace*, 32
Bretton Woods institutions, 3, 12, 31

Cambodia, 5, 21, 34, 48–72 *passim*, 77,
    79, 82, 83, 84, 86, 103, 111, 112, 121,
    138, 139, 144, 147, 149, 156, 161,
    162, 164, 165, 167, 168; aid flows to,
    124–5, 126; experience of war,
    50–3; health sector in, 63–5, 122–32
    (spending in, 128, 129, 131, 132;
    lack of staff in, 141); lack of
    sovereignty, 74; rehabilitation
    assistance to, 133–4
Cambodian Communist Party (CCP),
    53
Cassels, A., 163, 168
China, 12, 50, 51, 52
Chopra, J., 79
chronic political emergencies, 155–7,
    170
civilians, vulnerability of, in conflict,
    20, 29
Clapham, Christopher, 3, 9, 10, 16, 17,
    18, 57, 96

Cliffe, L., 46
Coalition Government of Democratic Kampuchea (CGDK), 51–2
Cold War, 1, 8, 11, 21, 30, 41–2, 52; end of, 26
communism, control of, 13
community health agents (CHAs), 65
complex impact of conflict, 25
complex political emergencies, 19, 46
conditionality *see* aid, conditionality of
conflict: deriving from underdevelopment, 37; international costs of, 26; resolution of, 3, 7, 38, 44, 73
continuum, concept of, 42
Control of Diarrhoeal Diseases (CDD), 141
Cooperation Committee for Cambodia (CCC), 78
Coordinating Committee for Health (CoCom) (Cambodia), 82, 86, 164
cost recovery measures, 146
Cox, R., 14, 15
Cuba, 34

DANIDA agency, 109
data, lack of, 166
debt: burden of, 18; clearance of, 160
Declaration on the Rehabilitation and Reconstruction of Cambodia, 75
decolonization, 4, 9–13, 22
demilitarization, 167
democracy, 11
Department for International Development (DFID) (UK), 31
dependency *see* aid, dependency on
Dessalegn, R., 56, 89
developmental aid, 37, 73, 113, 155
developmental approach, 159
developmentalism, 8, 9–13, 19, 157; and economic crisis, 13–15 *see also* aid, developmental
disbursing of aid funds, problems of, 102
disease, control of, 94
distribution of aid, 80
division of labour, international, re-analysis of, 29–31
doctors: brain drain of, 67; numbers reduced, 63

dollar, devaluation of, 13
drought, 36, 66
drugs: lack of, 136; spending on, 136; supplies of, 138, 140, 141, 149, 169
Duffield, M., 18, 19
Dunlop, David, 167

Emergency Recovery and Rehabilitation Programme (ERRP), 93, 94, 95–7, 137, 138, 143, 164; as source of drug supplies, 135, 136
environmental protection, 32, 33, 172
ERA agency (Ethiopia), 102
Eritrea, 20, 27, 40, 54, 57, 137–8
Eritrean Liberation Front (ELF), 54
Eritrean People's Liberation Front (EPLF), 54, 137
Ethiopia, 5, 20, 21, 27, 40, 48–72 *passim*, 111, 113, 137–8, 140, 142, 143, 147, 149, 164, 166, 167, 168; aid to, limited, 55; as Federal Democratic Republic, 90; effect of war on, 53–8; health sector in, 65–6, 87–103, 122–32; health spending in, 128, 129, 131, 132; Ministry of Planning and Economic Development (MOPED), 89; Red Terror in, 55; rehabilitation assistance to, 134
Ethiopian People's Democratic Front (EPRDF), 87, 88, 89, 90, 91, 93, 102, 126
Ethiopian People's Democratic Movement (EPRDM/F), 57, 58
Ethiopian Socialist Party, 56–7
European Commission, 20, 34, 35–6, 55, 58, 79, 85, 93, 112, 145; 'Linking Relief, Rehabilitation ...', 33; relief provided by, 27
European Union, 101; Common Foreign and Security Policy, 33
Expanded Programme of Immunization (EPI): in Cambodia, 86, 141; in Uganda, 105, 108, 109

Family Health Project (FHP) (Ethiopia), 97–8
famine, 95; in Cambodia, 52; in Ethiopia, 55, 126; Wollo camps, 57
Fitzgerald, E., 78

floods, 36
food: imports of, as aid, 18; production of, in Africa, 18
France, disengagement from Africa, 31
functionalism, 14
FUNICPEC (Cambodia), 85

governance: good, 172; poor, intolerance of, 24
Green, Reginald, 25
Gunneberg, C., 138

Haile Selassie, 54
health care, 48, 49, 61–8, 121; impact of conflict on, 62; in Cambodia, 63–5 (policy aims of, 80, 81); in Ethiopia, 65–6, 87–103; in Uganda, 66–8 (policy, 105–10); involvement of governments in, 70; market research for priorities, 163; minimum levels recommended, 167; payment for, 99, 139, 146; policy, in transition, 98–103; primary (PHC), 99, 106, 107, 133, 144 (in Uganda, 135); investment in, 135; traditional, 68; vulnerability of spending on, 124
Health Policy Review Commission (Uganda), 107
Health Policy Task Force (Ethiopia), 99
health sector: rehabilitation of, 48 (in Uganda, 103–10); sustainability of (in Cambodia, 122–32; in Ethiopia, 122–32; in Uganda, 122–32)
health workers, incomes of, 139
health care
Heng Sarim, 51, 52
HIV, 66–7
Horn of Africa, disasters in, 94
hospital-based approach to health, 135
human rights, 33; violations of, 2, 17, 159, 160
human security, 7
humanitarian approach of NGOs, 84–5
humanitarian intervention, 2, 20, 28
humanitarian relief, 41–5

Idi Amin, 59–60, 125
Inayatullah, N., 17, 120
incrementalism, 165–6

infrastructures, repairs to, 132, 134
inter-agency coordination, lack of, 163
Inter-Agency Standing Committee on Humanitarian Affairs (IASC), 43
International Bank for Reconstruction and Development (IBRD), 12
International Committee of the Red Cross (ICRC), 28, 64, 85, 112
International Monetary Fund (IMF), 60, 77, 97, 104
Iraq, 26; sanctions against, 2

Jackson, Robert, 3, 4, 11

Kampuchean National United Front of Salvation (KNUFNS), 51
Kaplan, Robert, 38
Keen, David, 39
Kello, A., 142
Kenya, 55
Khmer Rouge, 50, 51, 52, 53, 63, 77, 124, 141
khum (commune, Cambodia), 83
Korean War, 12
Kurdistan, Iraqi, 28
Kurds, refugee crisis, 28

LaFond, A., 139, 165
Lanjouw, S., 63, 64, 77, 86
Leftwich, A., 45
legitimacy, 47, 48, 49, 50, 70, 120, 121; dilemma of, 6, 73–119; of Ethiopia, 58
legitimate intervention, 10
Liberia, 39
Lomé agreement, 55
Lon Nol, 50, 51

Maastricht, Treaty of, 33
malaria, 64, 86
Marxism, 13
McNamara, Robert, 15
Médecins Sans Frontières (MSF), 83, 85; MSF-Holland, 136
MEDICAN (Cambodia), 84
Mengistu Haile Mariam, 54, 56–7, 88, 92, 93, 102, 123; fall of, 58, 89
migration, 38, 66; aid and, 34; causes of, 34
military spending, 123, 124, 167

modernization, 13; theory, 11, 14, 39
monetarism, 15
mono-economics, 16
Moore, D., 161
mortality rates, 65, 66
Mozambique, 19, 156, 164
Museveni, Yoweri, 60, 104

National Resistance Army (NRA)
    (Uganda), 60–1
National Resistance Council (Uganda),
    104, 105
National Resistance Movement (NRM)
    (Uganda), 103–4, 112, 125, 128, 140
neo-liberalism, 17
Netherlands, 140, 160
neutrality, 159
neutrality of aid agencies, 43, 86
non-governmental organizations
    (NGOs), 73, 76, 80, 84, 86, 89, 102,
    103, 109, 112, 114, 132, 137, 139,
    140, 141, 154, 164; as channel for
    aid, 18, 103, 125; funding supplies
    of drugs, 137; growth of, 78; in
    Cambodia, 140; investing in, as
    donor strategy, 85; seen as threat to
    national sovereignty, 102
non-aligned nations, 30
North Atlantic Treaty Organization
    (NATO), 2
Nyerere, Julius, 60

Obote, Milton, 59, 60, 125
Office of Transition Initiatives (US), 30
official development assistance (oda),
    32; as part of strategy for security,
    21; Cold War rationale of, 1;
    decline in flows of, 1, 25; decline in
    support for, 24
Ogaden war, 55
oil, rising price of, 13–14
Olsen, I., 122
Organization for Economic
    Cooperation and Development
    (OECD), 3, 15; Development
    Assistance Committee (DAC), 27,
    33, 34, 42; *Guidelines on Conflict ...*,
    33; Task Force on Conflict, Peace
    and Development Co-operation, 33
Oromo Liberation Front (OLF), 88, 89

Paris Accords, 75, 79, 81, 144
Pavignani, E., 164
peace, 172; enforcement of, 2
Peasants' Associations (Ethiopia), 56,
    89, 90
People's Democratic Organizations
    (Ethiopia), 91
pharmaceuticals, supply of, 97
Pieterse, J., 13
post-conflict, use of term, 42
poverty, 123, 136, 148, 156; alleviation
    of, 160; as factor in conflict, 34, 39;
    as factor in weakness of states, 120;
    in Third World, 120; of state, 49,
    121;
prisoners of war, disabled, 66
privatization, 68, 87; of aid, 20; of
    health care, 141; of relief aid, 36
prostitution, 66
public policy, problem of locating, 162

quasi-states, 4, 5, 15–21, 23, 36, 41, 46,
    47, 57, 120, 149, 156; health care in,
    61–8

recovery: aid for, 108–10; context of,
    48–72
redistribution with growth, 14
refugees, 34, 38, 64, 81, 86, 94, 95;
    Cambodian, 52; Ethiopian, 57;
    Kurdish, 28; reintegration of, 42
regionalization of aid, 101
rehabilitation, 85, 139, 162, 165, 166;
    investment in, 142 (patterns of,
    132–40); nature of, 143–5; time-
    frame for, 165
Rehabilitation and Development Plan
    (Uganda), 105, 106
rehabilitation assistance, 6, 163, 167,
    168; lack of evauation of, 150; non-
    conditionality of loans for, 143;
    priorities for, 5; to Cambodia, 133–
    4; to Ethiopia, 134; to Uganda, 133;
    weakens state institutions, 121
relief: as strategy for aid engagement,
    19–21; blurred boundary with dev-
    elopment, 41–4; critique of, 26–9;
    distinguished from development
    aid, 36; linked to development,
    158–61; manipulated by warring

parties, 29; transition to
development aid, 48, 49, 73
relief assistance: and war, 36–7;
critique of, 24
relief programmes, premises of, 19
resettlement, in Ethiopia, 56
resources transfer, US resistance to,
11–12
REST agency (Ethiopia), 102
Riddell, R., 25
Robinson, M., 164
Rostow, W., 11, 13, 14, 18
Rwanda, 28

Sadruddin Aga Khan, 35
salaries of health staff, 138, 139, 142,
169
sanctions, 2
sanitation programmes, 168
Save the Children Fund (SCF), 105, 110
self-determination of states, 10
self-reliance, 40
Serbia, sanctions against, 2
Sierra Leone, 39; peace enforcement
in, 2
Sihanouk, Prince, 50, 51, 52, 75
Smithson, P., 122, 148
Somalia, 26, 28, 38, 55, 87, 101
sovereignty, 8, 16, 19, 28, 42, 53, 55;
becomes conditional, 2; buying
into, 124–6; definition of, 9–11;
empirical, 47, 49, 53, 73, 74, 111,
120, 159 (financing of, 126–30; role
of international aid, 130; reduced
by rehabilitation, 147); juridical, 44,
74, 110, 111, 112, 158, 171;
negative, 10, 22; of Cambodia, 75;
questioning of, 21; reinforcement
of, 11–13; unconditional respect for,
4, 8, 10, 45 (demise of, 20, 22)
state: necessity of presence of, 158;
poverty of, 49
state–society relations, affected by aid,
161
statehood: crisis of, 8; criteria of, 9;
empirical, 11, 48; juridical, 48;
legitimacy of, 47
structural adjustment, 14, 15–18, 22,
40, 105, 112

structural stability, 7; as goal of
development cooperation, 33
Sudan, 21, 28, 55, 57; embargo on aid,
43
Suhrke, A., 35
Supreme National Council (Cambodia), 75, 76, 77, 78, 79, 86, 87, 112
sustainability, 48, 87, 121, 145, 161,
169–70; of assistance, 40; definition
of, 122; determinants of, 142;
organizational, 140–2
Sweden, 55
Switzerland, 164
systems of aid, 73

Tanzania, 60
taxation, 123; collection of taxes, 161
Third World: deteriorating situation
of, 17; food dependence of, 14;
interest repayments of, 15; place of,
in Cold War, 16; underdevelopment
causes conflict in, 38; US policy
towards, 30
Tiger economies, 18
Tigray, 57, 88, 90
Tigrayan People's Liberation Front
(TPLF), 54, 57, 58, 90, 137
transition, 87–98, 103–4; aid in, 104–5;
health policy during, 98–103; post-
conflict, 5, 6, 48, 49, 110, 132, 155–7
(in Ethiopia, 92–8)
Transitional Government of Ethiopia
(TGE), 88, 91, 93, 95, 96
tuberculosis, 86

Uganda, 5, 40, 112, 113, 121, 139, 143,
147, 149, 161, 164, 166, 167, 168; as
colonial state, 58–9; Asians expelled
from, 59, 67; effects of war on,
58–61; First Health Project, 143,
144, 145; health sector in, 66–8,
122–32 (policy in, 105–10;
rehabilitation in, 103–10; spending
in, 127, 129); rehabilitation
assistance to, 133–4
Uganda People's Congress (UPC), 59
Uganda People's Democratic Army
(UPDA), 104
Union of Soviet Socialist Republics

(USSR), 50, 52, 55; aid from, 12, 124, 125

United Kingdom (UK), 3, 15, 41, 160; policy in Ethiopia, 92–3

United Nations (UN), 3, 6, 10, 19, 26, 28, 34, 37, 44, 76, 80, 82, 86, 93, 94, 95, 101, 102, 112, 164, 170; Appeal for Cambodia, 77; Charter of, 9, 28; creation of, 12; Executive Committee on Peace and Security, 45; General Assembly, 32; Office for the Coordination of Humanitarian Affairs (UNOCHA), 43; peace-keeping operations, 26; Resolution 46/182, 28; Security Council, 31, 32, 51; Special Emergency Programme for the Horn of Africa (SEPHA), 93; Special Political Committee, 34–5; Special Representative of the Secretary-General (SRSG), 75, 76, 774

UN Development Programme (UNDP), 42, 81, 83, 87

UNESCO, 16; US withdrawal from, 16

UN Fund for Population Activities (UNFPA), 81

UN High Commissioner for Refugees (UNHCR), 38, 42, 43, 46, 86, 112, 145

UNICEF, 25, 53, 64, 65, 76, 77, 78, 79, 81, 83, 84, 94, 105, 108, 109, 110, 112, , 130, 142

UN Transitional Authority in Cambodia (UNTAC), 74–81, 83, 86, 87, 103, 112, 125, 145, 164

United States of America (USA), 3, 11–12, 15, 41, 50, 52, 55, 58, 69, 88, 92; aid to Cambodia, 51; as donor government, 111; devaluation of dollar, 13; disengagement from Africa, 31; foreign policy on Africa, 40; foreign policy interests of, 30;

withdrawal from USAID, 20, 30, 53, 85

Vietnam, 34, 52, 53, 82, 83; aid from, 124; invasion of Cambodia, 51

Vietnam War, 13, 50, 63

villagization, in Ethiopia, 55

violence: orchestrators of, 39; political, epidemiology of, 61; practised by children, 39

de Waal, Alex, 40

war: costs to international community, 61; impact of, 48–72; nature of, 37–41; relief assistance and, 36–7

war economies, complex dynamics of, 122

water programmes, 168

Were, Dr Miriam, 88

Whyte, S., 68

women, empowerment of, 172

World Bank, 6, 12, 15, 31, 42, 55, 60, 70, 81, 87, 92, 93, 105, 108, 110, 113, 126, 134, 136, 144, 146, 147, 160, 166, 167; Emergency Rehabilitation Project (ERP), 77; Family Health Project (Ethiopia), 134; Post-conflict Unit, 42; Project Implementation Unit, 110; Public Expenditure Review, 98; studies by, 65, 109, 133; *World Development Report*, 161

World Food Programme (WFP), 27

World Health Organization (WHO), 83, 84, 85, 86, 88, 94, 164, 165; neutrality of, 84; role in Cambodia, 82

Yasushi Akashi, 75

Yugoslavia, former, 26

Zwi, A., 61

Zed Books Titles on Conflict and Conflict Resolution

The hope that conflicts within societies might decrease markedly with the demise of the Cold War have been cruelly disappointed. Zed Books has published a number of titles which deal specifically with the diverse forms of modern conflict, their complex causes, and some of the ways in which we may realistically look forward to prevention, mediation and resolution.

Adedeji, A. (ed.), *Comprehending and Mastering African Conflicts: The Search for Sustainable Peace and Good Governance*

Allen, T. and Seaton, J. (eds), *The Media of Conflict: War Reporting and Representations of Ethnic Violence*

Cockburn, C., *The Space Between Us: Negotiating Gender and National Identities in Conflict*

Duffield, M., *Global Governance and the New Wars: The Merging of Development and Security*

Fisher, S. et al., *Working with Conflict: Skills and Strategies for Action*

Gopal, S., *Anatomy of a Confrontation: Ayodhya and the Rise of Communal Politics in India*

Guyatt, N., *The Absence of Peace: Understanding the Israeli-Palestinian Conflict*

Jacobs, S., Jacobson, R. and Marchbank, J. (eds), *States of Conflict: Gender, Violence and Resistance*

Jayawardena, K. and De Alwis (eds), *Embodied Violence: Communalising Female Sexuality in South Asia*

Koonings, K. and Kruijt, D. (eds), *Societies of Fear: The Legacy of Civil War, Violence and Terror in Latin America*

Lewer, N.and Schofield S., *Non-Lethal Weapons – Military Strategies and Technologies for 21st Century Conflict*

Lumpe, L. (ed.), *Running Guns: The Black Market in Small Arms*

Mare, G., *Ethnicity and Politics in South Africa*

Melvern, L., *A People Betrayed: The Role of the West in Rwanda's Genocide*

Moser, C. and Clark, F. (eds), *Victims, Perpetrators or Actors? Gender, Armed Conflict and Political Violence*

Ohlsson, L., *Hydro Politics: Conflicts over Water as a Development Constraint*

Pirotte, C., Husson, B. and Grunewald, F. (eds), *Responding to Emergencies and Fostering Development - The Dilemmas of Humanitarian Aid*

Shiva, Vandana, *The Violence of the Green Revolution*

Suliman, M. (ed.), *Ecology, Politics and Violent Conflict*

Turshen, M. and Twagiramariya, C. (eds), *What Women Do in War Time: Gender and Conflict in Africa*

Vickers, J., *Women and War*

For full details of this list and Zed's other subject and general catalogues, please write to: The Marketing Department, Zed Books, 7 Cynthia Street, London N1 9JF, UK or e-mail: sales@zedbooks.demon.co.uk

Visit our website at: http://www.zedbooks.demon.co.uk